Fool's Gold

FOOL'S GOLD

Why the Internet Is No Substitute for a Library

Mark Y. Herring

McFarland & Company, Inc., Publishers
Jefferson, North Carolina, and London

LIBRARY OF CONGRESS CATALOGUING-IN-PUBLICATION DATA

Herring, Mark Y., 1952–
Fool's gold : why the Internet is no substitute
for a library / Mark Y. Herring.
p.   cm.
Includes bibliographical references and index.

ISBN-13: 978-0-7864-3082-6
softcover : 50# alkaline paper ∞

1. Computer network resources — Evaluation.   2. Web sites — Evaluation.
3. Libraries and the Internet.   4. Libraries and electronic publishing.
5. Libraries — Forecasting.   6. Library science — Forecasting.
7. Electronic books — Forecasting.   I. Title.
ZA4201   2007013548

Cover photograph ©2007 Photodisc

Manufactured in the United States of America

McFarland & Company, Inc., Publishers
Box 611, Jefferson, North Carolina 28640
www.mcfarlandpub.com

To Anthony (Tony) J. DiGiorgio, without whom
this book would not have been written.

Suaviter in modo, fortiter in re.

Acknowledgments

I have many people to thank for this book. I have some hesitancy in mentioning them by name only because I really don't want them to be implicated by what I say here. As with my last three books, Bessie Meeks, once my administrative assistant, and now back working in her first love, teaching, read most of this manuscript. Any felicities of language I owe to her. Ms. Meeks has been teaching English for more than a quarter of a century and I rely on her keen eye to catch my blunders. Her successor, Mrs. Genevieve Sparacin, has helped enormously on the project as well.

The *Quellenforschuung* for this book, the source-hunting, could not have been more ably done. I am indebted to the library's Access Services librarian, Carrie Volk. I have always asked one of our newest librarians to help me on any book if for no other reason than to help them become familiar with the process of research. All the librarians who have helped me on my books have done a great job, but I asked Ms. Volk to undertake more this time, and she responded in superb fashion. She is incredibly well-organized, efficient, brilliantly familiar with the Web, and infectiously enthusiastic about every task. Ms. Volk did yeoman's work (or is that yeoperson?) and I cannot thank her enough.

To the president of my institution, Anthony (Tony) DiGiorgio, my thanks are in surfeit. Tony has turned our institution around and positioned it to reach even higher. His suggestion, for better or worse, that I come up with talking points led, in a roundabout way, to this book. Of course he cannot be held accountable for any of it, but I proffer my thanks here for giving me the chance to work with so many fine people.

Finally, thanks go to my wife, Carol, a woman of indefatigable good will. For more than thirty years she has made it possible for me to pursue these book-long interests, often at the expense of her own work and pursuits. She has done so without complaint. She also read about a third of this book and helped iron out my written obfuscations.

Contents

Preface

Writing a book is always a difficult task, but writing a book like this one is very nearly impossible. It isn't because the information for this book proved especially difficult to locate. Some of it did turn out to be contrary, but most of it, like digging about for knowledge on any given subject, turned up in the usual places. Rather, the difficulty of this book is its subject matter. I chose to write about the defects and demerits of the Web, and the recurring but preposterous notion that it has already, or will one day very soon, replace conventional libraries. In the meantime the Web, or the Internet (however one wishes to refer to it), has made all libraries obsolete.

I may as well have written why moms are an especially perverse and curmudgeonly class of people, why apple pie is an egregiously classless dessert choice, or why the flag, Old Glory, is a stupid symbol of an even stupider nation. In other words, I could not have chosen a more difficult if not impossible task to write about with any hope of persuading the tens of millions of people who use the 'net daily, and all but worship it, to at least reconsider their Web fideism.

Worship it? Let me illustrate. In the early nineties, a colleague of mine was giving a talk about the Web. For librarians, as with everyone else, the Web was a new and untamed animal and access to it proved a bedevilment unlike any other. But we foresaw its eventual onslaught, and many of us began to make preparations to usher it into the library. Besides, it appeared clear that delivery of some, if not most, services would eventually be delivered over this new electronic beast. The colleague talked on (and on and on) about URLs, domain names, dot.coms (there were but a few), Pine mail and the coming HTML. In the midst of his talk, as he waxed and waxed about this new animal, he interrupted himself with the words, "Oh my God, how I love talking about this stuff!" His sincerity could not have been more genuine, and his adoration no more complete. I have since witnessed his worship in a thousand others over the years. Pick up any magazine that talks about the Web (or Google) and you'll notice by the second sentence (possibly the first) that only hierophants and sycophants need apply.

We love our technology, and we Americans are especially in love with it, and cannot possibly live without it. Criticize my wife or my children, even kick my dog, but don't dare say anything negative about the Web! Oh, we enjoy the typical bitchiness we share with one another: "I have hundreds of e-mails to read whenever I take a day or two off!" we exclaim with exasperation but not without some pride. It means we're important people. (We'll die first before we add, "of course, about 75 percent of those are spam.") For Americans, technology is one of the highest expressions of our greatness and we adore it with studied pride. For most men, technology even has sexual overtones: we must have the biggest, best, fastest, newest, most important, and even the most expensive technology possible or we feel somehow less virile. Business, we understand now, means technology, and we'll match size (and number and cost) with anyone!

The evolution has been a rapid one. In 1965, businesses spent exactly zero dollars annually on automation. In thirty years, by 1995, businesses were spending, in the U.S. anyway, *one billion annually*. Today, that figure is even higher and there are of course no limits to how much more we'll spend. There cannot be any limits, because if you want to do business, you must have technology and lots of it. It's impossible to do business otherwise.

Well, yes and no. We have forgotten that only fifteen years ago, almost nothing was being done on the Web by businesses, much less by the rest of us. No one, so far as I have been able to ascertain, felt in any way deprived, shortchanged, disenfranchised or otherwise cheated. The only people working on the "Web" (it had a different name back then) would have been Department of Defense employees or others in scientific professions seeking to share knowledge (as distinguished from information) with one another. In fact, before the Web "went public" the original Web worked quite well as a knowledge-based entity, but then, very uncompromising restrictions governed its use.

Others who attempted to create Web pages back then did so with painstaking detail to a foreign language of codes. To create even one page to display on the Web might take an amateur several hours, an accomplished designer more than one. The codes had to be precisely right, and even one comma or one bracket placed in the wrong spot could cause the page go haywire, make it look like one of Picasso's famous faces when you didn't want it to.

Berners-Lee changed all that when he developed HTML, HyperText Mark-up Language, in 1992, only to follow that with the creation of domain names in 1993. The invention made it possible for anyone to create a Web page easily, or certainly much more easily than before. With the release of WordPerfect 10, one could simply type a page as one would a letter, click on a button and, presto, a Web page would appear, or at least a rudimentary one.

Elaborate Web pages with all the bells and whistles still require technical expertise but not nearly as much one might suspect. Even someone new to the Web (such people exist but not many in this country) could be trained to create a sophisticated Web page in a matter of minutes. A company without a Web site these days is thought to be antediluvian; indeed, an *individual* without a Web page must be a Neanderthal. Well, that may be stretching it a bit, but certainly everyone simply *must* have Web access of some kind, not to mention high-speed, broadband digital access, cell phone digital access and so on.

So what's the problem? Now everyone can use it and we are all so much the richer for it. The problem is that the Web has become something of a behemoth that, like the Blob, the great late 1950s sci-fi thriller, gets bigger and bigger each time it swallows something else (most often a human). Moreover, the Web's lack of quality control creates something of a blessing and a curse, but more often the latter than the former. Finally, its gigantesque proportions, magnified by the ubiquitous Google, have suggested to some of the more ardent worshippers that we could do away with libraries and simply digitize every book there is and "zap" it to all who want it. Indeed, Google is doing this even as you read. But how did I get involved with all this?

As I thought about the problem in early 2000, the man to whom I ultimately report, Anthony J. DiGiorgio, asked me to put together talking points for a new library building we were proposing to the state in which I work. It seems he was running into this argument that buildings aren't needed any more because we, well, we could "zap" stuff back and forth. I pondered the issue for about a week and sent him a list. I fiddled with it a bit more, turning it into an article for *American Libraries* called "10 Reasons Why the Internet Is No Substitute for a Library." The piece then took on a life of its own.

The article was requested as a reprint so often that the ALA placed it on its permanent Web site (an irony to some that I'll address momentarily). After so many requests for reprints had reached me (and many had not, but violated copyright and reprinted anyway), after the article had been translated into eight different languages that I know about, after it had appeared in publications in Egypt, Great Britain, France, Germany, Denmark, and elsewhere, I turned the article into a poster. More than 3,000 have been distributed all over the world. Sometime after that Robert Franklin asked me about a book, and so here it is.

"Dissing" the Web

Although it will seem so at times, this book is not about "dissing" the Web, to use somewhat current vernacular. I know better. One cannot complain about the Web and not get criticized, and for good reason. I really don't want to be thrown into the same camp as the Unabomber just because we both raise objections to the Web. This book is about dangers the Web has raised and my concern that we do something about them. It is also about the fear I have that because the Web is everywhere, and because Google and others appear hell-bent on making everything digital, these concerns may be ignored. Later on in the book I make mention of Robert Shattuck's *Forbidden Knowledge*. One of the many salient points Shattuck makes is whether we should do something just because we can. I over-generalize his brilliant book, but the gist of one of his arguments is present in my formulation. I use it in regard to our mad rush to mass digitization. I worry about what we doing, whether we are doing it correctly, whether any standards are being observed, whether we're saving any dollars for re-digitizing originals, and whether anyone really understands that digitization is *not* preservation. All of these issues and more are tackled in this book.

I Am Not a Crook, and Neither Am I a Luddite

Quoting the late Richard Nixon may not be the wisest thing I've done, but perhaps it will serve a good purpose. Both points are true but I focus on the last one. As I point out elsewhere in this book, I have been using the Web since 1992 and I use it every day; and as will be obvious, I used it to do some, but by no means all, of the research for this book. My arguments here do not dismiss the value of the Web. Obviously, the Web has great value and will continue to have increasing value. As I say repeatedly in this book, none of my arguments are to "get rid" of the Web or to contract its use.

Rather, they are meant to help us refine and refashion our thinking about it so that it will become what it was meant to be: a fine accessory to libraries, not an ersatz one. Because we worship our technology, and because too many of us are overly dependent on it, some readers will quickly dismiss this book as "something by a Luddite." I imagine a few of them will be readers in my own profession of librarian. Indeed, one librarian (and the only person so far with a negative comment about it) after seeing the poster exclaimed that the "library was nothing until the Web." This will be news to roughly 95 percent of all civilizations that managed, and surprisingly well, without it until now. We moderns too often and too quickly forget we really are midgets sitting on the shoulders of giants, as Robert Burton had it in the *Anatomy of Melancholy*.

Now there is an irony here that some will perhaps contend vitiates my claims. If the Web is so bad, why do I use it here? I address that in the book, but suffice it to say for now that one can complain about health care while still getting an annual physical. One can even have health care insurance and still not like the structure of it, its abuses, its defects, and its seemingly blatant disregard for the very people it purports to serve. My point in this book is not that the Web is without value.

Of course the Web has made some improvements, though I do not see it as many do: as the best and most spectacular invention of all time, of all civilizations. I view with a much more jaundiced eye because I see firsthand its many drawbacks, its numerous defects. Delivery of serial information via the Web is a great boon to everyone who uses a library. While it has done nothing to reduce costs (and has, indeed, increased them), it is far better for users to be able to get at information online than to wait until the library opens. For twenty and a half centuries we managed to be able to wait and during that hiatus from dawn to dusk produced some astonishing works of scholarship that are still used today (some of them even used instead of the Web). Still, not having to wait (and apparently it is our fate not to want to wait for anything, ever) is seen as one of the 21st century's grandest inventions, and so the Web turns everything into... now.

What this book is about are the dangers inherent in our unwillingness to wait for anything and our Web-cacoëthes. If this book does anything, I hope it will slow us down a bit, if only to get our bearings straight, and open a larger discussion about what we're doing, why we're doing it and what latent and manifest drawbacks we are creating for ourselves and for future generations.

What Is Covered Herein

So, what's in this book? The introduction sets the stage for the overarching fear I have about the perilous times libraries are in today. I'm not much of a prognosticator, but I see a number of things coming together and none of them look like they will make the climate for the future of libraries anything but bleak. Our K–12 education systems may well be the most expensive white elephant ever known to man. We balk at $500 toilet seats for the Department of Defense but seem to be content to pay $1,200 for chalk for teachers, or rather, fund endlessly bad teaching ideas that do not appear to help any student anywhere. I'm not the first to point this out, and even many educators are beginning to agree. The No Child Left Behind Act is yet one more expensive effort to improve what has remained intractable. But what has this to do with libraries?

Just about everything. Amid all this has come the Web, boasting just about everything it can and delivering not quite half. Among my own profession are those who wish to get rid of books regardless of what patrons want. With less than 5 percent of all books on the Web, many are saying we can be done with them. This decline in teaching coupled with a growing and alarming decline in reading have led to a decline in overall literacy. The point the introduction makes is one that I fear most: the generation that built grand libraries has left them to a generation that does not care for them, doesn't understand what they're for, and thinks everything is on the Internet anyway. Libraries are obsolete and let's be done with them, or so it would appear is the attitude to which we are heading.

Chapter 1 tackles the information available on the Web. We seem to be unable to make a distinction on the Web between information — random data — and knowledge, the latter something libraries have always collected and organized. The chapter looks at the Web's disinformation and how abounding it is. Next up is the Web's misinformation, and it appears to be even more overwhelming. This is followed by the Web's uncanny ability to revive hate groups of all kinds so that some offbeat group with ten followers, once on the Web, can gain hundreds. A number of examples are given. Finally fraud is treated: in e-mails, in business, in medicine and so on. Fraud is everywhere electronically because electronic access is everywhere. The problem is now a billion dollar business loss and threatens us more each day with loss of dollars, loss of identity, and loss of just about everything else.

Chapter 2 looks at how the Web presents so-called information. The first time we do a search using a search engine and see 5,100,000,324 hits in 3.2 seconds, we are exhilarated and shout, "Wow, fantastic!" Then we begin wading though the first twenty and shout something else, more likely an "expletive deleted." I point out that the same can be done with any library. If a patron asks any question at all, anyone could point to a library and say, "It's in there." Bad reference librarians notwithstanding (and there are some), that's not really an answer. And a jillion "hits" from search engines aren't either. I point out that much is not on the Web, search engines do not search all the Web, bias is everywhere in searches, relevancy ranking creates it own mare's nest, and that any fool can put anything up on the Web — and with more than 8 billion pages on the Web, it would appear that just about every fool has… at least twice. My point here, as in all chapters, is that this medium, the Web, really in its infancy, isn't ready to do the work of a real library, and it is doubtful that it will ever rise to that level of importance.

Chapter 3 treats the single most popular content on the Web: pornography. We have, as a nation, always been awash in pornography. With the advent of the Web, we are now a planet drowning in it. No sane individual really believes that the First Amendment allows or protects pornography. I treat in this chapter the incredible filthy glut of the Web's pornographic reach, its perfidious value to sexual predators, and its gormless encouragement of all of us to seek our lowest common denominator. For all the putative good the Web has done for businesses, my guess is that it has done an equal amount of harm, what with employees surfing porn when they aren't playing games, checking athletic events, or e-mailing the insipidities from the Web's latest, YouTube. The Web isn't democracy in action; it is the fulfillment of a kakistocracy, a rule of the worst. The scope of this book does not allow for a full treatment of filters but I mention them in this chapter. The unwillingness of libraries to filter is silly and wrongheaded. If they continue I predict it will be their undoing.

Chapter 4 treats a little known problem on the Web, link rot. Link rot, as might be guessed by its name, is a process whereby links to important facts simply disappear. For those who track such things, the duration of most links on the Web is between 18 and 36 months. Like root rot, link rot threatens to erase the good that the Web provides by making most of that good writ on water. Certainly its presence on the Web does not bode well for preservation, unless we wish to redefine preservation as saving something for only 36 months. Proprietary databases do not have link rot per se, but some of them simply choose to cut off the footnotes as too bothersome to piddle with.

Chapter 5 examines Google's capture of just about everything digital, worries about placing too much control in the hands of too few, and then closely examines the idea of mass digitization, brought to the foreground by Google's desire, really from its inception, to digitize all the world's books. The blatant disregard Google has for copyright and for preservation, along with a few other details, makes me wonder why we are rushing like mad to this dubious goal. Bear in mind that Google is a company that plans to bring us ubiquitous enlightenment via these books, and then goes out and spends more than a billion dollars for a company that runs clips of the stupidest stunts known to humankind. Frankly, I'm not encouraged, but I'm sure I'm missing the sheer intellectual value of an overweight white principal trying to learn to rap or an idiot teenager trying to set fire to his own flatulence.

Chapter 6 reminds people like me that all of this will work because, by golly, e-books will make it all happen. All the disadvantages of Web-based books are set free by the "onslaught" of e-books. We'll just digitize a book and presto, everyone will have it. In a word, no. E-books have been around for sometime now but have been going nowhere. Even at the height of the dot-coms they could not get off the ground. While they have a kind of niche in reference materials delivered over the Web, things like almanacs and statistical sources, all data one can view to date indicates that few individuals like them, want them or will read them.

Chapter 7 focuses on the grand "paperless society" we were promised about thirty years ago and are still nowhere close to today. The trouble with most Web-based information is that after three pages — if that long — most of us hit the print key. I talk about the process and physiology of reading that means this is inherent in our makeup rather than being merely an issue of which we humans are used to. Perhaps in 100 or more years we'll be able to read online, but for now anyway, we can't do so for long. And by the way, where's a tree-hugger when you really need one? With all the paper being generated by computers you'd think someone from Al Gore's camp would have said something by now. Trouble is, Al invented the Internet, so go figure.

Chapter 8 looks at two things: first, the shallowness of the Web. It may stretch from here to eternity but it really is by and large a mostly modern repository. This is not so much a criticism as it is an observation, but it is one that many users forget. While you can find something twenty years old on the Web, the vast majority of information is recent — about ten years or so. This will continue to change but the current pattern is to drop a year while adding a new one. The incentive to keep really old things on the Web is simply not present in its makeup. The historical record of our culture is being more and more truncated as each year passes. We're not dwarfs sitting on the shoulders of giants. We've simply removed the giants. They were bothersome anyway and tended to make us look smaller than we think we are. The more serious problem with the Web as treated in this chapter is its "snatch and grab" mentality. Thoughtful reflection is really not part of the Web's weltanschauung: it's all data, random bits of information and something for the now of our lives. If it takes more than ten seconds, move on. I look at this phenomenon in connection with reading literacy and how this helps or hinders what our children are doing. In a word, the picture is not a rosy one. The Web isn't the only culprit either, as expensive proprietary databases also suffer from short term memories, rarely archiving more than about 10 or 15 years.

Finally, chapter 9 sums up all that has gone before. I point out that the penetration of the Internet into the world's population is really much smaller (less than 20 percent) than one might think, despite all our protestations to the contrary that everything is on the Web and everyone is, too. I raise concerns about expensive bandwidth, the cost of hardware and software and so on, with the prediction that the saturation of the Web into people's lives will for many never happen. While about 1 in 8 may well be addicted to the Web in this country according to recent studies, in most of the rest of the world, they're just addicted to staying alive. I also point out that Web-based everything will mean nothing for many, and that continued rising costs for its support and continuance could well result in another bubble burst. This is followed by a fairly lengthy survey of what we're really doing on this most indispensable tool. What turns up from looking at about two dozen lists of the "Web's best sites" is not very intellectually encouraging.

Introduction

In a career in academic librarianship that now spans nearly three decades, seldom has a month gone by that some pundit somewhere has not pronounced the book ill, terminal or long since dead as automation grows. Time and again, prognosticator after prognosticator, like so many Daniels reading the wall for all us dimwitted Belshazaars, has declared the book as a format finished, kaput, gone, or going, the way of all flesh. And month after month, year after year, decade after decade, all have been very sadly mistaken. At the very least, the book's staying power has made them look hysterical. Not even the old saw of a stopped watch being right twice has rescued our would-be Nostradamuses. But every age has witnessed the same upheaval about some new technology putting an end to a tried and favored one. As one writer has it, "The rub is, of course, to find any such times," meaning, of course, that all ages have been fraught with peril.[1] The resiliency of the book has proved unbeatable to date, bouncing back again and again, its putative death rattle really a rallying cry.

Predictions Aplenty: Television as the Universal Educator

Not a few technology predictions seemed to have it right, too, but all proved errant in the end. For example, in the fifties, there was the rise of public television. Soon everyone would be able to sit down and learn from the masters: math from whoever the contemporary Einstein was, creative writing from whoever the current Shakespeare happened to be. Gone would be the need for teachers, professors, universities and certainly all libraries. Television would be the great leveler and all would learn from the greatest minds in whatever the age. Of course there was little in the medium then that should have elicited such pronouncements. Was it the sage advice of Gale Storm in "My Little Marjorie" that provoked such ruminations? Could it have been the sagacious barking of Shasta from "The Thin Man" that turned the heads of otherwise intelligent men and women? Who knows, but the prognostications rolled in surfeit. By the time television was giving us "Sock it to me! Sock it to me!" and the imbecilities of "The Six

Million Dollar Man," even the most blockheaded of the prophets knew that medium to be washed up for all but the narrowest of educational purposes.[2] Still, hope springs eternal and every time the Corporation for Public Broadcasting puts together some highbrow version of Dickens's *Bleak House* (the most recent of which was filmed in an odd chiaroscuro patina making it appear that it was filmed by candlelight), orgasmic-like squeals issue from academe as if some great event is now underway once more. Of course those squeals could be less from academe and more from high school students who see it as a chance to avoid reading the book.

Television did little, however, to quash the book-is-dead-doomsayers, and with them, libraries.[3] Not too long after television-as-the-intellectual-messiah came microfilm (and later microforms) as the be-all and end-all of books and libraries. Soon, pundits told us, *everyone* would have a library the size of the Library of Congress (LC), carrying it around in a shoebox, akimbo. No longer would library buildings be needed. No longer would we need those pesky librarians — what was it they did, anyway? — and every home could exchange the great books simply by mailing them to their friends in small envelopes, smaller even than a postage stamp. Oh, what a brave new world we all would live in!

More Predictions: The Library as Shoebox

Soon, however, the idea of Library-of-Congress-as-postcard began to wane when we had to use microforms. They did not prove altogether that easy to use. They were certainly portable, all right. If you wanted to — and only a cataloger would — you could carry around the entire National Union Catalog, and *all* its supplements, in your purse, or oversized wallet. The rub came when you had to read any of those forms (film, fiche, cards). Readers rarely came any smaller than those 19th century armoires not unlike the one C.S. Lewis used to launch the Pevensey children in and out of Narnia. The only difference between those armoires and those readers was that the readers were generally much heavier. Call it catch-22, call Houston with "a problem," but microforms did prove a bit unwieldy.

Undaunted, however, microforms raged on with the addition of reader-printers. This proved something of an improvement. At least one could have a paper copy instead of relying on one's ever diminishing returns known as memory. Still, that "portable library" weighed more than a baby hippopotamus, unless you read it on the book's staple, paper. Even with the poor prognosis, some librarians rushed to meet the new technology as the new messiah by discarding one-of-a-kind documents.[4] Over time microforms became more and more problematic. Of the scores of libraries that bought enormous editions on microforms (or worse, microcards), few used them, and none ever realized anything like a return on investment. Nevertheless, microforms persisted, not as they should — as a means of preservation of rare items that should not see human contact — but as a replacement for them. Silver halide film did not last the hoped-for eternity, but it did last longer than the public-television-as-universal-educator.

Libraries as the Snows of Yesteryear: Compact Disks

"*Nihil Desperandum!*" said the scryers with their ever-cloudy crystal balls. Compact disks rushed to the rescue. *These* disks, we were now told, would usher in not libraries the size of shoeboxes, but the size of credit cards![5] These compact disks unfolded in somewhat hilarious ways. Many libraries purchased huge journals offerings via ProQuest (now a respected Web-based entity). Rolling into libraries was a set up that, like the proverbial 500-pound gorilla, needed a room of its own if you intended to read anything. Often taking up a small corner of the library, these CD-ROM Mini-Cooper-sized reader-printer stations and 200+ CDs proved, let say euphemistically, unwieldy.

Oftentimes the index did not work at all, or pointed to the wrong disk. Of course it was always the *only* disk needed, so retrieving it proved a fun afternoon of sleuthing, not in the typical reference librarian manner, but more in the technobrarian manner. Anyone could do it, so long as he had the patience of Job. When sleuthing was not required — one experience of which lasted a lifetime — the "no image" problem replaced it, meaning that the desired image could not be found, whether by the machine or the disk or both, one never knew. Lost, not yet in cyberspace, but in near-cyberspace, the image could not be retrieved. Risibly, these images might appear once or twice on command only to be invisible a third or fourth time, not at all. The new mini library apparently had been written not with invisible ink exactly, but sporadic invisible ink — now you see it, now you don't — a kind of disappearing ink all the same.

Fixes for such errors never came in what one could call small packages. One might replace the machine one week, the computer the next week or request replacement disks in week three. In an Abbot and Costello "Who's on First?" comedy routine, these disks might work perfectly, or nearly so in year one but not at all in year three. New disks might work new machines, but disks purchased only three years earlier, on no machine known to man. Library life proved a most interesting time, as our Asian friends are wont to say.

In a thing-that-wouldn't-die sci-fi scenario, prophets of the compact disks reminded us ever so frequently not to worry. When blips occurred, and they did, we were told not to worry, just to be happy. When data created on machines five years earlier could not be fully retrieved five years later, all, we were told, would work out. Everything will be fixed ... in the future.

Today's New Education Messiah: The Web

And sure enough, now it has. We enter the 21st century and all has been replaced by the Web or Google or both. It's hard to convey the joy that this age has ushered in for libraries, so readers will be advised to hum Beethoven's "Ode to Joy" or Handel's *Messiah* to prepare themselves appropriately. We are in such a new, such a brave world that many can hardly contain themselves. Libraries will no longer need to be large, no longer need to be in one place. In fact, they may no longer need to be at all. Period. The Web or the 'Net or Google or some facsimile has changed everything!

Perhaps this time, our prophets are right, and that's what worries me. This brief overview has been purposely drawn out, stressing the changes, the predictions and the failures, not to bore the reader but to underscore that claiming a doomsday scenario — something I'm about to do — is not anything anyone should do lightly. Over the past thirty years doomsayers have come and gone in librarianship and almost all of them have been wrong. If not outright wrong, they have certainly been off-base, premature, untutored or all three. The role of the doomsayer is not a role anyone should relish or seek.[6] Librarianship has now come to a point in our history, however, where a doomsayer may be just what's needed. What has changed is not so much new technology that is better or more powerful than technologies in the past. The technology is still just as unreliable as ever. What has changed is our culture. And for that reason, one can approach this crossroads in our history with a furrowed brow with respect to the future of libraries.

Doomsayers Proven Wrong: Another One Bites the Dust!

Our culture? Hasn't every doomsayer of every stripe said this? "Among all the forms of mistake," writes George Eliot, "prophecy is the most gratuitous."[7] Shouldn't restraint be the order of the day since so many naysayers have been wrong? Hasn't life always been going to hell in a handbasket? Why is now any different? Because the evidence, which has been scanty heretofore, appears overwhelmingly unmistakable now. A young man can go to his physician and be warned about genetic factors, cholesterol, fatty foods, weight gain. But at twenty or even thirty, he is still immortal. At forty and certainly at fifty, when cholesterol levels are now seven times our age and our waistlines nearly exceed in inches our ages in years, the handwriting, so faint on the wall at twenty, now seems unmistakably large at fifty even without our bifocals.

Likewise, symptoms of our cultural malaise twenty years ago may have seemed overdone, overdrawn or simply over our heads. For example, in the early eighties, *A Nation at Risk* warned about "the rising tide of mediocrity."[8] Although the report cautioned that our country was more vulnerable to this rising tide than to a menacing power, not much, beyond more words, appeared. Today, however, as we shall see below, the evidence of this report is everywhere around us. While *A Nation at Risk* warned about K–12 failures, the late Allan Bloom's *The Closing of the American Mind* warned about the college-age students and their decline in critical thinking skills. Bloom's book sold millions but apparently only as a coffee table book and not as a prescription for remediation. (Did *anyone* really read it?) Again, as we'll see below, the evidence of most of his claims (and those of others) has come true and is everywhere around us.

What has this got to do with libraries? Only everything. If as argued here the culture favoring libraries has changed to an unfavorable one, and significantly so, the future of libraries, at least as we have always known them, appears increasingly in jeopardy. While some may argue that this may not be a bad thing and yes, the *traditional* library might not survive but *some* form of it will, it is the argument of this book that the technologies competing for that replacement — and make no mistake about it, they are competing — are not at this juncture in our history the right ones to replace anything, and certainly not a library. A time in the distant future may bring a technology that will adequately replace the library and all its services with the right sort of substitution. It is the argument of this book that that time is not now, not yet and definitely not with this technology.

Our Culture, Our Selves

Most astute observers know that our culture has changed. That is not necessarily a bad thing. Times change, people change. But when it comes to libraries, change may well follow the great 18th century historian Edmund Burke's proviso about change: "When it is not necessary to change, it is necessary *not* to change." In the case of our current technologies, changing the library to fit the technology is precisely the wrong way to go. *Adapting* our technology as a tool to serve the library serves both us and the library perfectly. If you look back over our list of prophets, two things jump out at you. First, how many librarians stood ready to jettison the library as if its present state were no longer acceptable. Second, in every case the current technology emerged from the Frederick Taylor school of change: *the one (and only) best way.*[9] This proved the undoing in every case. The library was and is the constant to which one may apply various changes and adaptations, but its core functions remained (and remain) the same. Forgetting this led to the eventual collapse of all newcomers.

Why then is the argument here that we may be witnessing the library's final collapse? First, the culture in which libraries once thrived is disappearing at a rapid rate, replaced by a culture that doesn't want them or understand their importance. Second, those touting the latest new technological panaceas at the very least encourage, if not outright desire, the disappearance of libraries.

Totems to the Totality of Knowledge

At the core of the culture of libraries is, like it or not, reading. As we shall see later, reading (i.e. books) is what most associate with libraries anyway. Our own history has not been scholarly, and even from the beginning of modern librarianship, the warning was clear:

> It is the peculiar vice of librarians more(even more characteristic than their propensity to talk shop(that as they know intimately the backs of so many books, they are likely to persuade themselves that they know its contents as well. The temptation is subtle and powerful, and its operations are not confined to the custodian of books. Let no one deceive himself into thinking that because he knows the royal road to learning, its guide posts, its directories, its ins and outs, the various vehicles that carry men on it, he is necessary [sic] travelling thereon himself. There is no virtue and no praise in this knowledge, if it is not applied to help either oneself or another to actual progress.[10]

That today's librarians have become more technicians than scholars is hardly surprising. But that we persist in eschewing that which makes us what we are — bookmen and women — remains a mystery. If what has made us who we are, if what has given us the first name of our profession begins to falter, the library as a cultural icon may well go with them. But librarians turned info-techs, turned cybrarians, is not at issue here. Should some or all librarians move away, far away from books, others who understand and relish them will take their place. While it is admirable that there are those among us who call for more stress on enthusiastic intellectualism "to improve the deplorable amount of misinformation, or no information, given by at least some reference librarians," the stress here is less on the intellectual make-up of the profession and more on the culture we serve.[11] Should that very culture turn from (or turn on) books, the very usefulness of libraries will ultimately be called into question. What libraries face today is a monumental threat, not only in the guise of a lack of education, but in the transmogrification into a banality of mind.

The Symptoms of Decline: Literacy

We need look no further than supposedly literate young people, whether high school and college graduates, or what passes for same today. Here's but a partial list of what both young people and young adults do not know, as variously reported over the last twelve or so years:

- Two decades following *A Nation at Risk*, reading proficiency of nine to thirteen-year-olds continues to decline;
- Less than 10 percent of all high school juniors can write well enough to meet national goals;
- Some Midwestern states accept agriculture courses as fulfillment for traditional physics and biology requirements;
- Only one in eight thirteen-year-olds can understand and apply intermediate scientific knowledge and principles;
- According to the National Assessment of Educational Progress, only 3 percent of American fourth, eight and twelfth graders can write above a "minimal" or "adequate" level;
- Only 15 percent of college faculty say incoming freshmen are adequately prepared in mathematics;
- Out of 22,000 students tested, 60 percent of high school seniors could not define the Monroe Doctrine, did not understand the political concept of containment, or knew what the term "Camp David Accords" referred to;
- Only one in five nine-year-olds can perform even basic mathematical operations[12];
- Young people can name all or nearly all the seven dwarves but only one or two of the nine Supreme Court Justices.[13]

And this is only the tip of the iceberg. The director of the National Right to Read Foundation argues that, "[I]n practice, what the child believed and felt became more important than what he knew, and schooling became a process of changing students' fixed beliefs instead of imparting substantive knowledge."[14] While this may seem pertinent to a discussion of our nation's K–12 effectiveness (and of course it is), it is devastating news to libraries. On the one hand, it might be argued that such news is good news. Libraries can do what they have always done, act as the intellectual safety net for all whose education is subpar. During our Culture of Reading, however, libraries worked hand-in-glove and were more an addendum to education than its substitute. What one learned in schools could be added to, strengthened, and expanded by libraries. As will be shown, however, in our Culture of Kitsch, reading is no longer encouraged and is often constrained. Not only are young people unable to read, but they are encouraged through our national effort at symbology to favor sound bites, the Morse-code version of reading on the Web, and not to value reading, or at least not to value it in the manner that our culture has heretofore (more about this in chapter 8). Of course not all of these problems stem from the Web, but many are the product of an over-reliance on short bursts of nearly illiterate reading.

Even when we limit the discussion to college students' literacy at the nation's leading Ivy League universities, we find discouraging and disheartening results. Not only are fewer and fewer required courses in science, math and English on the agenda, but they are often replaced by courses that, while imparting a kind of knowledge, may be imparting a knowledge so severe and esoteric as to be very nearly perfectly useless.[15] And do let's forget all the nonsense that young people today are different from their parents or that this generation learns differently. Indeed, a new study now provides clear evidence that young people do not learn any differently, and that their protestations to the contrary, cannot multitask, cannot text message, watch television, listen to their iPods *and* study geometry.[16] Although a 2005 report by the Kaiser Family Foundation found that 60 percent of 7th–12th graders reported multitasking (music, online chatting, television, the phone, all while ostensibly studying) the new report indicates that not only can young people not do this, but they are learning *less because they are trying to do so.* It turns out that our brains have simply not "evolved" beyond where they were when stylus and papyri were the tools of the hour.

More Symptoms: Education as Political Ideology

Without entering the stramash over why these literacy problems persist (and even granting that some of the criticisms by opponents of current schooling methods may be overstated), all critics agree that the problems are real and that their long-term effects are critical to the future of this country.[17] Universities are racked by competing political ideologies that have recently begun to interfere, or at least impede, education.[18] Meanwhile, learning takes a backseat as more and more survey courses are taught by fewer and fewer PhDs in favor of their teaching assistants, or adjuncts who are on campus a few hours each day. Furthermore, we do know of at least one profession where this poor training is beginning to show up: teaching. Over the last decade more than two dozen books (see note 17) have been written chronicling the saga of teacher education schools and the inherent lack of intellectual rigor. These schools, in turn, are those that provide the pool of professionals charged with, among other things, the teaching of reading.

Administrators and some librarians opine that the library must change. Politics from the Right, the Left and the Libertarian seek to remake the library in their own image. As the Right seeks to remold the library politically in an epigone image, the Left seeks to make it the hotbed of social activism. Meanwhile libertarians rush to privatize everything in order to reduce state expenditures to zero, or near zero.[19] While these pressures are being applied, the pressure for the Web to conform to certain delivery modes continues apace, stretching it first one way, and then another.[20]

Although these external stakeholders are more obvious in public libraries, they are not altogether absent from academic ones.[21] When state legislators who fund institutions look for a place to cut, they invariably cut academic libraries because the feeling is mutually agreed upon: the Internet has made, or is making, the library obsolete. Your future is to look forward to working in "information joints," though it is not clear whether these are places to smoke, drink, or whether those who work there are driven to both.[22] Either way, these stakeholders make their presence abundantly clear.

Can all this really have any impact on libraries? It already has. While we see everywhere articles reminding us that young people are living in a digital age, that universities are going to be library-less in the future, we see one or two still clinging to the value of reading.[23] But what belies these articles about the importance of the library is the evidence countering the idea that libraries, and reading, are still valued at all. What is more, there is substantial evidence that not even librarians still value libraries and reading. Administrators, not to mention librarians, are calling for the end of buildings, of books, and calling for "the transmogrification of libraries."[24] The word choice is most interesting. To transmogrify, according to *Webster's*, is to "change completely," that is "to transform, especially in a grotesque or strange manner." And yet the library pundit quoted clearly thought this to be a good thing! Another pundit writes, "It's the end of the library as we know it, and I feel fine."[25] Meanwhile others gleefully "pack up the books" out of undergraduate libraries in favor of "information," as if the two are distinct. Books? Who needs them? Give me a sound bite (or is that byte?) any day.[26]

Yet Another Symptom: Get Rid of Books

This business of "packing up the books" is particularly distressing coming, as it does, from the pen of a library dean, now a library provost, one Fred Heath of the University of Texas libraries in Austin. Of course it should not have come as any surprise that he would not only recommend but actually jettison 90,000 undergraduate books since Heath made his intent known a decade ago.[27] Ten years ago, Heath spoke of "paradigm shifts" and the need to look to a new future of electronic access. It did not matter whether the shift was necessary, only that it could be made. Wrote Heath, "Success [of the new electronic venture he suggests] will require that library administrators around the country boldly step forward and 'blow up' the paradigm in which we now work."[28] Heath succeeded, ten years later, in blowing up the undergraduate library in which he worked. The metaphor is an odd one. "Blowing up" a thing is normally reserved for those things that are broken or pose a menace. Old buildings are blown up because they no longer serve a purpose. Enemies are blown up because they represent a menace, or have become one. Are libraries now one, the other, or both? Heath surely thought the metaphor a good one as blowing up a thing makes way for progress. We blow up mountains for new roads, wooded areas for malls, untouched areas for urban sprawl. More evidence is required, however, to contend that libraries fit any of these categories. It should be pointed out that the books no longer present are in storage and can be retrieved if needed. Of course we all know that they will not be needed (the reasons for which are cited below).

Some may object that the language is too harsh with respect to the explosion in Austin. Heath is certainly not the only one. Recently Valparaiso University in Indiana opened a newly built $33 million library facility, complete with everything, but also with 80,000 *fewer* books.[29] Even though the building is twice the size of the building it replaced, no ugly, old, beat up and useless books will tarnish Richard AmRhein's (dean of library services) new building. We're in a new age and it will not include books. Give us clear, clean new spaces with computers and electronic access, and heaven forbid, get rid of the books, hide them, or at least make them inaccessible.

The petard upon which Heath (and AmRhein) hoisted the undergraduate library has been characterized as such, not only in articles which did not quote him, but in all others that did. The message was clear: in this brave new world, books are no longer needed.[30] Indeed, the library staff in Austin "were taken by surprise" and feared speaking publicly for fear of their jobs.[31] Apparently in this brave new world, *anything* might happen, and if you don't happen to like it, there's the door. The story has a rich irony. A senior business major, a young person for whom such moves we are told must be made, assessed the matter this way: "[T]his is a library — it's supposed to have books in it. You can't really replace books." Au contraire, Virginia, not only is there no Santa Claus, there is also is no library with books.

When librarians doubt their very buildings themselves, we are in serious trouble. It is no secret, for those in the profession, how long and how often librarians have wrestled over their very name. Over the course of my career we have gone from being librarians to information specialists to today's cybrarians. Librarian is not enough any more. Books are inessential. Bytes or bits of *information* are clearly much more important. Ostensibly we did an excellent job of this as the market has now responded. The librarian — as a professional term — can count on making at least 20 percent less than an information specialist, who may well be doing the same job but over the all-important Web. Why many of us (though certainly not all have bowed the knee to Bill) have chosen to run from our well-known moniker is a puzzlement. Why most of us cannot see that this will only spell the doom of *libraries* in the long run is beyond me. Since there isn't anything ready to assume its place, we will see its eradication before we see its replacement (or resurrection).

Another Symptom: Libraries Disappearing

Find this hard to believe? So did media specialists in K–12. Who cared what you called the library so long as you called it something, right? Besides, media centers better described what the old term libraries once defined. Books were still there, of course, but they did not remain alone, or even in the place of preferment. No, alongside them, and soon crowding them out of place, came videos, DVDs, CDs, and computers. Meanwhile, in Europe, media centers, the birth of which prefigured their birth here, eventually replaced libraries in the K–12 equivalent there. Over time it became clear that books did not need to occupy a place of preferment, or even a place at all. Computers took over, along with all things Web-based. Libraries in the European version of the K–12 have all but disappeared.

Eventually administrators took the next "logical" step and decentralized media centers by placing media in the hands of teachers, first in their classrooms and later via Web connections. Slowly, but altogether too effectively, media centers began to vanish until today most K–12 equivalents have nothing that resembles a library at all, or at least only a minuscule version in which books are housed and circulated. Meanwhile, the same evolution grows inexorably in the U.S. Media centers continue to grow while media per se — the Web in particular — expands geometrically and libraries shrink. Most media specialists I have spoken to tell me they are not so much worried about funding as they are about existence.

A Deadly Symptom: The Internet as Ersatz Library

Internet-specific changes pressure libraries to conform to the Web's image. As content providers take over more control of content, as Congress tinkers again with copyright (about which more later), as the cost and need for bandwidth escalates, libraries are forced to decided whether they will buy books or more electronic access.[32] Some readers will doubtless see this as so much good news, as it is, indeed, often reported. But for every change in the Internet, the Internet provider, or the delivery mechanism for the Web, there must be an attendant change in those providing the delivered access. Imagine trying to provide readers access to electronic journals via dial-up! It simply would not work in today's environment. So libraries upgrade, buy new servers, change out memory, increase speed and replace machines every three to five years. None of this, even at reduced prices for hardware, comes cheaply. At the institution where I work we experienced a 500 percent cost increase *in one year* from our Internet provider. While changes have not been so great in recent years, every year we witness a rise in cost. Since many such costs are absorbed outside library budgets (information technology units or from technology funds, for example) these costs are not always figured into the delivery of so-called "inexpensive" access. For every new change in Web access or delivery comes a new round of calls for changes in libraries.

More than one legislator is on record as having argued that eventually there can be one book that can be digitized and "zapped" to all other libraries. Google's mass digitization project has, of course, only encouraged what is to a few a somewhat harebrained idea. But to call it that publicly risks being labeled a Luddite as otherwise intelligent individuals, even in librarianship, either make the same case, applaud Google or make equally absurd claims that libraries need to be more like Google. Long forgotten (but to the point) is the Benton Report funded by the prestigious Kellogg Foundation. Kellogg interviewed "libraries leaders" only to find that many of them either despised the library or did a superb job of hiding their love for it. Most could not wait for the new digital age that of course was "just around the corner." That corner is a long one as we are now nearly ten years since the publication of that report.[33] The fact, however, that many began singing a dirge for the library a decade ago is not a comforting thought.

Finally, the Fatal Symptom: The Decline in Reading

All of this might be discounted, however, as so many other dire predictions have been, if one other trend were not also present. I alluded to it earlier when I mentioned culture in general and now, more specially, let us say it explicitly: *the decline in the culture of reading*. A number of reasons exist for this, none of them passive, and none of them very encouraging.

Part of the blame, but certainly not all, can be put upon K–12 teaching. The teaching of reading, both to practitioners and to our nation's children, has seen some very rough spots.[34] While this is not the place to become embroiled in the reading wars that have wracked our nation's teacher preparation programs, suffice it to say that enough empirical evidence now abounds to prove beyond any shadow of a doubt that the Whole Language approach to reading (used by the vast majority of teacher preparation programs, and by nearly every school system in America), when used alone, all but guarantees a certain substantive amount of reading illiteracy. My own generation saw the beginning of this approach in the famed "Dick and Jane" readers that touted the "look-say" approach.[35]

In *theory* it works, or rather it should. In practice it does not, and students end up hopelessly frustrated bad readers. Most such "readers" cannot read above a very juvenile level and many are intolerably bad spellers. They cannot be entirely blamed. When one has not only not been taught how to spell sounds, but specifically prevented from learning them, devilishly difficult but common English words are mangled at every attempt and eventually avoided. Anyone who has ever taught freshmen English in the last twelve years can attest to this.

Parents, too, must share some of this blame because they do not necessarily model good reading behaviors, and take a decidedly studied lack of attention in their children's school work, though there are some signs of hope to mitigate both inferior schools and confused parents.[36] It may be too little, too late.

Aiding and abetting all this are television and the Internet. We've all known for some time that television is a mindless activity that leaves its worshippers gormless after only a short while. But new evidence reveals that three hours on television and three or more on the Web makes Johnny mostly illiterate.[37] The National Endowment for the Humanities released a shocking study barely two years ago showing a rapid and sharp decline in reading over the last 20 years. Most of that decline occurred over the last ten years.[38] The percentage of adults who read literature dropped in the year of the study, 2002, to 46 percent, down from 57 percent just twenty years earlier. While this substantiates the claim above that parents are not modeling good reading behavior, the drop in reading of 18 to 24-years-olds is even greater. According to Dana Gioia of the NEA, "Literary reading in America is not only declining rapidly among all groups, but the rate of decline has accelerated especially among the young."[39] Gioia goes on to point out why this is important to libraries if it isn't already obvious: "Reading a book requires a degree of active attention and engagement. Indeed, reading itself is a progressive skill that depends on years of education and practice." Years of education and practice. When we lose this in our culture, we lose the will to build places that hold books. We lose the will that requires there be places to house books to engage our minds in a progressive fashion.

Some might argue that literary reading is a different kind of reading and so should not be too alarming. Who really *wants* to read *Wuthering Heights, Erewhon, Vanity Fair* or any number of other "boring" books? But it is the very interconnectedness of reading that makes it important. When one puts down a book as too troublesome or hard to read, he will later put down a newspaper. With the newspaper gone, so go newsletters and any other means that cannot be digested quickly, easily and in sound bite fashion. Indeed, the NEA survey found that "total book reading is declining significantly."[40]

Just how bad is this decline? From almost 60 percent in 1982, to 2002's abysmal 43 percent, young people have all but quit reading. While one cannot say with certainty why this is, the most obvious reasons for this decline are that students simply cannot read well, combined with an increase in both television and Web surfing. Mark Bauerlein, project manager of the NEA report, blames "the proliferation of Internet, e-mail, iPods, and Blackberries."[41] Meanwhile, if all of this were not bad news enough, studies of college-age students reveal similar findings: students do not read, do not want to read, and find reading a labor when they are required to do it.

Although anecdotal, informal surveys I have conducted of faculty who teach honors students reveal the same sad findings. This concurs with the honors students I have taught. Require more than 50 pages a week and one is certain to endure a riot. When combined with the now known fact that the college-aged watch more than three and half hours of television a day (not to mention the same or more hours of mindless Web-surfing), the danger of both disaster and illiteracy is very high.[42] When they aren't watching television, they are blogging, or at least most are. Estimates of the almost 32 million blogs on the Web contend that nearly 60 percent of them are run by 13 to 19-year olds.[43] Read any 100 of them and literacy, or budding Jack Kerouacs, do *not* come to mind. NetGeners are a vocal, sometimes self-absorbed group, but they are not readers or writers in the traditional sense. Before someone argues that that's just the point — they are meant to be unconventional — bear in mind that these unconventional habits are drawing them away from literacy. *We live in an age where the culture that built libraries has been inherited by one that does not, or cannot, use them, and is increasingly seeing them as useless.* That some are seeing libraries as pointless should come as no surprise.

Nor is it just reading, or its lack, that should trouble us. Many of these same young people are not volunteering, not involved with anyone else, and are not well-versed with the real world going on around them.[44] For example, among high Internet users in the young adult category, only 11 percent use it to keep up with the news. The remaining numbers (82 percent) say they watch television. About 20 percent still read a newspaper every day compared with their peers in 1972, of whom almost half did. Of incoming freshmen at UCLA, only 34 percent see keeping up with politics as important, about half as many as their hell-no-we-won't-go peers in the 1970s.[45] This might come as good news if only we could be sure the news they do get is not entirely limited to "The Daily Show with Jon Stewart" and others like it.

Should we think that this loss in reading is not so big a deal, that same NEA report indicates that declines are present in what many would consider related activities: museum visits, volunteer work or visiting historic sites. While 96 percent of the adult population surveyed watch at least one hour of television a day (and almost half watch three hours or more) only 45 percent have ever *read* a play, only 17 percent were ever *seen* a play or an opera, and not even a third have seen a live performing arts activity.

Some will doubtless complain that this is simply a snob factor, a measure of elitism. Only the hoity-toity bother to do such things anyway, will be the brush-off. This is just a report indicating that people are no longer elitist, we'll be told. This charge may well be true, but it is the contention here that visiting libraries is, for better or for worse, considered an "elitist" activity. Furthermore there is now evidence that this decline in reading and in cultural activities in general is affecting other areas specifically. A new report from Great Britain reveals what many have long thought: children are less able when compared to their peers of yesteryear, especially in math skills and scientific knowledge.[46] The report indicates that in the UK 11- to 12-year-olds are now on average two or three years behind where that same age group was only 15 years ago. Does anyone need to be reminded that 15 years ago neither this country nor the UK was routinely generating many would-be math or science geniuses? To say the picture is a bleak one for the future of libraries is an understatement.

Declines in Reading Mean More Overall Educational Decline

But the picture is bleaker still. New reports indicate that while young girls may be lagging in the hard sciences, young boys are behind in nearly every subject. A national hand-wringing has occurred over the lack of young women entering the hard sciences but so far only deafening silence over the academic state of young boys.[47] In a 100-plus-page report examining academic progress by gender, we find young boys are 50 percent more likely than girls to repeat elementary grades, more than one-third more likely to drop out of high school, and twice as likely as girls to be identified with a learning disability. In only ten years —1992–2002 — girls have out-performed their male counterparts in reading and writing by a widening and disheartening gap. By the time boys reach high school, assuming they do, they are far less likely to be considered "college material" than females. It's too early to say what the problem is precisely, but some early indications indicate that it may well have something to do with too much time in front of the television, too much time on the Internet and too much time with video games and iPods.[48]

Summing Up: What's It All Mean?

So, what, really, does this have to do with libraries? Let's see what we have. First, there have been many reports over the last thirty years about libraries and their decline. Over the last four decades more than one pundit has argued that libraries are changing and vanishing at the same time. Surely we need not worry now. We can be optimistic that, like all the other times in the past when critics have sounded the tocsin, the eventual result was the proverbial, "Where's the fire?" We've seen the so-called smoke before but with not attendant fire. Libraries and culture will remain the same as both always have. Don't be so sure.

During all these changes, *librarians* have been at the vanguard of the complaints about libraries. In many ways, the physicians of said buildings have complained that the patient is sick and in grave danger. On the heels of all these problems comes another: a generation whose reading preparation is dreadful to the extent that said generation is less and less likely to read at all. This generation, now grown, does not read as much as its predecessors and now has given birth to yet another generation with even poorer reading skills than before. Their models of behavior are parents with poor reading skills. Couple this with an educational system that does not discourage reading but has so ill-equipped them with the skill to read that they could not even if they wanted to.

Added to all this is a new culture consisting of some who do not speak English as their native language, and others who do not speak it well (though it may well be their native tongue).[49] Now mixed within our culture is a native-born group that cannot read well and finds even the simplest of reading matter a struggle, placed alongside a non-native English group that may not know even the simplest of English phrases. As was mentioned earlier, the culture that built libraries has now been inherited by a culture that does not know how to use them, does not know what to use them for, and does not see any reason for lamenting their passing.

In the midst of all this comes the Internet, a fast, easy-to-use means of getting around this problem temporarily: these individuals can simply surf to places of comfort: areas where they will understand what is there, remain unchallenged, and gather information, misinformation and disinformation at their leisure.

Undergirding all this change has been a legislative and political one that has discovered what librarians have known all along: libraries are financial black holes to operate even minimally. Calls to cut budgets, to raise taxes or both have pressured legislators to look for costly expenditures to eliminate. Libraries loom as large, distressing, costly enterprises begging to be cut. Costly libraries exist in a cultural climate where Web-fixated individuals no longer see their value and so do not bother to come to their aid.

Libraries Are Obsolete

If all of this were not enough, librarians, legislators, know-nothings and the rest rush to the fore to argue that *the Internet is making libraries obsolete because "everything" is on the Web*. It's one thing to hear legislators say this; it is at once humiliating and defeating to hear librarians say it, or say nothing in reply.

I see the juxtaposition of all these "planets" forming a deadly syzygy in the galaxy of libraries. I see these turn of events as so powerful, so overwhelming, that the life expectancy of libraries as we know them is doubtful at best, and their death a foregone conclusion at worst.

The remainder of this book is an argument against the idea that one of the most deadly of the choices, the Web, is the one best solution to replace libraries. I single out the Web and all its attendant glory because it combines so many symptoms together to make for serious disease indeed: poor reading, disinformation and misinformation, and ease of putative solution. But this book it is more than just a series of arguments outlining the defects of the Web. In point of fact, the Web, *as a tool and nothing more,* can aid us in the pursuit of better cultural health. As a tool, the Web is useful; as a substitute it spells out a terrible future. Unfortunately, the Web is rarely billed as a tool. Rather, it is being billed all too often as a magic pill to cure all of our diseases. So this book is an extended argument that we cannot, we must not, allow anyone to think the Internet is a substitute for a library. It is nothing more than a tool, and, as we shall see, a very flawed one at that.

1

Caught in the Web

It's Saturday, but it may as well be called errand-day because that's all you'll be doing. You're in a hurry and you've got lots to do. Soccer practice for Julie is in an hour. Jim's violin lesson is at the same time so you must drop Julie off at the field first. After that, it's the cleaning and the hardware store and the ... well, you get the picture. So you hop in your car, drive to the nearest and most familiar grocery store (you don't want to spend all your time wandering the aisles looking).

Morality Play

You rush into your favorite store only to discover a much-improved way of shopping. Everything is in a heap and you must find a free computer in order to choose what you want. At the check-out counter your groceries will be waiting. *Now this is more like it!* Or so you think. You rush over to the first open terminal, type in what you want, and, some moments later, hurry over to the checkout line. Before you can say, "Chateaubriand for two," you have enough food in your basket to make the feeding of the five thousand seem like lunch for two. Everyone around you is raving over this new system and even you think it has much to commend it. After all, you've done the week's shopping in less than five minutes.

Then you begin to sort through what you must take home.

The first item is not what you ordered. You asked for milk and you've got a "Got Milk" commercial. The second is close but it's still not exactly right — you wanted shampoo and instead you got the Warren Beatty DVD by that name. The third item, corn, is right but you discover it's just the shucking on the corn; there's no corn inside. Puzzled, you pull it back to discover it's *fake* corn, a joke. Hahahaha. The next item is an ad for erectile dysfunction you didn't even request.

All the nonfat food you ordered is mixed in with fat-filled food enough to kill an army, not of one, but of one million. The ripe dates you ordered are really a couple of guys from the back who were putting up stock. What the heck is your husband going to say!? Did you really just *pay* for them? Forget what your husband will say; what will the rabbi think?

Seriously confused, you jump about a third of the way into this morass of food and discover that some of the food is spoiled, some is plastic and some of it is really fodder, as in food for animals. Still, all around you people are raving over how great this is and how they wished *everything* could be just like this. If you even begin to raise an objection to point out some of the flaws, you are immediately cast as an anti-food-ite and frowned upon, even snickered at behind a sleeve or two. When you presume to say even one thing, even a small thing that's wrong, everyone you know, or almost everyone you know, rushes forward to tell you that you don't understand, you just don't get it, why are you living in the dark ages, and why don't you wake up and join the 21st century. They shake their heads and tell you you're just one more spoiled cumquat (which, by the way, you discover you've just paid for) on the food chain.

Embarasses des Riches

Some will wonder what this scenario is all about and what the heck it has to do with libraries. Others, seeking a theme, will complain that this is not how Google (or Hotbot, or Yahoo! or Lycos or ... fill in the blank) really works. Others still will dismiss this chapter as one more bit of evidence in the court's brief against the author's blatant Luddite tendencies. Some will blush with chagrin. "Oh my," they'll say, "and in *our* profession. Didn't twenty-plus years in this profession teach him *anything*?"

But is this really any different from our current state of Google-affairs? Consider the average patron who walks up to Google and types in a word or a phrase. Before you can say nanosecond, 1,546,765,326,872 hits are returned in 3.245 seconds in a list filled with what is purported to be information on the subject matter, *ad rem*. But is it? A quick aperçu reveals that the first thirty hits are a mixed bag of quasi-appropriate hits. Some are hate sites. Some are horseshoe close, but misses all the same. Some are outright misinformation while others are just woefully misguided. You cannot begin to fathom why some are there; they just turned up. Still others are right in many ways, but you have still have a sinking feeling that they are not really the best, just what turned up first. Besides, there are, literally, millions of them. After the hate groups and the — how shall we say this to prevent the Luddite charge? — the possibly usable but not quite right hits, you have the pornography, misinformation, disinformation and, eventually, some useful materials.

Only the Near-Best and Almost-Useful

Getting to useful information isn't quite so hard, but would anyone argue that even the useful information is the best? If a student does a search on abortion and finds www.naral.org near the first of the list, all is fine information if she doesn't want any balance on the subject. But balance is the last thing someone who wants information fast and easy is going to stress about. A search about abortion (or smoking or gun control) in Google turns up dozens of sites that are useful but only when used with their counterparts. This is easily done giving a student a book that looks at both; but much harder when he or she clicks on whatever comes up first or second and does not bother with third or fourth.

Too many hits is one of the smaller problems. Other problems abound, e.g., misinformation, disinformation, hate groups, fraud and pornography. We'll look at the first four of these in turn and save pornography for a separate chapter. But a brief word before we proceed.

Fending off the Luddite charge is never an easy one, and virtually (no pun intended) anyone who criticizes the Web, Google or both is sure to be labeled as such. Pointless as it may seem to some, let me hasten to say I not only use the Internet, but I use it daily, seven days a week, 365 days a year, and have since 1992. While I claim no techie's specialist knowledge of the Web, I know something about knowledge, and it is about knowledge that this chapter (and in large measure this book) holds its brief. If we define *knowledge* as any bit of datum, right or wrong, factual or not, fraudulent or accurate, then I accept the charge of Luddite because I do not define it as such. That is a definition of *information*. And if this is the definition of information that we want, then, yes, the Web should replace all libraries. On the other hand, if knowledge includes something about accuracy, appropriateness, balance and value, then the Web cannot arrogate to itself a place of preeminence to knowledge-seekers.

For example, if as a user I want to know where in Nashville, Tennessee, a street called Tammany Drive is, handing me a gazetteer is not going to rank high as an answer. Indeed, in many ways it is worse than an answer. It merely provides me with the answer to a question I did not pose. The more I use the Internet via Google or any one of a dozen other search engines, I find that the answers — millions of them — tend along these lines. Sure, the Internet is very powerful, it is very capable, and much of what you find on it *can be* useful and reliable. But not everything, and not even most things. Moreover, not everything, contrary to popular belief, is on the Web; nor is what's there the *best available knowledge*. And though it surely sounds heretical, the Web isn't always the fastest way to find some kinds of information. Some proprietary databases (though they, too, as we'll learn in a later chapter have their problems), such as *Academic Search Premier, InfoTrac, Lexis-Nexis* and many others that could be named, have far better information than the open, unfettered Internet; and the information there is far more reliable. The unfettered Web has significant problems, however, and it is to these problems that we now turn.

Missing Misinformation

When searching Google, information-seekers will inevitably come across an online, open access encyclopedia called *Wikipedia*. Once there, they often never go anywhere else. It's bookmarked on their computers for frequent, repeated uses. In classes I teach on searching the Web, I often ask students how many use *Wikipedia*. Three years ago, less than a fourth of those in any class polled indicated they used it consistently. In classes polled in late 2005 and early 2006, more than three-fourths did; and for over half it was the *only* source they consulted regularly. Out of more than 100 students I asked, *only one* knew anything about how *Wikipedia* worked, or that its information could be manipulated by those who did not know anything about the subject matter. This seems low for the college-aged, but what in the world are we to do about students not yet in college?[1] While picking on *Wikipedia* is easy, this holds true for any community-built reference work, and there are a few online. But *Wikipedia*, by synecdoche, will serve for all.

Wikipedia has more than 3 million articles in more than 200 languages. It's easy to use and covers just about everything from antiquity to contemporary popular culture. In late 2005 an entry for one, John Seigenthaler, Sr., a one-time administrative assistant to Robert Kennedy and now well-known publisher, set off an online brouhaha. Seigenthaler's biography linked him to the assassination of both Robert and his brother JFK.[2] How was such a thing possible?

Less than a week after the story appeared, *Wikipedia* tightened its submission policy and many would now say that we should no longer be bothered by it. Of course the question arose — and still remains — how many more articles are suspect, and whether there would have been any inquiry if the story had never appeared.[3] Welcome to the information superhighway!

What the *Wikipedia* story revealed is the flawed nature, not just of how stories are developed in that source, but the whole architecture of the Web. No one would argue that bad information does not get into books — the James Frey fiasco is a good case in point.[4] But *Wikipedia* serves to indicate that the Web as an ultimate or primary source is an untutored approach to looking for reliable information. In the interest of full disclosure, it should be pointed out that *Wikipedia* is not without merit, or that it is completely unreliable, at least in some contexts.[5]

Immediately following this information fiasco, *Wikipedia* addressed this concern of bad or false information interlarded with good accurate information in this open-source tool.[6] The new anyone-can-edit policy restricts some entries entirely, while making others partially restricted. While *Wikipedia* officials call the bogus or inaccurate information "a minimal problem, a dull roar in the background," it serves to point out how much information-seekers are willing to put up with so long as it's delivered over the Web. This charge of error does not address *Wikipedia*'s problem of poor grammar and inconsistent proofreading in many of its entries. If all these disclaimers were not enough, consider what one finds on the "Cite" pages of the encyclopedia. There appears the following note as if it were the most commonplace admission in the world:

> Most educators and professionals do not consider it appropriate to use tertiary sources such as encyclopedias as the sole source for any information — citing an encyclopedia as an important reference in footnotes or bibliographies may result in censure or a failing grade. *Wikipedia* articles should be used for background information, as a reference for correct terminology and search terms, and as a starting point for further research.
>
> As with any community-built reference, there is a possibility for error in *Wikipedia*'s content — please check your facts against multiple sources and read our disclaimers for more information.

Such a note is astonishing on so many levels that it's hard to know which ones to address and which to leave out. First, it's news to many educators and professionals that encyclopedias are not worthy reference sources. While the argument about *Wikipedia* can easily be made that *it* should not be the sole source, to make a blanket statement about all encyclopedias is to exclude about half or more of every reference collection in every library in the world. For example, the statement means excluding the *Encyclopedia Britannica*, perhaps one of the most respected sources for accuracy the world over. It would exclude Mircea Eliade's most important *Encyclopedia of Religion*, or his predecessor James Hastings's excellent *Encyclopedia of Religion and Ethics*. It would also exclude some single-source encyclopedias, such as the Frederick Hoxie's *Encyclopedia of North American Indians,* or Stanley Sadie's magisterial *Grove Dictionary of Music and Musicians*, or the fabulous *International Encyclopedia of the Social Sciences*, and so on.[7] If the preposterous assertion were true, it would mean that much of the work of the 19th and 20th centuries would be inutile. It would mean Diderot's famous beginning has come to a sad end. This may well be democracy at its most open and free, but it does remind one of the making of sausage: it's best not to watch.

But look at the other subtle but equally fatuous assertion that "as with any community-built reference" it cannot be relied upon. Outside of *Wikipedia*, there are no other community-built encyclopedias that allow open access for everyone to update as one sees fit. The *Stanford Encyclopedia of Philosophy* (SEP), for example, is a community-built encyclopedia, but it has made every right decision about that process where *Wikipedia* has made, so far as can be ascertained, every wrong one. For example, one could recommend SEP to any student without reservation; one could not recommend *Wikipedia* under any circumstance without numerous qualifiers and a promise that collaboration would be necessary for every entry. This is unfortunate because clearly *Wikipedia* has numerous well-trained and qualified scholars. But because it chose to add the chaff to the wheat, it has made all suspect.

Indeed, even after the Seigenthaler fiasco, *Wikipedia* came under the scrutiny of scholars about its accuracy.[8] One scholar, Alexander M. Halavais, had taken on an assumed name for the expressed purpose of undermining *Wikipedia*'s veracity. In all, before he called a halt to his shenanigans, he had hijacked more than a dozen articles. He knew no on would check his false credentials, and no one did. More telling than Mr. Halavais's ruse is the action of *Wikipedia*'s own co-founder, Larry Sanger, who has turned on his creation for another, *Citizendium*, a site that required scholarly research and the usual academic vetting. Here's a novel idea: is it possible that creating a reliable, trustworthy and scholarly tool requires scholars and funding? Could it be that reliable, trustworthy collections require libraries, librarians and funding? It's only in movies that characters can exclaim, "Hey, kids, let's create our own spaceship," and have anyone take them seriously.

For how many print encyclopedias have issues of accuracy, quality, and scholarship ever been a consideration, given the meticulous fact-checking that takes place? It is an odd confluence of events in the online medium that allows for the format of information to dictate to us our acceptance of it *regardless of its accuracy or reliability*. Granted, for many adults (but recall the study *Decline in Reading* in the introduction), *Wikipedia*'s shortcomings are easily overcome, or ignored.[9] But what about young people? Are we steeped in Google blood so far that we'll accept "less than accurate" as a definition of "information" (I'll dispense with the knowledge distinction)? It would seem so.

21st Century Flat-Earthers?

Recently I listened to an exuberant Thomas Friedman (he of the rightly famous *The World Is Flat: A Brief History of the Twenty-First Century*) extol Web resources as he made his compelling case disproving Christopher Columbus. He was speaking at the National Book Festival and applauding the virtues of *Wikipedia's* vastness and its ubiquity as evidence that the world is flat.[10] Amid all his hoorahs, however, he never once mentioned this flaw, or any others regarding the Web. Later that same week I listened to *Seven Revolutions,* a brilliant if depressing documentary about the future of the world. With equal enthusiasm, Erik R. Peterson quoted approvingly Nicholas Negroponte's claim that every issue of every volume of the *New York Times* since its inception could be delivered to laptops in every country on earth in a matter of seconds.[11] Again, all praise, no problems. The Web has, of course, the ability to deliver grand feats, and we are right to marvel at them. But it struck me that while it's true that all these *New York Times* issues can be delivered that quickly, going into even a modest library delivers ten times that amount of information in however long it takes you to walk into the building. The trouble with *both* scenarios is that you still have to read them *one at a time*, one word at a time, not to mention needing some way to access the best ones that address your inquiry.

Wikipedia is but one example. The greater Internet is a more serious problem. There are at least five causes of Web misinformation, including scholarly misconduct, a broad heading that includes falsification, fabrication and plagiarism.[12] The most celebrated recent case is J. Hendrik Schon's. A one-time shoo-in for the Nobel Prize for physics in 2002, Schon, it was discovered just before the prize was announced, had fabricated his data.[13] He did not receive the prize and was fired from his job at Bell Laboratories. While his scholarly misconduct was widely announced in print, even today one can find his research on the Web far more easily than one can find his dismissal, or even a recanting of that research. Even taking into account human error, the Web is far less likely to issue a recall as one would in a text (as for example Knopf did on Michael Bellesiles's book *Arming America*).[14] Of course one of the many reasons the Web is touted is its open access freedom. This also leads to one of its defects: lack of quality control. It is under no one's purview to track down the bad information on the Web and weed it out. Given the nature of Schon's work — light physics — even most adults would not be the wiser.

Abounding Bias

Other reasons for the Web's misinformation abound: bias, currency, unintentional removal, the Web's "anonymous and egalitarian nature" and so forth.[15] Currency as a defect will surely puzzle some, as the Web is often cited as preferable over print because *it is* so current. But any regular user of the Web will instantly recognize this as a problem. Some sites are left unattended for so long that information is no longer accurate or has become badly outdated. Because it's on the Web, however, many will think it current (see the Johns Hopkins case, below). This does not even begin to touch the problem of archiving information on the Web, or of accessing what is referred to as "the invisible Web" (more about this in the next chapter). Various electronic versions doubtless make their way onto the Web, but which one is the official, or more official, version and which one should be used as definitive?[16] Because it is still on the Web, it is there for the unwary to use. With more than eight *billion* Web pages and millions and millions of *daily* users, just how much misinformation are we sharing as fact?

Three examples illustrate the Web's misinformation problem. After the downing of TWA Flight 800, investigations began immediately. The most curious occurred when Pierre Salinger held a press conference to accuse the Defense Department of having shot the plane down during training. Most viewed this incredulously, and fact checkers proved them right when they discovered the information had come from a conspiracy site. Salinger eagerly rushed forward his "'Net-borne" conspiracy and embarrassed himself with his outrageous claim.[17] (What is equally disconcerting is the number of people who believed him to begin with!) A better known example is one surely known by all readers. Nearly every Web-connected user has seen the e-mail urging friends not open certain e-mails with key words in them because doing so will shut down their computers. It's impossible for a virus-infected e-mail to shut down a computer simply by being opened, yet many thousands *still* believe it and forward it to thousands of friends.[18] These examples only underscore how easy it is for even intelligent people to be fooled by the Web's ubiquity and currency of "information."

Stupid Web Tricks

Even major news organizations can be duped. In 2002, the highly regarded Associated Press reported that PETA (People for the Ethical Treatment of Animals) had outfitted more than 400 deer in orange vests so hunters would mistake them for other hunters and not shoot them.[19] Guy Lockey, a sporting goods store owner, offered a reward for each vested deer bagged. Although the story is just crazy enough to fit the usual PETA *modus operandi,* trapping a live, wild deer and fitting it with a vest is next to impossible. Moreover, Guy Lockey is a fictitious name. But if it came off the Web, so it had to be true, right?

The fourth example is the well known one that occurred at Johns Hopkins and represents the limits of the Web, falling under the heading of "what you don't know can hurt, perhaps even kill you." Ellen Roche, a seemingly healthy 24-year-old, volunteered for an asthma study at the well-known and highly regarded institute. After entering the study, she was given a drug protocol that had been vetted, or so it seemed, by the researchers. She inhaled a chemical treatment, hexamethonium, that led to the progressive failure of her lungs and her kidneys.[20] This sad case is made all the more tragic because it could easily have been averted. The supervising physician, Dr. Alkis Togias, made what appeared to be a thorough search of the literature. He approved the drug as did the ethics panel who reviewed his research methodology. But Dr. Togias relied heavily on PubMed, an electronic source that only goes back to 1966. A traditional print search would have found articles published in the 1950s that warned against using this drug in such experiments for the very reason that Ms. Roche died: rapid, progressive lung and kidney failure. Togias relied on PubMed and even did a Google search on hexamethonium. But his search did not reveal the inherent danger with his drug protocol, though the warning existed in the citations section of *Poison Index Toxicologic Management*. These citations are on the Web but are not easily found by inexperienced searchers.

Certainly many medical librarians would have found them doing the searches they normally do. Indeed, two medical librarians did re-do the search using only Web-based sources and found the warnings against the drug, though it was mostly easily and quickly found doing a print-based search. While this is admittedly a narrowly defined case, it raises a most serious issue. If we rush forward into cyberspace, ignoring the value of a full-service library, what other dangers, less deadly of course, are we opening ourselves up to? This is one case we know about. How many less deadly but nevertheless equally misguided cases will emerge as time goes on?

Pinchbeck and Ormolu

The anonymous and egalitarian nature of the Web is also a problem. Everyone knows how easy it is to put up a Web site these days. Indeed, it is so easy, even elementary school students are doing it. But nothing prevents pranksters from placing authentic-seeming sites online for the unwary to use. *The Onion* is a well-known and humorous Web site known by most, but not by everyone. Some of its most outrageous stories have been reported as true in papers in other countries. The well-known site about dihydrogen monoxide did not have to leave this country to dupe others. Some who stumbled upon the site began pestering Congress about the dangers of what turned out to be water.

Because the Web is so easy to use as a publishing medium, because there is no gate keeping, because there are no fact-checkers, misinformation is inevitable. Some may argue that these misprisions are small and on balance unworthy of our attention. But consider the work of the South Korean researcher Woo Suk Hwang. Hwang's ground-breaking stem cell research held center stage for many months. It was even used as evidence to criticize the Bush administration's policy on stem cell research, though that policy did not deviate from that of Bush's predecessor.[21] Only in late 2005 was it discovered that Hwang had fabricated his research. Lately, his taciturn partner, Gerald P. Schatten, has been implicated as well.[22] Some may see this as a marginal complaint against the Web; others will be rightly bothered when the Web's research begins to influence social policy. In a less Web-based delivery of information, it is unlikely Hwang's research would have made it through all the hoops before being reported as bogus. The Web's instant gratification attribute makes certain many bogus claims will be made before it is learned that they are, in fact, specious.

None of these are reasons for shutting the Web down, of course, and no argument is being made here for quality control. But these are serious enough offenses to surely give intelligent people pause. At the very least, these reasons appear more than adequate to explain why we do not want the Web to become our only or main information portal for serious research. These missteps should be enough to explain why we withhold our enthusiasm for the Web as a primary information resource as a rival to a good library. It's too late to put the genie back in the bottle, but perhaps it's not too late to point out that at least one of the genie's three wishes is a curse masquerading as a wish.

Deceptive Disinformation

A more serious problem for the Web is its host of disinformation sites. It's odd talking about disinformation in what is the freest, most democratic nation on earth, but apparently the "egalitarian" (I'm being diplomatic here) nature of the Web allows even the poster country for democracy to support, if only indirectly, disinformation as powerful as what was once commonplace under the former Soviet Union. Under the Communist regime, whether in the former Soviet Union or any one of its satellite countries, disinformation became a staple product. *Pravda*, the official Soviet newspaper, published disinformation daily as did many other government-backed news outlets. For example, when Gorbachev visited this country, he, along with other previous Soviet rulers, stared in disbelief at our ... supermarkets. The official Soviet line had been that most of our people could not get the most basic of products. When my wife and I taught English for a month in Hungary, we witnessed this firsthand. Our students were from Romania, Bulgaria, Georgia (the country, not the state) and many other former Soviet-satellite countries. They could not believe we could go to any number of stores to get staple products. One Bulgarian student thought my wife and me among the richest people in the U.S. because we owned four cars, one for each of us and our two college-aged daughters. When I explained that this was quite common in the U.S., she was incredulous. That's *not* what they had been taught.

Disinformation is a useful tool either to keep people ignorant, or simply to mislead. Unfortunately, the Web is filled with such sites, and unwary users of the Web encounter them all the time. Some readers, no doubt, have seen the e-mail arguing that hard coughing is a good heart attack preventive if one is alone and cannot get good medical help. This e-mail circulates from time to time. The American Heart Association does not endorse this as a life-saving method; yet only a month ago, I received it for the umpteenth time. While not unequivocally wrong, it is misleading enough to endanger the health of some who view it as a safe alternative. Chat rooms and Web sites provide information that supports those with eating disorders.[23] Sites like "Anexoric and Proud" and "Anexoria Nation" give out information that anyone can read and try for themselves. Does anyone think this disinformation is read and ignored?

But coughing to prevent a heart attack is an example of a more benign sort of disinformation. More serious are sites claiming that AIDS is a virus released by our own government to target certain race groups.[24] Has this crackpot theory been successful? Unfortunately, it cannot be dismissed as the harmless ravings of an overheated imagination. It is estimated that about 33 percent of African Americans believe it was created by the Department of Defense as a "genocidal agent against blacks" while *another* third are not sure if it's true or not.[25] That's more than half of all black Americans! This sort of disinformation not only increases the risk of those who practice unsafe sex, but further weakens already tenuous race-relations present in this country.

Some will argue that the Web cannot be blamed for this. The same sort of thing could have been done in print. Can it? Of course it can, but it is unlikely to get as a wide a circulation, or ever be as widely known as it is in its Web-based clothing. Even if printed, it would likely have to go the way of vanity presses and thus be immediately doubted by most. Moreover, no unsubstantiated claim would ever be included in a library. Most such claims come from the highly untrustworthy publishers that libraries avoid. Not so on the Web. See for example www.apfn.org/apfn/aids2.pdf, where readers are warned that they are being "hoodwinked" from this "manufactured virus." The site showcases as "proof" a Department of Defense appropriations bill for $10 million in 1970 that funded this research "concocted at Fort Derrick."

Spam, the *Really* Inedible Kind

Other such sites abound. Has anyone using the 'Net regularly missed getting the "Nigerian scam" e-mail? This purports to provide the reader with millions if he will simply reply to the e-mail with the appropriate information about his bank accounts. It cannot be argued that these scams are harmless (see fraud, below). Other sites argue that Bill Gates, the Microsoft genius, was murdered on December 2, 1999.[26] Why aren't these sites shut down or lawsuits filed? Most of these are of unknown provenance and with no names, there can be no lawsuits. Meanwhile, the unsuspecting Web user *will* encounter them. Meanwhile, the official professional librarian group, the American Library Association, not only touts the Web but encourages its members to make their library portals "more like Google."

Perhaps some will argue that even these examples are harmless. What is not harmless, however, is the number of Web sites that encourage illegal drug use — not to mention abuse — with little or no mention of any possible harmful side effects. The Web is full of sites that not only endorse illegal drug use, or campaign actively for the legalization of many illegal drugs, but also make drug use sound very glamorous. This happens because, as one *New York Times* article had it, "the Internet lacks a quality control mechanism, even in [discussion groups] that may ultimately encourage an activity that remains illegal for Americans of all ages."[27] Some cites may have an "I am 18" check box but of course this is a veneer to get around a loophole in the law. Regardless of such boxes, illegal drug use remains off limits for everyone until the law changes. How many libraries would accept print publications touting illegal drug use? Once again, what we would in no way endorse before the Web appeared, we now accept implicitly or explicitly because it is served up in digital form. As with all of life, everything settles to a lowest common denominator.

Don't Bogart That Joint

Discussion groups promoting illegal drug use are only the tip of the proverbial iceberg regarding disinformation on the Web. For every good discussion group such as one dealing with cancer — either for patients or for family members supporting another — there are scores more discussing the basest of human endeavors. In the past, many discussions that the vast majority would not have been privy to are, because of the Web, thrust in our faces. Some of these discussions are harmful. No drug from any pharmacy would ever be approved that killed half its users. Indeed, in some cases, if the population of users is small enough, even one death will make drug approval an uphill battle, if ever successful. But put it on the Web, and everyone can take it, buy it, or sell it. This is unlikely to change, too. Many see the Web's "anarchy" as one of its best features and would fight against any effort that would change this. Indeed, most civil libertarians argue that the Web is useful *because* there is no control, governmental or otherwise, and so favor everything that makes it more free — or anarchic — rather than less so.[28]

Earlier I mention the James Frey incident. Frey's book *A Million Little Pieces* created a firestorm when it turned out his book relied more on fiction than fact. Oprah Winfrey first defended, then excoriated, Frey because millions of her viewers had been "lied to" by his outrageous act. Apparently, for stories appearing in print, this business of deception is intolerable, as newspapers and magazines make numerous routine corrections to seemingly innocuous errors. With the Web, however, we're willing to change our view about deception, disinformation, or outright lies. Some readers will shout against my text, "But what about the First Amendment?" They will argue that the First Amendment protects these Web sites. We're not so tolerant when we see a lie in print; put it on the Web and everyone rushes to defend the "Pierre Salinger syndrome," or the willingness to suspend all belief if it's 'Net-based.[29] Again, the Web as a chief information resource cannot be a promising sign for an age that is producing a generation that will not read much beyond the sound bite. Most will miss the Web's amalgamation of misinformation and disinformation. "Information" is rapidly being defined as whatever's on the Web, right, wrong, or any combination in between.

Some will argue that my objections are the objections of an isolated Luddite. These things will work themselves out, they reassure us, and disinformation, or any of the other Web versions of same, will compete in the market for attention and truth will out. But does it? Not according to Robert McChesney:

> [T]he likely result of the digital revolution will be the withering — perhaps the outright elimination — of the media giants and a flowering of a competitive commercial media marketplace the likes of which have never been seen. Indeed the rise of the Web threatens not only the market power of the media giants but also the very survival of telecommunication and computer software giants.[30]

Some will argue this is a good thing, but let's be sure we're not throwing the baby out with the bathwater. Do we really want to turn over all our news, all our "information," to anyone who can host a blog or put up a Web site? Some will doubtless argue that the Web, and specifically blogs, are already a boon to democracy.[31] Yet for every good occurrence — the Smoking Gun and its claims against Frey, or the Drudge Report and some of its scoops — there are dozens of others that counteract that claim. For every Instapundit one can cite, there are scores of "MySpace.com" types that are awash in the worst form of narcissism since Narcissus first saw his reflection in the water.[32] Combine the misinformation and disinformation, along with spelling and grammar which prove a *pons asinorum* for many, and you have, not a boon to democracy, but a boondoggle. Add to this the commercial journalist enterprises on the Web, and the recipe for failure on a ubiquitous scale is suddenly more probable than merely possible.

This is not to argue that the Web cannot — is not — being used for much good. But its grand defects are being ignored, or discounted to the extent that many find it impossible to name even one.

Disinformation also weakens the Web's catchphrase "death-of-distance" we hear so much about. Indeed, one the Web's grandest attributes, we are assured, is its shrinking of space, of distance, making our world flat. For commercial interests, surely, this has its advantages (as pointed out below). But the death-of-distance argument is again, as with most of the benefits on the Web, a double-edged sword. One can also spread lies, deception, disinformation, and the like over many millions of miles, and to every corner of the globe.

In the AIDS example above, the odds would have been very small that more than a handful of individuals would have ever purchased a book of nonfiction that claimed the AIDS virus was a genocidal scheme of the Department of Defense. With the Web, millions see it, and of that number, many more are influenced by it. What future impact this will have on citizenship is anyone's guess. Some argue it will reduce nationalistic tendencies. The 21st century has so far seen little evidence of it, however, while at the same time witnessed a rise in the sharing of bad ideas.[33]

We have been down this road of fragmentation before. "Our daily lives," writes Andrew Shapiro,

> were first drastically reordered by radio and then television. The spread of broadcasting, of course, knit diverse audiences together in ways that simply were previously impossible. And, more recently, in a process far more complete, the proliferation of specialized stations and channels, especially in the United States, has a reversed the trend, fragmenting listeners and viewers into smaller, perhaps more homogenous groups. *Strikingly, well before this shift from broadcasting to "narrowcasting" is anywhere near complete, yet another, potentially transforming, change in communications is occurring through the Internet.*[34]

Most see this new transformation as a cornucopia filled only with benefits, and there can be no denying that there are many. But the Web's defects nevertheless remain significant enough to disqualify it as a chief or primary *knowledge* tool. Do we want to foster not only a more fragmented society, but also a more misinformed one?

Misinformed? Indeed. Consider a more serious form of disinformation: conspiracy theory Web sites. Conspiracy theory Web sites have a serious impact on the public square. We may have dreamed once of an ideal public sphere that the Web has given life to, but is anyone making the argument seriously anymore? Trust, equality, inclusivity and the other ideals about a giant "town hall" meeting that once marked potential Web discussions have been replaced by conspiracy theories, hate groups, vile and violent language and just about any other human antipathy one can name. The Web, as one pundit has argued, "is not a medium for propaganda, but for conspiracy."[35] Imagine a literal town hall in which the local town drunk, while fully intoxicated, is given a voice equal to the local political philosopher, and that's today's Web as a public forum. There are no boundaries on the Web, and few who want to recognize this defect, much less suggest any remediation for it.

Knocking on Heaven's Gate

Heaven's Gate is a good case in point. A religious sect, if we use the term "religious" loosely, Heaven's Gate mixed New Age psychobabble with outrageous science fiction and near–sexual asceticism. The group, by anyone's definitions, held strange, even bizarre beliefs. Left to its own devices and *without* the Web as a vehicle for misinforming others, the selcouth dogmas that forbade sexual relations among its members would have sent it to an early, one-generation death. Few would have been the wiser. Using all the merits of the Web — ubiquity, egalitarianism, open access, no boundaries — the group managed to attract nationwide attention before finally endorsing, and then committing, mass suicide. How many of the unwary, especially the highly impressionable at whatever age, were roped into this insanity because of the omnipresence of the Web? [36] Do we chalk this up to, as ALA's *Intellectual Freedom Manual* puts it, the dangerous way life that is ours in freedom? Or do we rather regret that we have been hoisted on our own Web-based petards? Laws that prevent one, willy-nilly, from driving intoxicated on the highways because that behavior endangers others, are nonexistent for regulating the "drunks" on the information superhighway. Given this, can we at least quit touting the Web as the panacea meant to replace libraries?

As one famous politician once said, let me be perfectly clean about this. The contentions here do not discount the value of having at one's fingertips what amounts to "the great books." Sites like MIT's Greek and Latin Loeb's Classics make available "at home" texts which, it is true, are available in almost any library of 50,000 volumes or more. The convenience for those who want them is a phenomenal timesaver. Even convenience like this does not, however, address the educational ramifications of bad literature made widely available. No one reads more than three or four pages on the Web at a time anyway. Beyond that, most are likely to print any Web-text over three pages (where's a tree-hugger when you need one?); this creates a serious ecological issue not being addressed by anyone. Any academic institution will readily reveal that printing costs have doubled, tripled, and even quadrupled with the advent of the Web, adding to their expenses, not reducing them. Most of these institutions have had to place limits on once limitless free printing. These increases in printing do not account for employees madly printing everything.

Furthermore, given students' penchant for looking for an easy way out, great classics on the Web, regardless of language, are generally rifled for needed information, not read for their literary contributions. Bear in mind that these texts are being made available to a generation already allergic to reading. Indeed, this appears to be at least one feature of Questia, a virtual library of 50,000 or so texts made searchable for free but providing text access at graduated costs. Is this our future? We buy lines or passages of Shakespeare, not his complete works. If this is progress, it is a 21st century definition of it that does not bode well for our future.

Finally, reading as a cognitive process gets lost in all this sound-bite literature. As anyone who has studied reading for very long knows, it is the *process* of reading that makes you better at it, Evelyn Wood's speed-reading courses notwithstanding. In the same way that memorizing multiplication tables enlarges the mind's ability to understand computations, reading enlarges the mind's ability to comprehend texts. We have already witnessed what calculators have done to computational skills in a generation of children who now cannot make change from a cash register without a calculator. It now appears we are not content with that loss but will now add compromised reading to our list of educational failures as well.

If U Cn Rd Ths

While they do not fall neatly into one of the categories defined here, online degree mills have multiplied like so many pages from a Xerox machine. Yes, of course, there are legitimate ones; but as many states are now learning, there are many others that make any number of undergraduate and graduate degrees (including the doctorate) available online. Many cheer this development as yet one more merit of the great Web. But now states like Georgia, and others, are learning that pay raises, merit raises and promotions have been based on the attainment of advanced degrees earned fraudulently from online diploma mills. Laura Callahan of the Department of Homeland Security illustrates this problem well.

A perfect match for the computer conglomerate she had to oversee, Callahan had supposedly worked with computers since the mid-'80s, and had outstanding credentials, including a PhD in computer information systems. As senior director and chief information officer of that department, she pulled down six figures. By March 2004, she was exposed "not [as] a skilled IT executive, but an unqualified hack."[37]

Degree mills have, of course, been around for a long time, but the Web has made diploma mills readily available to anyone wishing to advance in his or her job with little effort. While such diploma mills as the one Callahan used may be easily dismissed, places like the University of Phoenix and their ilk survive because they are in cities in close proximity to vast conventional library resources. Thus, the thousands in tuition one may pay at an institution of higher education for a degree in residence now also supports those working on online degrees who pay nothing, by providing them with free library resources.

Online universities will argue that the Web has made research possible, but anyone pursuing one of these degrees will tell you otherwise. No one can pursue a creditable degree without access to costly proprietary databases such as *Academic Search Premier* or *Lexis-Nexis*. Although most academic libraries password-protect their resources from the free Web (though none are hacker-proof), anyone walking into a state-supported academic library will likely have access to most, if not all, of these very expensive resources, free of charge. To argue that this is *their* problem is to fail to understand the logistical impossibility of prohibiting such uses. In order to do that, it would have to be nearly impossible for students who have paid to use them via their tuitions to use them conveniently.

Why Can't We Just All Hate Each Other, Virtually?

Perhaps we can dismiss disinformation and misinformation. Perhaps, too, conspiracy Web sites are merely hysterical forms of communication that can be ignored, too. Intelligent people, because they know better, will avoid both. Even diploma mills we may dismiss because they were around long before the Web and would continue, less easily of course, without it.

But can we accept an information source that also promulgates the worst bile that humans have to offer? Would we be so forgiving of non-Web sources if everyday we opened our newspapers, or turned on our radios, tuned in our televisions, to venomous hate groups? Recent laws have been enacted to condemn further those who are guilty of crimes if those crimes have been committed out of a provable deep-seated hatred for specific groups. Yet searches on any search engine will lead the unwary to sites that purport to provide sound advice masked in HTML-code that looks innocent enough but veils a putrid combination of misinformation, disinformation and outright despite for certain groups. Apparently, if this is delivered over the Web we are willing to suspend all the rules of civility.

The Turner Diaries, for example, were of course available in print long before the Internet. But that same ubiquity that gives us news at our fingertips now makes *The Turner Diaries* as readily available as *The Complete Works of Shakespeare*. As the Klan, skinheads and white supremacist groups waned over the years, the Web has now rejuvenated them for a whole generation of young people who might otherwise have missed them entirely.[38] Some have argued that this is a good thing because they are now out in the open. But this is an odd stance for a country that shut down the apple industry because eating 700 alar-treated apples every day for 70 years *could* cause cancer and might hurt children. With a clear and present danger in the form of thousands of hate groups spewing out their poison everywhere a computer resides, why is there little or no concern?

Take for example the site martinlutherking.org. Here is a site that purports to be a favored site for finding information about the impavid civil rights leader. Doubtless it lures thousands to it, especially during Black History Month. As it turns out, the site is run by a white supremacist group. Using a mix of fact and fiction, the site hides its hatred of blacks amid its concern for "civil rights." At a time in our country when race relations are not at their best, such sites make any hope of repair perhaps not impossible, but certainly far more difficult than would otherwise have to be. Add to this, sites using the 9–11 tragedy to exploit hatred of Muslims, gays, Jews or any other marginalized group, and the recipe for disaster is as omnipresent as Microsoft Windows. Although hate crimes statistics have leveled off to about 8,000 a year, the number of crimes committed by individuals whose views have been molded, created or reinforced by what is available over the Internet has risen.[39]

Thanks to the Web, the palpable hatred these groups spread is now available worldwide, and to an audience without boundaries. The Internet site Strromfront welcomes the Web. "The Internet is a major breakthrough for us. It's a significant advance to developing a White-rights movement in [the United States]," according to Don Black, Stormfront's creator.[40] Racial fears and misguided individuals now have a friend in the Web. Many who would hold their insipidities in darkness, or whisper them in secret to one another in unnamed alleys, may now resort to cyberspace where they are told, "You are *not* alone. There are millions like you. Join up and we'll change the world by ridding ourselves of these undesirables." Add to this, thousands of blogs that are unhinged in their private hatreds, and even the most urbane of individuals might be persuaded. Hate blogs are only the beginning, too. Less internecine, but equally mischievous, are so called "black blogs" that single out a candidate for office whom the writer or writers of the blog happen to dislike. These can sink a fine candidate in no time at all.[41]

Another site, one of the Web's many Holocaust revisionist ones, is Charlemagne Hammerskins. This group, in addition to its vile disinformation and repulsive anti-Semitic content, features a rather chilling reminder that even though Hitler was defeated in World War II, his idiocy lives on, warning, "Be assured, we still have one-way tickets to Auschwitz."[42] Other sites are designed, it seems, to attract younger users, offering games that feature the killing of blacks, Jews or homosexuals. The Simon Wiesenthal Center, which tracks these sites, reports that there are more than 2,300 such sites, most of which are mounted on servers in America because hate laws in Europe would shut them down.[43] With the unrestricted Web, we have become the "Land of the free, and the home of the racist."

Moreover, we misguidedly think, because we allow First Amendment absolutists to make these decisions, that thousands of such sites will do little or nothing to the body politic, much the same as we continue to delude ourselves that a country awash in pornography will feel no effect on its sexual mores. The only avenue open now to eliminating these are the aforementioned anti-hate laws in Europe. One celebrated case occurred when the French government took Yahoo to court.[44] This touches only those sites that can be traced. Many sites use anonymous remailers that strip off any identifying information in an e-mail by replacing the point of origin with a random number. By using these techniques after encryption (referred to as chained remailing), the sender or senders will likely remain untraceable.

Just Send Me Your Checking Account Number and...

One of the rightly highly touted benefits of the Web is its entrepreneurial spirit of e-commerce. Not so many years ago, a young, inventive person would have had to jump through many hoops, look for venture capital, and put in endless days, nights, weeks, months and years, only to see his or her dreams of a business never get to opening day. Of the few who did get to "opening day," hundreds did not make it to the end of opening week. Location, location, location killed off most, or they managed to hit upon the unhappy mix of being a barbershop in a town of bald-headed men. In other words, their new widget, their better mousetrap, had managed by the luck of the draw to be in a place where no one wanted it.

For example, my daughter has a site on the Web. Hers is a business that would have been impossible years ago as a conventional one, or at least without exorbitant start-up costs. Her site features a clever mix of knitted or hand-sewn items and her passion, philosophy. As a conventional business, she could have tried this in a thousand physical locations and never found the right fit. Located in cyberspace, she receives enough traffic to keep her busy (etsy.com).

With the Web, location is everything, or rather I should say *everywhere*. Put up a link and anyone can sell anything, as eBay proves daily. But these very features make the Web vulnerable to miscreants and those seeking a fast buck or an easy way out. Before the Web, buncombe artists had to go door-to-door, or play shell games on street corners, all the while keeping a nervous eye out for the police. Scam artists and con men looked for retirement communities or other seemingly easy prey to victimize. Today, they sit in their pajamas and order online, as that famous credit card commercial reminds us.

Earlier in this chapter I mentioned the Nigerian scam e-mails. With the remailing features mentioned above, dozens of these go out to millions of addresses on the hour. The same technology that makes the location-mantra for businesses unnecessary makes the con man's game child's play. He no longer goes door-to-door. We inadvertently invite him to our dens, our bedrooms or our businesses.

"No longer can people say," writes Carol Ebbinghouse, "'I got it off the web' and blithely assume that this makes purported information more, *rather than less*, reliable."[45] Of course as we now know, liars are liars, whether in person or in cyberspace. The virtual reality is that liars are able to lie more often, to more people, and in less time than ever before. With fraud, as Ebbinghouse points out, we're not talking about slip ups, spoofs or the "Homer nods" sorts of mistakes we all make. We're talking about what appears to be reliable information *meant* to mislead.

Combining the statistics of the Federal Trade Commission, the National Fraud Information Center, the Better Business Bureau and complaint centers for Internet fraud shows that fraud and deceit on the Web have skyrocketed in a way that makes Enron look like child's play. Although the number of claims dropped in 2005 from 2004, the dollar amount was larger. Internet fraud accounted for more than $5 million in losses in 2004, but nearly tripled in 2005.[46] In 2001, individuals lost some $117 million to Internet scams.[47]

During 2004, Consumer Sentinel received almost 400,000 fraud related claims (Internet and otherwise) totaling more than half a billion dollars.[48] But it only gets worse. The most recent figures indicate that fraud is at an all-time high, surpassing the $800 million mark.[49] Of those scammed, the average dollar loss was nearly $2,000. The scamming comes in many forms, too: auctions, money offers, fake checks, lotteries or lottery clubs, phishing (e-mails claiming to be from reputable sources just to get your personal information), advance fee loans, work-at-home plans and Internet access services.[50] Internet identity theft still accounts for many of these fraud claims. Identity theft began offline, but the Web is now the preferred method of cons using this mode to misrepresent.[51] The sad conclusion is that if one chooses to use the Web as his or her preferred means of doing business, he or she *will* eventually become a victim of Internet fraud of some kind.

Some might argue that those who get scammed get what they deserve, but that argument could be made about many of life's tragedies. Often on the Web, however, it is the innocent or the unwary who get hurt most. While there is a way to recover one's losses, it isn't easy. The trouble is, Internet fraud is disaggregate, and so does not occur in one company with one group of people, but everywhere the Web reaches, which is to say everywhere. Moreover, fraud is not limited to businesses. Charities are now the target of Internet scams.[52] The real key is avoiding fraud altogether, an impossibility if the Web figures largely into one's business.

It's hard even for a trained eye to spot some of the investment frauds available over the Web. Do names like *Investor's Chronicle* or *Stocks to Watch* sound reliable? Well, they're not.[53] Often such sites tout worthless stocks and securities or bogus companies. Getting a "stock" tip from one of these sites, from a spam e-mail or a chat room, is as good as holding your open wallet out a car window. Getting your money back is next to impossible. Stocks are hyped, earnings are boosted that are nonexistent, "cybersmears" (false stock or company advertising) employed, or trademark and antitrust violations used to delude the wary and the unwary. In the case of cyber-smears, a con artist or just a disgruntled employee uses the Web to take a stock's price down, or to allow short sellers to do the same.

So rampant has Web fraud become that the National Consumers League established a Web site just for businesses.[54] Ebbinghouse points out that the problem is so vast that it may no longer be possible to trust any rumors of expansion based only on a company's Web site for fear it may be just a "pump and dump" scheme, a ruse of fraudulent sales practices to unload "house" stocks. Online auctions are yet another scheme. Before buying it's best to check out the FTC's Web site (www.ftc.gov) first.

When businesses aren't the subject of fraud, deception runs amok. On the millennium's New Year's Eve, almost 9 million people in the United States watched Dan Rather and CBS cover the gala events in Times Square.[55] Or so they thought. CBS had taken the feed from NBC, technologically erased its peacock and inserted its famous eye, somewhat blackened in recent years owing to this and the later Bushgate shenanigans. CBS claimed that this was part of the brave new digital world but conceded that some might find it deceptive. When hundreds of irate calls later came in, it underscored that hunch.

Elixir of Life, Really

Business fraud isn't the only kind of fraud on the Web. It may be just a little hyperbolic to speak of medical fraud, but only barely. Medical information sites are everywhere on the Web and WebMD is one of the best. But bad medical advice is also on the Web.

In the case of medical information what you don't, or do, know may well kill you. The Web is filled with blatantly misleading medical information, medical misinformation, and hawkers selling nostrums (not unlike the quacksalvers who peddled useless medicines door-to-door in the late 1800s and early 1900s), illegal prescriptions and more.[56]

Do-it-yourself sites allow patients to go online, answer a handful of questions and diagnose themselves. This brings to mind the old saw that he who has himself as a doctor has an ass for a patient. With more than 100,000 medical sites to choose from on the Web, the possibilities are endless. The emergence of these sites has impacted the doctor-patient relationship. Patients appear in physicians' waiting rooms with reams of Web-printed information pages about drugs, possible treatments, and prognoses. Woe to the physician who would dare question the Web, too. The American Medical Association has issued warnings from time to time about the Web's medical information and the possibility that it could well pose a threat to the health of unwary users.

Even in reputable sites, trouble lurks. When former surgeon general C. Everett Koop lent his name to a Web site, surfers flew to it expecting only the best. In most cases they were not disappointed. In one well-known link, however, the site listed the best, most innovative hospitals in the country. So far so good. But the fine print indicating that the named institutions had paid more than $40,000 each for the listing was never posted.[57] Since the Web must use innovative uses to secure much-needed revenue, such pay-back schemes are hardly uncommon.

Spoofs and counterfeit sites on the Web are also abundant. For years, mistyping "Infoseek" as "Infosheek" returned a semi-pornographic site. But other such sites, while unlikely to be misused by the educated, are easy prey for the less sophisticated. Sites like Microshaft and Washington Pi**ed (for the *Washington Post*) along with scores of sites ridiculing political figures pose trouble.[58] The World Trade Organization (WTO) now has a counterfeit site, www.gatt.org, to contend with.[59] The official Web site for the WTO is www.wto.org. The former site is filled with anti-WTO information. The site is so well done that most would pick the counterfeit site over the real one. As mentioned earlier, politicians have received their share of spoofing or counterfeit sites: President Bush, former vice president Gore, as well as those who might want to be president, or already think they are (see the Bill Gates for President site, for example). Sites claiming whales in Lake Michigan; addictions to various, outrageous commonplace items or products; along with wrong-headed or just wrong information abound.

Sit Here

Cybersquatting also poses a problem.[60] Cybersquatting occurs when a domain name is either snatched up quickly or bought after lapsing, for no real purpose other than to charge a fortune to those who might want it. While rampant in the mid- to late 1990s, it is less of a problem now, though it lingers still. A chamber of commerce in a Kentucky county, for example, allowed its domain name to lapse and so lost it to a porn site. Getting it back cost thousands of dollars. A child's well-known Web site lapsed and the same thing occurred. Some better known victims were Avon, Hertz, Panasonic and Fry's Electronics.[61] Even reputable Web-based sources such as Amazon have defrauded us in some manner. Have we forgotten Amazon's noto- rious "dynamic pricing" scheme that set the price levels for DVDs based on income levels or past purchases?[62]

A letter or two can make the difference, as when Nancy Yanofsky typed ".com" instead of ".org" in the address of her pro-choice group and ended up at abortionis- murder.com instead.[63] Cybersquatting is not, of course, a serious matter, save to those few trying to get their domain names back. But for many surfers it represents just one more annoyance in the search for information. Imagine picking up a *Britannica* and looking up an article on "nature" only to find it is about a nudist colony. No buyer would tolerate such nonsense, but when it happens on the Web, either we ignore it, downplay as meaningless, or agree it happens and continue to praise the Web for all its other benefits. It is as if we have shut off our minds at the point-and-click stage.

Conclusion

Some reading this chapter will complain that too much has been made of the Web's inability to deliver reliable information. Moreover, some will claim that it's disingen- uous to complain about the Web and then cite information that comes from the Web. Such arguments are spurious and silly. To argue that one cannot cite the Web while complaining about it is the same as arguing that those driving cars cannot complain about vehicular accidents.

The attempt in this chapter, and this book, is to present as compelling a case as can be made that the Web poses many serious problems that should vitiate it as a chief source of information. Without putting too fine a point on it, the very benefits of the Web are also the very causes of its defects. We cannot turn a blind eye to these defects any more than we would to a physician who lost as many patients as he helped owing to his own carelessness. To argue that the Web poses significant dangers as an informa- tion source is merely to point out the obvious. The Web cannot replace a full-service library. In fact, *it cannot even compete*. To ignore the problems of the Web, as valuable as it is, is to open ourselves up to grave dangers.

Thoreau once warned that industrialization threatens to make us "tools of our tools." No better example exists of this than the Web. The Web is no better (and no worse) a tool than any of the hundreds of other information sources available to us. But it is a tool with many flaws. The argument here is not for putting the genie back in the bottle. The argument here is to understand that the genie is rarely one that always grants good wishes. Our velleity that it become the perfect, one-stop shop for all our information needs will not make so.

We must not forget that only a decade or so ago, we did not have access to the Web and were none the worse without it. We forget this and all too easily. A colleague wrote me recently (March 2006) complaining that I had written too negatively about the Web. "The library wasn't a library before the Web," she wrote. How soon all of us, even those of us who should know better, forget!

2

Forget the Needle.
Can You Just Tell Me
Which Haystack?

The exhilaration of that first Google search is generally unmatched by the second, third or fourth. Retrieving 1,345,678 "hits" in 3.025 seconds does make one rather heady. To misapply an old "Seinfeld" line, we instantly feel as if we have become masters of our information domain. And we're masters of that domain for about as long as Elaine and Kramer were of that "other" domain. Everyone feels powerful that first time. It's only after running through one of those lists looking for a usable something that we come to understand what the phrase "pig in a poke" really means.

Your Research Is the Needle; the Web Is the Haystack

Okay, is that really fair? Even seasoned searchers gripe about Google, are hot-tempered about Hotbot, go a bit loony over Lycos, or yell at Yahoo. It isn't that we can't find what we want but more, perhaps, that the expectation has been raised to such a pitch that we feel we should find *right away* whatever it is that we're looking for. When we don't, and we often do not, we get a little steamed. For those who work at reference desks in academic libraries, the stories are now proverbial of students who come to the desk, some practically in tears, desperate over why they cannot find some simple bit of information, *even after looking for hours on the Web*. User error of course plays into many such failures. But as this chapter demonstrates, the needle in the haystack is hidden for reasons that often remain a mystery to the user yet are part of the design of the search engine itself. Moreover, for all its putative vastness, the Web isn't as large as it may appear to be. Claims that the Web is as large as or larger than the largest of libraries are untrue.[1] When one factors out the spam, advertisements and disinformation, it is fundamentally false.

Much has been made in earlier chapters about the dumbing down of rising generations and that remains true for a number of reasons, not the least of which is the deterioration of education in K–12 for the last thirty years. Careful readers will complain, however, that while some of this is the fault of the Web, very little, perhaps none, can be placed at the feet of search engines. *Au contraire*, as the French are wont to say.

In December of 2005, the National Center for Education Statistics published a report on adult literacy.[2] Literacy among the college-aged to interpret complex texts proficiently fell from 40 percent in 1992 to 31 percent in December 2005. The test, as Mark Schneider, the center's commissioner of education statistics, points out, isn't designed "to test your comprehension of Proust, but to test your ability to read labels." The good news, if you can call it that, is that we are not alone. Similar studies reveal an equal failure in the United Kingdom, where professors there believe that current students are not only less prepared, but also less teachable.

What has this to do with search engines? Blame exists in large enough quantities to go around just about everywhere, but many point to the Web, and specifically to search engines. Because Google, and others like it, produce results — please note the lack of qualifier here — young people are happy with whatever they find, whether it's right or not. As pointed out in chapter 1, Web results are as likely to be disinformation or misinformation as something accurate. Indeed, so bad has the problem become that a group of researchers have come together to form credible online information.[3] Their Web site (http://credibilitycommon.org) is an attempt to develop techniques "for assessing the credibility of information on the World Wide Web. The idea is to direct users to either credible information, to skilled Web researchers (reference librarians) or both. (We'll return to this question of literacy and the Web in chapter 8.)

To give some example of this decline and the need for making credible information easier to find, *graduate* students at Tel Aviv University, hardly a run of the mill institution, were asked to find on the Web a picture of the Mona Lisa, the complete text of either *Robinson Crusoe* or *David Copperfield*, and a recipe for apple pie with an accompanying photograph of same. Sounds easy enough, but they were given no time limit. Only 15 percent succeeded in finding all three!

Of course there are many attenuating factors we could bring to this example. Some blew it off, some didn't bother and some, of course, couldn't find them all. But any percentage below the 95th percentile should be considered a failure, so easy is this test. Once again, we're victims of our own success, or, as Oscar Wilde once put it, "nothing exceeds like success."

The Web: First and Only Research Stop

Is there an over-reliance on the Web? Surely you jest! Ten years ago students I taught would have said no, and they would have been right. Now, it's hard to find even one who does not rely exclusively on the Web for all his or her information. In 2000, a study on how people sought out information revealed that search engines were the top resource used, resorted to almost 33 percent of the time.[4] This would not be troubling if information seekers sought out other sources, but that happened only rarely and in a bygone age. When university students come to our reference desk and ask for information they have been agonizingly looking for, for hours, they are dumbfounded when our reference staff finds it in a matter of seconds, usually in an almanac or some other "ready reference" source. They are amazed that some "stupid print source" could out-perform the Web.

This isn't new. About twelve years ago I was a helping a student at another university locate an article. We had access to one of the early Neanderthal tools, a CD–type version of full-text articles. Our machine was down, again, and I mentioned to her that in this particular case we had the article in paper. "That's okay," she said nervously, "I'll come back when the machine is working."

The point here is twofold. Not only is not everything on the Web, but it is getting increasingly hard to convince students — or anyone else for that matter — that not only is not everything on the Web, but what's there isn't fully searched by search engines, or cannot be "seen" by them. That is, search engines perform inadequate searches because they cannot find and index what they find efficiently. They also do not search all of the Web.[5] Furthermore, most information-seekers think that if it isn't on the Web, then it cannot be legitimate when in fact, the situation is more likely to be just the opposite.

Making the Invisible Web Visible

So how can it be that search engines do not search all of the Web? One reason is that part of the Web is invisible to search engines altogether. This part of the Web, sometimes called the "invisible Web" or the "Deep Web," is simply not visible to search engines because of the way search engines work. The information maintained on the invisible Web is incredibly useful, as we shall see.[6] The other reason is that in study after study, search engines really only search, at best, only about 20 percent to 40 percent of the Web at any given time.[7] If this is the resource to which information seekers turn when looking for information — and we know it is — then users should know what they are not getting. Imagine buying the latest best seller, rushing home, and finding the first 30 percent exciting and entertaining and the remaining 70 percent full of blank pages. Of course no one would tolerate such a turn of events, but let the Web deliver it and we're all quite happy, thank you very much. So part of the reason the needle — your research — can't be found quickly is that search engines can't see the haystack in which it resides. But other reasons abound.

Part of it has to do with the evolution of the Web.[8] Many know that the Web (or the Internet proper) began as a project by the U.S. Defense Advance Research Projects Agency (DARPA) in 1969. The idea was to have a communications vehicle that would let allow the researchers used by this agency to share information while they worked either on the same project, or on similar ones from various locales. Early versions ran Gopher, a kind of directory or index that allowed one to fish about for what one was looking for. It was not very user-friendly, but then the audience for it was small and very much familiar with the technical know-how to make it work. And that proved to be its problem. While one could search, in a manner of speaking, Gopher servers, once there one had to hunt and peck for what one needed. Before we had cyberspace, we had "Gopherspace."[9] To search these Gopher servers, other tools were created, but it wasn't until Tim Berners-Lee created the Web tools all of us know today that the Web began. He first created HTML (HyperText Markup Language) in 1990, and with that invention, the Web *per se* really began. This language allowed certain users who knew how to use the codes (and later everyone) to create webpages. Berners-Lee also created HyperText Transfer Protocol (HTTP), a set of rules that allowed any computer to link and retrieve Web documents automatically. Finally, he fashioned what he called the Universal Resource Identifier (later Universal Resource Locator, the URLs of today) that provide the unique Internet addresses familiar to us all.

This becomes important with respect to searching because many search engines do not search anything but HTML documents, making many PDF files, Flash files or just data residing on back-end databases of unlinked Web pages inaccessible or ignored.[10] The development of the Web led to some inherent searching problems that have not been fully resolved.

Most current search engines use tools referred to as robots, spiders or crawlers, which "crawl" the Web looking for answers to inquires. And therein lies the problem. Search engines build directories in one of two ways, open or closed.[11] Google is an example of an open directory builder, Yahoo an example of the closed kind. Closed directories place a great deal of their internal control on editors who select what goes into the categories. Open directories rely mainly on algorithms and/or volunteers. Both have problems. Open directories are now preferred because they can be done more cheaply but are fraught with quality control issues, as we saw in chapter 1. Other problems can also occur.

For example, size matters.[12] Because the Web is vast, these directories can be small in comparison to the overall Web. The categories can be well-chosen but limited either by the knowledge of whoever is compiling them, or by the preferences they have chosen. Get ten people in a room and ask them to look at 100 different items. At the end of the day it would not be surprising to have ten different sets of categories.

But size, while it matters, isn't always the most important factor. It doesn't help much if there are thousands of sites on the Web, but the search engines being used can only find some of them. Imagine consulting your accountant at tax time only to discover that, yes, you owe, but he's not sure how much, or can't tell you, or can only tell you part of what you owe. (Perhaps if he did this over the Web it would be all right.) An abyss separates what is on the Web and what search engines are able to deliver.[13] And like hidden treasures lost at sea, information-seekers are often content just knowing that "land" is out there somewhere, whether they can find it or not.

Human Bias, Even on the Web!

Index-building can lead to bias. We're all human and what I choose as a category is doubtless governed by my background, my likes and dislikes. Another person might well choose differently owing to her different biases. Then there is the problem of the social politics of the work environment.

Another kind of bias also intrudes and it has to do with what the categories are called or labeled. One editor may choose a category as a "catchall" and put many things in it that another editor might break down into several categories. Whatever a search engine has as a broad general category (and one cannot always know) may not really be reflective of what is on the Web in that area.

Finally, generating revenue for a search engine may govern not only how well it retrieves, but it also may govern what it retrieves *first*. This is not to say that all search engines are expected to be altruistic endeavors. Of course they cannot be. But a search engine that has sites come up on the first page because they have paid to be there is definitely different from a search engine that pulls up the qualitative best that is on the Web (and yes, there are some, see below). In other words, the deck may well be stacked against the information-seeker to go to, or at the very least see first, sites that have paid a higher premium.[14] This is like voting for the politician who raises the most money; er, well, you know what I mean.

As anyone who uses the Web regularly knows, currency is a problem. Building these directories takes time and in the ever-protean World Wide Web, change is the reigning philosophy. Keeping everything current is impossible. Although smart crawlers are being utilized today, the process of crawling the Web is very expensive and very time consuming.[15] Experts estimate that there are more than eight billion pages on the Web (with the number higher, no doubt, by the time you read this). Regardless of how good a crawler is, none of them is good enough to crawl all of these, index them, and do it quickly every day.

Schedules, rules, and other internal decisions govern when (and even if) a page gets crawled, or is examined for new content. If a page is created one day, it may not be re-crawled by the same search engine for a good while (time lengths vary from search engine to search engine). If the page is changed between crawls, any new data will not be available to new inquiries unless and until that page is crawled again. The cost of crawling the Web not only accounts for why so little of the Web is actually crawled, but also why search engines are not all the same. Crawlers (or spiders) can be tricked, too.[16] They return results based on the inquiry but something on the page, for example, metadata or something else, made the crawler or spider "think" the page relevant to the inquiry when it isn't. The only way for the avid researcher to get around this problem is to find out what the eccentricities are for each search engine and adapt each for its best use. Although once thought to be the "holy grail" for search engines, metadata has now come under attack because its successful use relies so heavily on who's writing it, what its purpose is and whether the vocabulary is controlled or not.[17]

Because search engines do not search all of the Web, what each retrieves does not necessarily duplicate what the others retrieve. Because some engines use popularity or relevancy ranking (something very easy to do with the 18.5 billion blogs on the Web, and one new created, according to some sources, every second), more and more popular pages will end up in search engines while very good, very useful pages will remain either overlooked completely, or covered by only a few.[18] Relevancy ranking, really only understood by those who create the algorithms for it, takes away from information-seekers and all others the knowledge of what's happening in a search.[19]

As Google points out with every search how quickly it returns information, speed is preferred over how carefully it matches the inquiry with the results.[20] Google has already highlighted some of the Web's failings by creating separate categories for information sources, Google Image and Google Scholar, to name but two. These would not be necessary if the returns were based on quality instead of number. To solve that dilemma, the index searches only a certain kind of file.

Most search engines are geared to text because it's easier to search and index text than it is any other type of file. Google Scholar is an attempt to answer a long-standing criticism of the Web in general: it's simply become too commercial and much too over-crowded with junk. While still undergoing development at this writing, Google Scholar represents a small improvement. Right now it has mainly scientific and medical content, most of which is easily found elsewhere, but that will doubtless change. But Google Scholar does represent an admission of sorts that the popular Google search engine is simply overwhelmed by built-in biases that cannot be easily corrected.

Obviously, proprietary databases such as *Lexis-Nexis, Academic Search Premier* and others are not searchable by search engines or by any Web tool. Libraries purchase these materials for their clientele and all are very expensive. A given author may choose, if he or she owns copyright, to put an article up on a searchable page, but the vast majority do not, or cannot, because they do not own the copyright. Even information once found on the Web may not be found when searched for again at a later date.[21] Because proprietary databases are paid for, the information retrieved from them it is of a higher and much more expert quality than what is available freely on the Web.

Instant Experts

I know almost nothing about neurosurgery but I can put up a page on the Web about it in a matter of minutes. I might simply make something up, or I can get a volume on neurosurgery and add some fancy language that makes it appear not only to be legitimate, but also that I also know what I'm talking about. If I sign the page "Dr. Mark Y. Herring," it will appear that I know more than I really do. And while I have a doctorate, I do not have a medical degree (and no, I didn't stay in that hotel to make it seem so). An information-seeker knowing even less than I do about neurosurgery may well think my page useful, and the "Dr." before my name may easily make him think "MD."[22] On the other hand, to appear in *Medline*, a proprietary database, I must first publish what I know in a peer-reviewed journal, not an easy task. Information there is far better than information on the open Web.

Another problem obtains. The Web appears to be winding down in size, regardless of what one may read. One reason for this is that most who were going to use the Web to reach certain clientele have already done so. Growth rates for the Web have been steadily declining. In 2001 and 2002, the Web actually shank in size. While the Web has been shrinking or leveling off in size, the rate at which sites disappear has increased. Finally, remove USA–based sites from the Web and it decreases by almost half; remove the English language sites and the Web decreases by over 65 percent.[23] One of the first criticisms of Google's mass digitization plan for 10 million plus books was that the selection process focused on English language texts, proffering only a handful of non–English titles by comparison.

Google Bombing

If all of these criticisms are not enough, we now encounter "Google bombing," a neat trick that uses Google's algorithm against itself to create jokes created by those on the political right and left. For example, last year you could type in "miserable failure" and the first hit was the official White House biography of President George W. Bush. But Bush isn't the only one being bombed. Hillary Clinton, the porcine Michael Moore and unlicensed poet Jimmy Carter have all been made victims. Even countries get "bombed" by the Web. Type in "French Military Victories" and you'll get an error page asking "Do you mean French Military Defeats?" So, whether your politics run conservative, liberal, moderate or libertarian, chances are the Web has bombed someone you love.[24]

The way this works is simple. With nearly 20 billion (yes, that's a *billion*) blogs on the Web, if enough of them reference a page, Google (and others like it) begins referencing it. The more, the merrier. Just citing will not get it, because the page citing must be an influential one. While bloggers do much that's good, they a love a joke as much as the rest of us so it doesn't take many to get a link established. Although Google has made some adjustments in its algorithm to reduce this likelihood, it has not closed the window on fresh content, especially if the site updates regularly, such as a news site or, again, a weblog. Once again, the more the merrier, and another link is established.[25]

This is all fun and games, and the results, especially the first time, are hilarious if one remembers not to take his or her politics too seriously. What is troubling, however, is how this gamesmanship is used to skew results on other, more important matters. We already know that results can be manipulated by the site itself, the Web address or the metadata. It would not take much to use these tricks to do more, substantive skewing that would take information-seekers not only to wrong information, but to wrong-headed information as well.

Even accounting for these factors, any search engine's results are still a matter of the information-seeker wading through those millions of hits to find the best ones. If the returned results contain the answer on the first two or three screens, perhaps it will be found. If the answer ends up on screen ten, however, only the most persistent searcher (i.e., your local librarian) will find it. (Think back to the example in the previous chapter of the Johns Hopkins tragedy.) I've asked classes consisting of freshmen, sophomores, juniors and seniors how many of them got beyond the *first* screen. So far, one student admitted to doing so, and she was a woman in her fifties.

It's important to stress that none of the things are reasons not to use the Web or any of the search engines available, and that point needs to be stressed repeatedly. Killing off the Web or shutting it down is definitely not the point being made here. Clearly, online searching is here to stay, as are online courses, e-learning and the panoply of e-based courses now available.[26] What is being hammered home, however, is that searching the Web should not be the only research tactic, or even a primary one. It isn't a silver bullet, a one best way. It is one way, and a somewhat inferior one to more traditional ways of searching. To think otherwise is simply to be grossly mistaken about what constitutes good and bad information. It would be wrong to dismiss the problems listed here, however. "Search engine indexing and ranking," write Steve Lawrence and C. Lee Giles, "may have economic, social, political and scientific effects."[27] For example, one company that gets placed on a higher relevancy ranking may put its less Web-savvy competitor out of business for no other reason than it understands better the chicanery, or eccentricities, of search engines. No one would rely on *Star* magazine for valid information on celebrities. Yet Web results on diseases, racial groups, events or political issues may well be a *Star*-equivalent for their medical, racial and political counterparts. Late or misdated scientific information could well turn the direction of a given scientific bent based entirely on search engine happenstance, and a bad one at that. It would appear that nature of scientific material on the Web is reaching critical pitch.[28] The tension between public access (for the public good) and dollars to make such ventures profitable has escalated to levels that threaten to leave scientific access to those who have, while removing it completely from those who have not.

Several references have been made in this chapter to the invisible Web. It is not the scope of this book to ventilate that subject thoroughly, but some further mention should be made. Sherman and Price's *The Invisible Web: Uncovering Information Sources Search Engines Can't See* (2001, see notes for the full citation) is one of the best to examine, and there's no reason here to reinvent the wheel. But the source — along with the authors' Web site (http://invisble-web.net, or available at http://www.searchwise.net) — is an invaluable site to examine, as are others, such as the librarian's index (see below).[29] As they point out in their book, very valuable kinds of information are not easily found by commonly used search engines.[30] Another very useful tool is the *Librarian's Index to the Internet* (http://lii.org). Both of these, and others, provide access to the invisible Web and also list new site information that allows one to keep up with whatever is new on this part of the Web.[31] Granted, these sites do not contain anywhere near the number of sites major search engines examine (in most cases fewer than 20,000 sites); but they do contain highly valuable information.

For example, they provide access to things like weather data (not sites like the Weather Channel but sites with weather data in them), patents (which are devilishly difficult to tract anyway), out-of-print books, most library catalogs, grants and philanthropic information, translation tools, demographic information and more. One site on the invisible Web, for example, allows you to track flights in real time, so you'll never rush to the airport to pick up your mother-in-law too early (or too late). Since this information is generated by air traffic controllers, it is far more accurate and up-to-date than calling the 800-number, pushing a half dozen buttons, only to discover the time is the same as it was an hour ago when you knew the flight was late getting out of the gate.

But not knowing that popular Web search engines cannot "see" the Deep Web means users will never locate much of this information-rich content. The information is "hidden *because search engines have deliberately chosen to exclude some types of Web content.*"[32] Search engines will doubtless get better at finding this information, but what do we do in the meantime? Imagine going to a library and having the librarian say, "Some of our best information is behind the that door but I can't let you see it just yet. You have to wait until some later date, but when I can't tell you."

Error 404 — Page Not Found

For all the reasons given above — cost, crawler errors, editor errors and so on — even if the problem could be corrected it might not be for the best. If search engines could find everything available, it could easily make searching for what information-seekers want even more difficult than it already is. Although certain parts of some PDF files are searched, most are not.[33] These files are often very long and too large to be indexed. While this is not a highly critical problem today, it will be as more and more Web sites begin using this kind of file type. For example, dynamically generated pages are very problematic.[34] These are pages that have been created by a program that makes its choices from various options in order to generate a page. Since some programs can of course be made to do certain things — not all of them useful — search engines creators are wary of searching them. Should dynamic content become more commonplace on the Web, as it likely will, this problem will have to be overcome. At some point, Google *et al.* will have to decide, if they haven't already, whether they will index for the popular user, the serious user, or both. So far the decision appears to favor unanimously the popular user, and for all the obvious commercial reasons. This means that serious users — researchers, professors, students, physicians, attorneys and so on — will have to look elsewhere. As indicated earlier, Google has already admitted this with the rollout of Google Scholar. It's clear that if this venture is not successful — i.e., at the very least self-supporting — it will not be continued. Serious information-seekers should be aware of this and know that when they do a search in any of the commercial search engines, it is only the beginning, and a very tentative one at that.

What we sometimes fail to see is that while search engines have made our Web lives more simple, they have also made them more complicated. Inadvertently, they have generated a number of unintended consequences. The issue of information literacy is far more complex and difficult to assure as more and more "stuff" appears on the Web. For example, the vendor which supplies access to the online catalog where I work, Innovative Interfaces, is considered by many in our profession to be the Cadillac, the Rolls-Royce, of automated systems. It is for good reason that it has acquired this reputation, because it supplies many much-needed improvements each year. Recently, however, it announced a new interface for young children that relies almost completely on images.[35]

I'm sure this seemed like a good idea at the time, but I view this with the same despondency I did when my daughters, now 28 and 30, were in grade school and their math teacher encouraged them to use calculators. Much to their dismay and their teacher's, I made them learn their multiplication tables. I wanted to be sure they could make change from a dollar without a calculator. Often in our rush to make things easier and better we create more problems, often ones that will not be apparent until later. Creating an interface of mostly images for young children will do nothing to help develop their reading skills. It may in fact harm them. Oftentimes we make life much too easy by providing well-intentioned workarounds that short-circuit the learning process, now or in the future.

Illiterates of the World, Unite!

Sure, young children need to use the Web, one must suppose, but do they have to at the expense of reading? Here is yet one more nail in the coffin of general literacy (I am sure I will be roundly criticized as a Luddite for saying so). But what is the harm of forcing individuals to learn something much more important first? Reading is a skill that must be learned early in order for it to become a skill that will be forever fine-tuned. We humans are an interesting lot, and if something hard can be made easy, it is likely we'll never learn the hard thing very well.[36] (For more on this, see chapter 8.)

Search engines have made the life of information-seekers far too easy. It has also made them much too complacent and far too easily satisfied. We think searching 40 percent of the Web "good enough" so long as we are allowed to think it is "everything." And almost nothing is as gratifying as finding *something* in a matter of seconds compared to finding the *right* thing with more effort. For now, the gratification of finding the right information on the Web is reserved for the more experienced Web user. Still, so long as we think we're doing something we're content with our ormolu information, that is until we try to put it to use.

Meanwhile, the traditional library disappears. The library as place is not only diminished by the Web's ubiquity, it is also disappearing as a matter of fact, freeing up space for more computer access.[37] But, what, me worry? as Alfred E. Newman made famous. With the baby thrown out with the bathwater, we don't have to listen to that infernal crying any longer. As long as this remains the case, the library will vanish over time (as, recall, it already is doing in elementary and middle schools). This will not change now, and will only worsen (ingravesce, as physicians would say) as time inexorably passes.

3

Weare18.com[1]

Vice is a monster of so frightful mien
As to be hated needs but to be seen,
Yet seen too oft, familiar with her face,
We first endure, then pity, then embrace.
— Alexander Pope

It's impossible to surpass Pope's lines in describing concisely and accurately the history of our nation's relationship with pornography. Pope wrote for somewhat tamer times than our own though it cannot be said that pornography was unknown even in his less lutulent era. On the contrary, Pope surely knew much of it through the Hogarthian chronicles, and may well have been aware of medieval poems like the "Land of Cocaigne," wherein priests retrieved wayfaring flying brothers by playing like drums the bare bottoms of nuns. If anything, Pope understood the dangers of pornography or vice much better than our own more "enlightened," anything-goes times. Today, apparently, one cannot read anything remotely religious for fear of breaking down that fictive "wall of separation" that our ostensibly fragile Constitution cannot exist without, if we are to believe those wall-of-separation proponents.[2] On the other hand, viewing of fellatio is an inalienable right, again, according to those Constitutional absolutists.

From Brown Wrappers to "In Your Face"

In my own lifetime spanning barely a half century, pornography has gone from its once infamous brown paper wrappers to today's most revered and protected form of "free speech." Sadly, the American Library Association (along with the usual suspects like the ACLU and First Amendment absolutists) have gone to great lengths to protect everyone's right to view any kind of intercourse with any kind of partner anywhere. In its infancy, television did not hint at sexual misconduct (most *married* couples slept in *separate* beds) and mainstream movies had to pass the rigorous Hays Commission standards. Today, gratuitous sex is rampant in mainstream movies, even when those R and NC-17 movies lose millions.[3] Meanwhile, television sitcom characters snigger about everything from sexual innuendo to blatant declarations of every kind of sex known (and some unknown) to humankind. *Sub rosa* storylines, even in commercials, titter like junior high–schoolers over erectile dysfunction or vaginitis. Oh, we have come a long way, baby! One can no longer be sure that even while watching the evening news, stories about prostitutes loving their jobs, or commercials reminding us of the annoyance of itchy yeast infections, will not intrude. Sex is everywhere.

The so-called stuck-up fifties gave way to the liberated seventies, and now sex, because it is a very substantial part of life, must be talked (and talked, and talked) about. We went from to a nation that could not whisper the word sex, to one that ostensibly cannot shut up about it. Furthermore, our coverage of bodily functions does not end with sex. We're so brave, so new in our world, so uninhibited that we drone on in public about pubic irritations, diarrhea run amuck or uncontrollable urination, as if no one knew these were problematic and embarrassing matters. We have become, over the years, a most scatologically fixated culture. Hollywood appears unable to make a "serious" movie unless someone has gratuitous sex of some unhinged kind, or the main (or lesser) character doesn't treat us to his or her Technicolor eructation, apropos of nothing.

Whether in movies, television or the Web, sex, scatology and the rest, and lots of it, cannot be avoided. To write in this manner is of course to be branded as a pecksniffian prude who wishes to invirtuate all of life, to talk euphemistically of storks while ignoring the real grit of living. I would gladly accept the charge if it resulted in only one less minute of a woman advertising vaginal refreshers, one less man joking about someone earning knee pads, or one less wisecrack about some female's overdeveloped bosom. As Pope predicted, we first endure, then fondle, then can't shut up about it.

But all of that begs the question. Sex is everywhere, so why pick on the Web? Is Web-based pornography really that big a deal? Is it fair to complain that the Internet fails us again, this time because it's awash in pornography? Are we as a nation awash in voyeurism because the Web has made it so readily available?

Web-Based Porn: Pond or Ocean?

If statistics are any indication, it would appear a foregone conclusion but let the reader decide. The argument here isn't that we have only recently discovered pornography. As almost any book or article is quick to point out, pornography has been around quite a long time. Livy records that certain Roman emperors spent their leisure hours viewing or reading it. Diogenes of Sinope, that quintessential liberal figure, fought against the customs of his day by eschewing manners, dressing shabbily and masturbating openly just to make a point.[4] But the argument here isn't that pornography is new but that its nonstop ubiquity is owing to the Web.

We have changed our tolerance not only of the subject matter but also of what we are willing to allow *because* it is delivered over the holy grail of the Web. And so, herewith, yet another reason why the Internet is no substitute for a library. Horace writes somewhere that the eye is more easily led than the ear. Horace's truism is proved daily by the Web's pornographic content. We librarians want to have it both ways, it seems. We want reading to matter and pornography on the Web to be inconsequential. We argue that what we see and read changes us in very significant ways *unless* what we read or see is pornographic. Then great hordes rush forward to discredit the idea that anyone can really be changed by watching nude men and women (and animals) in whatever configuration have at one another in all sort of sexual acrobatics. The argument of this chapter is that we cannot have it both ways, so to say. Either we are changed by what we read and see, or we're not. If we are, then we are being changed most significantly by one of the Web's most prolific single issues: sex.

Pornography worldwide is a 60+ *billion* dollar industry, 12 *billion* of that alone coming from right here in River City.[5] Adult videos, many of which are available for viewing on the Web or can be ordered online, account for $20 billion. Sex clubs on the Web account for more than $5 billion; with escort services, magazines, cable or pay-per-view services, phone sex, CD-ROMs and novelties making up another $25-plus billion. If all of this were not enough, uncategorizable sex offerings account for another almost $2 billion. But this is only the beginning.[6]

About 15 percent of all Web sites are pornographic, a seemingly small amount; but its influence is far-reaching, as we shall see. The Web boasts of nearly 400 million pornographic pages. Nearly a third of all *daily* searches (close to 70 million), however, are for pornographic retrievals. About 10 percent of all e-mails are pornographic (nearly 3 billion). Almost 40 percent of all downloads are pornographic in nature (nearly 2 billion) and close to 120 thousand daily requests to Gnutella, a file sharing network, are of the unquestionably constitutionally illegal child pornography kind. More than 100 thousand sites on the Web are of children in pornographic repose.[7] Kazaa, another file-sharing network, has been downloaded more than 200 million times, with more than 4 million users sharing and searching files at any given time, many of which are pornographic in content.[8] We are a nation that does not discriminate, either, as about three-fourths of all men and a quarter of all women admit to visiting pornographic Web sites annually. Not to put too fine a point on it, more than 50 percent of all men who are members of the religious group Promise Keepers (and who have pledged to stay away from such things) tap into the pornographic cesspool regularly.

Peer-to-Peer Smutloading

To discover the extent to which pornography in general, and child pornography in specific, is available on peer-to-peer networks, the Customs CyberSmuggling Center used three search terms to find child pornography in 2003. Of some 341 files returned, nearly half were child pornography while about a third were adult pornography.[9] The Government Accounting Office (GAO) did a similar search in 2001 and had similar results. Just over forty percent were child pornography, just over a third adult pornography, while about a fourth were nonpornographic.[10] The GAO discovered that child pornography on the Web was easily found, abundant in number, and ready to be downloaded in easy fashion. Given that a good portion of file sharing (though certainly not all) violates copyright, and a significant amount of it is pornography, one must wonder why restrictions on file sharing are so slight. Certainly the legitimate sharing of files among scholars could be accommodated on a Gnutella-like server with coded access. The rest would have to resort to old-fashioned means, by illegally using snail mail. If such a policy would make the sharing of pornography obsolete, or at least much more problematic, it would be worth it for our children.

Law enforcement is beginning to crack down on child pornography on peer-to-peer networks, but so far the efforts have been negligible.[11] To ask law enforcement to curb one head of the hydra-monster called pornography while its other myriad personas go unchecked is like asking FEMA to repair a breached levee *during* a raging hurricane. The effectiveness of the efforts will be, on the balance, hard to tell. Operation HAMLET (a global investigation) and operation MANGO (on pedophiles living in the safe haven of Acapulco, Mexico) have both had successes in breaking up child pornography rings.[12] Again, unfortunately, these two massive operations were mere drops in the proverbial bucket. The main difficulty is the ease with which peer-to-peer file sharing makes the distribution and sharing of child pornography ubiquitous and without consequence.

Porn: The Cash Cow

It is estimated that the pornography industry takes in more revenues than CBS, NBC, ABC, ESPN, CNN and FOX News, *combined*. In 2003, MediaDefender, a filtering outfit, discovered that in a given 48-hour period, more than 6 million pornographic files were available for download.[13] Put the number in perspective. The six million figure alone exceeds the number of holdings of our largest academic libraries, and is about a fourth the size of the largest library in the world, the Library of Congress. The American Library Association has a great deal to answer to its membership (many of whom have young children) for its defense of pornography. To argue that the First Amendment must be absolute, and that we must accept this measure of perfidiousness in order to preserve the greater good, is patent nonsense, especially when a simple solution, like filtering, remains readily available. ALA should express its contempt, if it has any, for smutographers by calling for the filtering in *every* library, not just public ones, and not just in children's areas. Such an act would go a long way to exhibit its concern for the enormity that is pornography, whatever the kind.

Thankfully, some librarians are calling upon ALA to do this very thing. The celebrated case in the Minneapolis library is but one where librarians, tired of working in what was the equivalent of an adult bookstore, so bad had violations of the unfettered Web become, filed suit. Dorothy Field, director of the Orange County (Fla.) Library System in Orlando asks, "How do we justify offering pornography in the public library? Is it just something that comes with the total package? ... Where is the justification? Common sense tells us there is none."[14] Indeed. Too few librarians are weighing the cost, and many are finding, only too late, that the price of unfettered Web access allowing for pornography is a loss of public support.[15] Once public good will is lost it is almost impossible to get back. Imagine what would happen if all libraries took to heart one professional's call to catalog pornographic sites the way librarians do everything else.[16] Talk about capitulation!

Recently, a young 8-year-old St. Louis child was allegedly sexually assaulted by ten first and second grade boys on the school's playground.[17] The victim and her brother both contend that the other young boys were trying to sexually assault her. The ten boys consisted of one 6-year-old, five 7-year-olds and four 8-year-olds. All have been referred to the city's family court on misdemeanor charges of first-degree sexual misconduct and third-degree assault. Even the court administrator remarked at both their delinquency and ages. Does anyone really think the ubiquity and easy availability of pornography now on the Web did not have anything to do with this? Without the ubiquity of pornography streaming into homes, such stories would be unheard of.

Already we know that recent studies prove 13- and 14-year-olds are more accepting of premarital and extramarital sexual relations between unmarried partners after seeing videos of the same.[18] Of course unblocked adult channels contribute to this, as do adult-content movies young people gain untutored access to. But so does the Web, and the Web is far easier to access. Is this the legacy we want to leave to succeeding generations? If 13- and 14-year-olds already feel this way, how will they feel in college and beyond? Thankfully, Republicans and Democrats are coming together in an effort to find a solution. We can only hope they are not doing too little, too late. The argument here is not that it will be an easy fix; the argument here is that a fix is available if we have the will to enforce it.

So, is pornography a problem, and is it specifically a *Web* problem? To coin a phrase a former president once made famous, it depends on what how you define "problem." Among our *cahier de doleances* against the Web, pornography, and all its twisted sisters, ranks chief among them. While the Web did not invent pornography, it certainly made its longevity and ubiquity a certainty. In other words, we are awash in pornography, and men, women, and our children are its witting and unwitting victims. While all of this has not been made possible by the Web — yes, it was there before the Internet — clearly the Web has made it ubiquitous, more readily available, and more likely to be part of *everyone's* Web existence, whether they want it or not.

Our approach to pornography *vis-à-vis* other potential dangers is a curious one. For example, mention children in any sentence with any other remotely dangerous entity and instantly a battalion of opponents will arise to support its removal. Whether it's alar in apple juice, fluoride in water, or transformers near an elementary school, if there is one chance in a million that a child somewhere in the world will possibly be made uncomfortable, millions of individuals appear ready to take the offending monster down.[19] Yet when it comes to pornography, we are slow to respond to a *known* vice that has no redeeming value. Some argue that pornography is "appropriate" for adults, but no one has been able to say what it is appropriate for, and no one has outlined its putative beneficial effects. For a short time, some argued that pornography might improve the sex lives of couples, but even that argument — with the rising tide of men who are addicted to porn — has fallen in the gutter where it belongs. One would think the simplest thing in the world would be the elimination of porn on the Web. Lamentably, at just about every turn, the American Library Association has been there to cavil against any possible solution under the guise of its absolutist First Amendment interpretation.

While it is not the purview of this book to address filters, one brief aside is in order. ALA has been the chief opponent of them in any library but especially public libraries, the single largest provider of free online access outside the home.[20] The stated reason is often that they do not work. This is curious since ALA knows perfectly well that filters do work *at least* as well as all other automation now used in libraries. For example, proprietary databases routinely drop titles without notice, have trouble allowing the printing of graphics, and drop footnotes (see chapter 4). One would think this would vitiate the source, or at least elicit calls for improvement, but in more than a decade and half of following the literature I have not seen even one article raise this as an objection for having them. Yet a filtering source, effectively blocking 85 percent to 95 percent of offending sites, is considered inutile because it does not block 100 percent of the possible sites 100 percent of the time. No other library automation is required to be this effective.

The arguments about filters over- and under-blocking (blocking too many, or not blocking all) are cited by ALA as reasons for making their uses wrong in libraries. That is, if one good site is blocked (never mind that nearly all filtering software allows sites to be added, or sites to be unblocked), it should not be used. It does not seem to matter that only fifteen years ago, all these sites that we cannot live without now, were unavailable at all. No one then felt deprived or felt then that the First Amendment was being butchered. Now that we can get to them, miss even one and the First Amendment is being scuttled, or so we are to believe. For ALA, to lose even one good site in return for the blocking of 100 pornography sites remains, incomprehensibly enough, unacceptable.[21]

Why, however, does ALA care about the possibility of one Web site being lost to either over- or under-blocking in the first place? It seems disingenuous. Google, ALA's poster child for the best sort of search engine (indeed, ALA routinely comes out with statements about how all library OPACs should search like Google), does not even search all the Web (recall from the last chapter that it searches only about 30–40 percent of the Web). Although this does not make Google useless, you can bet that if filtering software showed up as this ineffective it would be ridiculed mercilessly. Of course it would be wrong to argue that ALA wants to use the First Amendment as an abattoir for morals, and yet its apparent desire to protect pornography is, at best, curious; at worst, perfidious.

Web-Based Porn Ubiquitous, but Is It Illegal?

This raises the big debate of whether pornography on the Web is illegal. While it is illegal to traffic in it, or to allow the underage to view it, most hide behind the

Supreme Court decision of *Miller v. California* (1973) where only obscene speech is banned for everyone. This is odd, too, because a close reading of *Miller* proves that pornography is illegal. The three-part test of *Miller* argues that if sexual (or excretory) acts are explicitly prohibited by state law (and all states have some law against them), if material depicting these acts appeals only to prurient interests and is "patently offensive" as judged by a reasonable person using community standards, and if there is no serious artistic, literary, social, political or scientific value, the material is illegal.[22]

All child pornography is banned for everyone. The Web, of course, has both of these types of sites (yes, and including excretory ones!) and yet banning pornography appears next to impossible. Some contend that there is no "place" in cyberspace and so community standards cannot be ascertained. But this is to split hairs in a more Talmudic way than even Talmudic scholars would. Regulation or outright banning of this kind of pornography is granted under *Ginsberg v. New York,* which upheld New York's ban of the sale of same to any minor (under the age of 17).[23] The case reads like a description of any pornography Web site: nudity, sexual excitement, sexual conduct, sadomasochistic abuse that is shameful, morbid, appeals to prurient interests, is patently offensive to prevailing standards in the adult community as a whole, and is utterly without redeeming importance. One would think that using this, the "Ginsberg" speech rule, would make it easy to eliminate pornography; but a quick view of the Web will prove this untrue.

Some have argued that because some sites' practice of requiring that you click on "enter" after agreeing that you are 18 or older is a satisfactory workaround. Yet using Google's Image search gets around all of this quite easily without clicking on any checkbox at all. Almost any term put in the Google's image search engine (even using common female names like Cindy, Jane or Carol, or using the names of flowers such as Rose or Violet) will provide salacious images of oral, anal and group sex, simulated rape and more. (Curiously, using Google's own SafeSearch in its "medium" mode reduces offending sites by more than 90 percent. We miss sites anyway with each search so why not just make this the common search mode?)

Lawmakers have, of course, tried to prohibit pornography, both the commercial trafficking of it and those who abuse others in it. Everyone knows that porn is everywhere on the Web, too. For example, the Communications Decency Act came about because of the ubiquity of Web porn although the galvanizing report, a 1995 Carnegie Mellon study, proved flawed.[24] Even so, the effect might well be said to have been McCarthyite. When Joseph McCarthy argued that there were Communists in high-ranking government positions, the only thing he got wrong were the numbers. Unfortunately, his hyperbole, which was of course regrettably overkill, is all that anyone remembers. The Carnegie Mellon report got the ubiquity of Web-porn right; it just got the percentages hyperbolically wrong, and that has done enough damage to slow the banning of Web porn down to a snail's pace, if that fast. Whenever porn is brought up, soon the argument will be made that it's not all *that* bad. The Communications Decency Act passed and President Clinton — the irony is acute — signed the bill into law.

No one who has used the Web for more than ten minutes can doubt that Web porn is readily available. Most (ALA excepted) do not even doubt that it should be strongly regulated if not banned outright. What appears to be the bugbear in this case is how to do that. Most writing about this subject would argue that part of the problem is that pornography is hard to define and generally revert to Justice Potter's familiar quip that "I know it when I see it." But pornography is really not that hard to define, and the court in both *Miller* and *Ginsberg* have made strong efforts in that direction. Others would argue that the First Amendment means accepting speech you may not like. But this is like saying the Fifth Amendment really means you cannot defend yourself. Since the mind is more easily swayed by the eye than by the ear, why not simply ban all sorts of sexual antics (the list is long but it would include fellatio, cunnilingus, anal intercourse, fisting [no more need be said], group sex, masturbation, scopophagia, bestiality, any simulation of these things, child porn, nudity and so on) on the Web?

What proponents of porn (one is at a loss how else to refer to them) have yet to show is what good it does anyone: men, women, children or animals. The Web has made pornography a concern for everyone. Before the Web it remained a problem — and the sole financial responsibility — of those addicted to it. They were forced into dark alleys, forced into scrimy theatres, and forced to get their porn in brown wrappers (though the postal regulations prove effective in making even this difficult). One cannot find on the Web *any* pornography that is not utterly without any social, cultural, literary or political merit. While there are those sites that try to get around this by shooting mostly women, but also some men, in libraries or bookstores, one would be hard-pressed (no pun intended) to make a case that this fulfills the literary claim.[25]

Underused Laws

To forestall child pornography, law enforcement has not been without its tools, though as soon as they are in place, the courts (whether state, federal or the Supreme Court) are quick to erase them, or otherwise make them impotent. Chapter 110 of Title 18 contains provision for civil and criminal penalties for the production, distribution, sale and possession of child pornography. This act set the legal limit at under 18 years of age. The Child Pornography Protection Act of 1996 (CPPA) amended this to include three other aspects: a visual depiction in which a child appears to be engaging in a sexual act, a visual depiction that has been modified to make it appear a child is so engaged, or a visual depiction in which a child is promoting or advertising explicit sexual conduct. CPPA enlarged upon already present provisions to specifically tie them to Web-based or computer channels.[26] But the Supreme Court declared in April of 2002 that the second provision, in which a child appeared to be engaging in explicit sexual conduct, was unconstitutional.

The Child Protection and Obscenity Enforcement Act of 1988 and amendments of the Child Protection Restoration and Penalties Enhancement Act of 1990 added other requirements to Title 18. These requirements call for the pornography industry to essentially verify that models and others who "perform" in their movies be documented to be 18 years of age or older. The kinds of records are specified and the records must be on hand at all times and shown to police when required. Obviously these protections were enough (hence, the Web site that is the title-onym of this chapter), so Congress tried again.

The Children's Internet Protection Act (CHIPA, or CIPA) and the Child Online Protection Act (COPA) both looked very promising for a few years following the defeats of CDA I and CDA II.[27] Thanks in large part to the ever-present American Civil Liberties Union (ACLU) and in no small measure ALA, hair-splitting about what the law actually says chilled the potential effectiveness of both laws. COPA (designed to "fix" CDA) failed in large part because it imposes sanctions on Web vendors who knowingly provide material harmful to minors. Smutographers will not turn themselves in, and securing violators and proving they knowingly provided materials — even though common sense demands that they know — is apparently impossible. COPA also failed because courts found that its injunction "harmful to minors" placed an "impermissible" burden upon protected speech.[28] COPA, while it remains a statute, is still ineffective.

CHIPA's reach to public libraries has already been challenged and struck down by a federal district court.[29] Its application to schools on the receiving end of federal funding remains. Both addressed themselves, not to adults viewing questionable materials, but to minors, or those under seventeen years of age. Again, the guidelines are clear to anyone not employed by the ACLU or work in ALA's Office of Intellectual Freedom: obscene materials of prurient interest that are patently offensive to the average person. Yet even when restricting the reach to minors alone, First Amendment absolutists will stop at nothing to ensure pornography's place in the public square.

Although CHIPA only went into effect in July of 2006, both ACLU and ALA are already looking for loopholes and workarounds. One important case that may force the Supreme Court to take a long look is the argument that filters block adults from accessing constitutionally protected material.[30] But this pits the rights of one group against those of another, arguing that libraries cannot be required to have filters because it will deny the right of free access to constitutionally protected materials for adults. If the courts agree with this argument, they will in effect be saying that what adults want matters more than what harms minors, a stand they have rarely taken before. The argument that pornography is protected free speech is a lost cause. Pornography fails in a number of respects but chiefly on its claim of redeeming value.

The Children's Online Privacy Protection Act of 1998 (COPPA) "prohibits the collection, maintenance and use or disclosure of personal information from children under the age of 13 on commercial Web sites" whose aim is for children, if the operator knows the child is 13 or younger, or if the information is collected without verified parental consent.[31] The idea behind COPPA is to prevent the collection of personal information on children that could be used by the site itself or by others hijacking the information on that site.

In the end, however, the Web remains unfettered and unembarrassed by its flagrant and blatant violation of the law. Child pornography abounds and sites not using children but adults in every conceivable and inconceivable arrangement of men and women (and even animals) remain. What ALA, the ACLU and other organizations must answer to, however, is not whether pornography is protected — it is clear it is not — but why they continue to shield it as something of redeeming value.

The emphasis on the redeeming value of pornography is an important one because even in these challenges, no attempt has been made by the ACLU, or anyone else for that matter, to make a reasonable case for the good that it does. All we have so far are the destroyed lives, whether of those who pose for it, or those who buy it. Pornography can be likened to harmful cholesterol. No one argues that it is "good" for you, or that it's good for any age group, even children. No one contends that we need not worry about the fat content in children's food because they are too young for it to harm them, and of course no adult would make the case that certain high levels are fine. With pornography, unlike cholesterol, there has yet to be identified a "good" pornography provides, yet still it remains.

If cholesterol does not seem like a useful metaphor, swimming pools may be substituted.[32] Swimming pools pose a threat to children wherever they are. Although they provide great benefits to owners, especially adults, they still pose significant, even deadly, dangers to unsuspecting children. Hence, owners are forced to put in fences, pool alarms or locks on the access to them. Most are required to drain them in the winter. Yet although education will generally work with most children — teaching them how to swim — it will not when it comes to surfing porn. Pools do not have a way of suddenly appearing while a child is playing video football, or video baseball. The cholesterol metaphor appears more accurate, as nothing about bad cholesterol is good for anyone, whereas learning how to swim can not only provide excellent aerobic exercise, but could save lives.

"There's lots of junk on the World Wide Web," writes one pundit. "And there's lots that's worse than junk. Some of the stuff, for some people, is offensive or worse. The worse includes material deemed obscene or, and this is a very different category, 'harmful to minors'— aka pornography."[33] The pundit, in this case, is no mere mortal but the very well-known and rightly respected Lawrence Lessig. But even Lessig exhibits the sad behavior about the Web criticized throughout these pages. Later, in the same passage, Lessig admits that pornography is awful and child pornography is of course illegal. After making his usual strong arguments, he brings up censorware and without batting an eye, writes, "And obviously, if the choice is no Internet or a filtered Internet, it is better that kids have access to the Internet."[34] That is not, of course, the choice, and to imply that it is, is silly.

To Have the Web Means Having Porn?

It's hard to think of a more irresponsible statement made by a responsible scholar. Does Lessig seriously mean that it's better to let children be subjected to pornography than to have them surf on a restricted Web, a Web that none of us had a decade and half ago and were none the worse for wear without — and possibly better off? This is the equivalent of saying that we should not try to curb drunk driving for fear we will subject the abstemious to an undue infringement of their rights. But in a pluralistic society, that is exactly what we do. In order to guard the weakest and the least able to defend themselves, we often restrict the behaviors of all. Those who refuse to abide by these strictures are subject to legal penalties. This is the way it has worked for all our laws — that is, until we are faced with trying to make Web-based pornography illegal. If we are such an irresponsible society to believe that our only choice is to leave the nation awash in pornography of every conceivable and inconceivable description *or to allow that portion of the Web to be cleaned up,* then we deserve the hydra-headed problems it brings.[35]

So far every effort to remove or prohibit pornography is stymied by those who argue that our Constitution is too fragile to withstand its loss. The argument tends to be that if this goes, a whole host of other constitutionally protected speech would go as well. Yet when did the Constitution begin protecting patently offensive speech? No one denies that the Constitution protects all kinds of speech, even speech that only a handful of people would find offensive. However, First Amendment cases have found certain kinds of speech — libel for example, or crying fire in a crowed theatre when there isn't one — should not be protected. It has been the Court's wisdom that not only are they *not* protected, but they also must be *prevented.*

As indicated earlier, COPA (1998) followed on the heels of CDA and tried to limit the availability to minors of unseemly materials on the Internet.[36] The pointed language in COPA unmistakably targeted Web-based pornography. COPA provided for penalties for anyone "Whoever knowingly and with knowledge of the character of the material, in interstate or foreign commerce by means of the World Wide Web, makes any communication for commercial purposes that is available to any minor and that includes any material that is harmful to minors."[37] Even those who trafficked in smut and had not yet made a profit found themselves shackled by COPA. Again, COPA flounders owing to the usual suspects who rushed to the defense of their *ne plus ultra* views of the First Amendment.

Senator John McCain, future presidential hopeful for 2008, pushed CHIPA very hard and by 2000 had pushed it through both houses. Again with an irony that should not be lost on anyone, President Clinton signed it into law in April 2001.[38] The tack taken by CHIPA was that libraries and schools would prevent pornography at least to minors through filtering. ALA once again stepped up to the plate and through innuendo and outright fabrication created such an atmosphere of doubt about filters that many librarians gave up trying. CHIPA remains but is in litigation limbo.

We're Awash in Porn

"Today our society is awash in graphic sexually explicit materials," write Dick Thornburgh and Herbert S. Lin,

> that are widely available in nearly every medium of communication — print, audio, and video — and in nearly every imaginable setting from home and school to overnight lodging. Much of the material with which this report is concerned was clearly violative of the obscenity laws a decade or so ago, but seldom are prosecutions brought in the 21st Century.[39]

Yet it does not seem to matter. We would rather be a country awash in this cesspool than risk losing one byte from the Web. In many ways, we get what we deserve from this irresponsible approach. The idea of seriously policing these materials without taking into account the manner in which the Web has made it ubiquitous is ludicrous. Pornography is intrusive and virtually impossible to avoid because the Web has made it everywhere available.

This rich, supposedly unprecedented educational and information resource that will putatively replace libraries routinely delivers the worst that humankind can offer. It's important to remember, however, that pornography is not only available in millions of Web pages, but also in chat rooms, e-mails, alternative groups, FaceBook, MySpace, Friendster and other so-called "social communities." Moreover, the local child molester who might not have shown his face twenty years ago shows it in every community in America, thanks to the Web. The anonymity that the Web provides makes it easy to prey on the young and unsuspecting without the risk of capture, much less prosecution, that would have been true when those of that bent were forced to seek pleasure in the open.[40] MySpace, especially, has become a haven for pedophiles and porn.[41]

In fact, MySpace has become so bad ("skanky," as the *New York Times* puts it) that even corporate sponsors such as Weight Watchers and T-Mobile are either pulling their ads or threatening to do so. Some users are as young as 14 or even younger. Most of the profiles are so base that they cannot be repeated here. Some of the "more presentable" profiles include young girls "practicing to be porn stars" or the sharing of pictures of the anything-goes porn star Tera Patrick, and others. If you think pedophiles have missed this opportunity, think again. They are there and trolling for the wary and the not-so-wary. Some schools are now in the business of trying to prevent harassment, or trying to make certain their students know who the real administrators are and who the imposters are.[42] Some principals and other school leaders are learning that MySpace has creative "profiles" of them that, while clever in some cases, are entirely fictional. Young people, being what they are, have had great fun with some of these profiles that have been taken seriously by others: other students, other school administrators or officials, and others in other states. The most serious problem continues to be predators, but fictional profiles are beginning to appear with more regularity and creating something of a nuisance for all involved. Not only school leaders but others are bullied, electronically of course.

Proponents of the unfettered Web have argued that a better approach is to use schools and libraries to teach good Internet use and avoid its abuse. But this seems wishful thinking. For the last twenty-five years our school system has proven itself incapable of teaching most children how to read and write, add, subtract, multiply or divide.[43] More recently we learned that we can now add geography to that list of unteachable subjects. To expect schools to undertake this new skill when they cannot accomplish their mission is foolhardy at best, and just plain foolish at worst.

Censorship: The *Bête Noir*

Of course censorship is on the minds of many, and ALA argues most vehemently about it. Censorship should not, of course, be taken lightly.[44] But to argue that we should accept everything for fear of censoring anything is a peculiar postmodern argument.

Libraries censor routinely, and often for the worst of reasons — price. Thousands of very good, very useful, very important books are missed by libraries every year because there simply aren't enough funds to go around. The materials those libraries have bypassed have effectively censored them from their patrons. Furthermore, librarians — and most of the rest of society — rightly have little trouble censoring hate speech. Why do we find it so hard to censor pornography we know is deleterious in every detail?

Since the Web contains, relatively speaking, a small percentage of pornography compared to the rest of what it offers, should there be any concern?[45] To date there are about eight *billion* pages on the Web. When all the pages and groups are added up, it may, depending on who is counting, account for about 20 percent that would fall into the pornographic category. Should we risk the other 80 percent for this relatively small amount?[46]

Holding that question at bay for a moment, one would have to recall that the remaining 80 percent is not all good, reliable information. As we have seen in the last chapter, not only is everything not on the Web, but even what comes up in searches is often not the best that exists on the Web, and some of the Web is not searched at all. Indeed, the "howling wastes of the Internet," a phrase used by one wag to describe the Web early on, may not have been far off. Librarians allow much over the Web that we have never before, nor ever would have allowed in print. Think for a moment: how many libraries can you name that offer free and unfettered access to photographs of sexual behaviors of every description, in every possible human (and animal) context? One? Two? If one of those is the Vatican's *Index Prohibitum*, is there another? Now, stop and think how many libraries of *any* description can be named that offered free and unfettered access to videos of these acts, with or without children? As Derek Law points out, the problems the Web brings suddenly make it seem much less than the "Holy Grail" we once thought it to be and that, sadly, some continue to think it today.[47]

Why can't we regulate Web-based porn? Part of the reason is because the real dangers of pornography are often waylaid by the imagined (read penumbral) violations of privacy. Take for example the government's subpoena of Google's search data.[48] In trying to carry out the provisions of the Child Online Protection Act, the government tried to persuade a judge to get Google to turn over million of search records. Google's three main competitors — Yahoo, America Online and MSN — have complied with the subpoena already. Google's showboating, cheered by thousands of conspiracy theorists who fear what their own government might do more than they do the real activity of child molesters everywhere, masks just how many young lives will be ruined forever in the meanwhile. Although there is *no* right to privacy in the Constitution, merely a "penumbra," or shadow of rights that Justice William O. Douglas thought he saw "emanating" from the actual rights, child molesters, pornographers and a host of other "undesirables" have been shielded by this fictive shadow from an actual law that should shackle them.[49]

It should go without saying that those who traffic in such things should not have the benefit of law. And responsible citizens, even though they are law abiding, may feel at least a pinch, however imperceptible, if they pursue wrongdoing by our system of justice. We see this in all other contexts. For example, when roadblocks are set up at various locales in an effort to apprehend drunk drivers, no one is more inconvenienced than teetotalers, or those who have enjoyed a drink well below the legal limit. Although such cases are coming under more and more scrutiny, hardly anyone objects, for we understand that in order to catch the few it is sometimes necessary to impose upon the many. No reasonable individuals would argue that they would rather see drunk drivers take the lives of dozens before seeing any law-abiding citizen inconvenienced for a moment.

Likewise, it seems, should be the case with pornography and the law's long arm to catch its creators since it is adjudged obscene.[50] For the millions who have never visited a pornographic Web site, having their anonymous records examined is meaningless. For those that surf recreationally, so much the better that this behavior may be curtailed or even constrained. And finally, for those using the Web to troll for smut, or even looking to ensnare the young, their days will finally be over. If truth be told, only a small percentage of those records would ever be examined closely, and then only for individuals who have *repeatedly* looked at or visited sites specializing in child pornography. To disallow even this paucity of intrusion is tantamount to protecting child pornography, child molesters and all those who traffic in these and similar lurid occupations.

While CDA and its variants, CHIPA and COPA, have either been rebuked or taken to a stalemate, other almost laughingly impotent laws remain unchallenged. Unsurprisingly, the Neighborhood Children's Internet Protection Act (NCIPA), a sister piece of legislation, stands unchallenged. It requires libraries in receipt of certain federal funds to draw up Internet safety policies. This is particularly vexing since child pornography is speech specifically *not* protected by the First Amendment and specially prohibited even inside the privacy of one's home.[51]

First Amendment Absolutists

One might expect that given this scenario, even die-hard defenders of the all-or-nothing interpretation of the First Amendment would at least see two things. First, that not all speech is protected. This is blatantly obvious, yet many, ALA included, appear not to understand this at all, or at least act as if they do not understand it. Secondly, it should also prove that even when it comes to those illusive penumbral rights glittering among the Bill of Rights, they, too, are not absolute. Obviously neither point resonates with ALA or the ACLU, as case after case pressed by these two organizations never reveals a working knowledge of the actual law. Only one point drives both organizations: the First Amendment is absolute or it is meaningless. ALA's position is, and has been for the last thirty years, that no speech is so offensive, so pornographic, or so sexually demeaning that it must not be preserved and protected. To do otherwise is to jeopardize our ever-frail, valetudinarian First Amendment.

Some might argue that NCIPA represents a step in the right direction, a move that would find common ground between libraries and the law. But it is not because the requirements of this law lack any observable function other than to send libraries to the drawing board to doodle out what will largely become unenforced, or unenforceable, provisions. The most that will come out of this law are a set of rules that can be posted for a generation that can no longer read, or certainly not read anything more than a sentence or two. In other words, NCIPA is meaningless window-dressing for it will do nothing to stop the spate of horrific sexual materials abundant on the Web.

It is odd, really, that frequently left-of-center solutions often bank their success on the one thing this postmodern society has taught us it can no longer do well: educate young generations. Given the failure of K–12 education in this country for universally agreed-upon necessities such as reading, writing and arithmetic, it would appear that young children do not have the cognitive ability (search strategies, typing skills) to navigate the Web independently.[52] Young adults (ages 13–17) probably do have the requisite cognitive abilities, but teaching young males not to surf sites that are full of free pictures of nude women having unbridled sex would be harder than teaching new tricks to old dogs. Add to this age the inherent braggadocio of showing off such pictures to peers and you have an impossible educational scenario.

Posting acceptable Internet use provisions or giving a tap on the shoulder does little to stop pornography in the library, and nothing at all to retard its ubiquity on the Web. Monitoring is another favored tactic, yet only if it does not involve technologically monitoring what a person views. For example, an individual library employee may randomly visually monitor what patrons are doing but not actually remotely monitor technologically. To monitor using technology would be an invasion of privacy, that sacred, even sacrosanct rule that allows us to sacrifice our children in favor of molesters to prevent undue "privacy" intrusions. While it is technologically possible to monitor keystrokes, sites visited and the like, First Amendment absolutists remain foursquare opposed.

Furthermore, while some may argue that public institutions cannot filter the Web, at least private ones can. Some might argue that if an individual has a "problem" with unfettered access, she can do her work in private libraries. But even this is no guarantee. Although there is no Constitutional right to unfettered Internet access in private libraries, some state constitutions, such as California's, trump the Constitution's, or a private institution's reach. In the case of the Golden State, students at private institutions can expect unfettered Internet access, too.[53]

Ubiquitous Porn Means You Can't Just "Turn the Channel"

Some may grant that many may find pornography offensive and so should just steer clear. But making that claim, and doing so, are next to impossible. If any other criminally intentioned individual preyed so openly on his victims, ALA and the ACLU would be the first to cry foul. For example, imagine the din of hue and cry that would ensue were the police to use the tactics described below to entrap criminals? Yet pornographers are not only exculpated but defended by others for doing it.

The inadvertent intrusion of sexually explicit pictures into almost *any search* is a very strong likelihood.[54] Pornographers prey upon misspellings. Misspelling even a familiar Web site can land a minor in the wrong place. The most common misspellings have been acquired by owners of adult Web sites.[55] Domain name suffixes such as .gov and .com for once familiar sites are now well-known, the most familiar of which is www.whitehouse.com. A young person may not know, at least the first time, that this is a well-known pornography site. The same is true of www.firstwmendment.org. That site would naturally occur most readily to a 13- or 14-year old as a good place to begin a paper on the First Amendment. Even well-known children's sites have been bought up by pornographers after the original owners have forgotten to renew the domain name, or have been too slow to renew it. *Porn-napping,* as this is often referred to, is a common practice.[56] Of course the original owners can get the name back, but often at exorbitant prices that would, under ordinary practice, be considered a form of extortion. This occurred on a children's money management site, moneyopolis.org. Once taken over, visitors were sent to euroteensluts.org, obviously a pornographer's site.[57] Surely all the young teens on the site were over 18, of course.

Turning Porn Tricks

Cybersquatting, a trick referred to in chapter 2, is another favored method of pornographers. In this case the pornographer buys up the domain name legally and then switches the site. Some innocent sounding names in which this has occurred are civilwarbattles.com, eugeneoregon.com and tourdefrance.com.[58] None of these would ever indicate what awaited the visitor, even an adult. The same is true for the trick known as "doorway scams." This method involves constructing the site so that the content will appear high on the search results. For example, a search on "livestock" may result in a "hit" list with a porn site on bestiality. While most advertisers will not sell space to pornographers, this hasn't stopped them. Some have bought pop-up ads that give error messages or message alert boxes that lead, when clicked on, to pornographic sites.[59] I encountered one particularly internecine pre–Google trick that seemed tailor-made for the college-aged. After a search for a common term for a paper, a few hits resulted with just enough information that was close but not exact. In a box at the bottom of the search results was the following: "Not finding what you want? Click here." The end result was a site filled with so many pornography pop-ups ("looping," the industry calls it), one had to shut the computer down to clear them. Another feature is called "mouse-trapping," in which the mouse becomes useless. No matter what you do, you are trapped into porn pop-ups.[60]

Downloading is a favorite pastime of youth. Often, pornographers use this technique by providing what appears to be searched-for information. Once the download command is clicked, the user ends up with porn on his computer, a technique called a "Trojan horse." This can happen when downloading something as innocent-seeming as a calendar or even a puzzle meant for children.[61] A "dialer" is another pornographer-favored trick. which hides an expensive dialer on the computer following a download. Each time it's used, expensive downloads of porn ensue.[62] The Federal Trade Commission has taken legal action against this last form, but it has not disappeared completely.

Besides, paying a fee, even a large one, is not much of a deterrent to a company that stands to make tens of millions from well-placed dialers.

"E-mail spoofing" is another favored trick. Although most wary Internet users do not open an e-mail from an unknown source, pornographers have managed to use various techniques to replicate one's own address book. The e-mail then looks like it's coming from a known and trusted source.[63] Finally, P2P (peer-to-peer) file sharing, mentioned above, is a common pornographer's practice today. So far, nothing has been done to make this illegal, or to stop the abundant flow of smut from one computer to the next, whether one wants it or not. To reiterate a point made earlier in this chapter, Google's image search is the quickest way for a user to find sexually explicit pictures. In a search performed in late 2005 by the author on horses, the resulting *first* page displayed two images of women engaged in oral sex, and sexual intercourse with a horse.

While these are not all the tricks of pornographers, these are enough to illustrate the problem the Web has wrought. Even with the innocent pursuit of information on the Web, chances are high that users will end with pornography. Indeed, it is has become proverbial among wise users of the Web that to know the latest in Web-based technology, one only has to visit a pornography site to see what will be more widely used in the future. Pornographers know that they must stay on the cutting edge of the newest in technology to keep their poison ubiquitous. According to a recent CACRC survey, more than 25 percent of all minors have had at least one exposure to sexually explicit images, the most common of which is either nude pictures, or pictures of women involved in sexual intercourse of some kind.[64] Like the tobacco industry, pornographers know that if they can entice young people early enough, they will keep them coming back for more. Once a person, young or old, has been hooked, it is next to impossible to undo the damage, as porn-addicts can well attest. Arousal theory indicates that consumers of pornography must not only view more of it more frequently, but must view more extreme forms.[65]

Conservatives, joined by the most unlikely bedfellows — feminists — have with one voice condemned pornography. Both groups see it as not only bad for children and adults, but as demeaning to women, who are its most likely victims. The number of lives ruined by chance exposure to pornography continues to escalate and in its wake are ruined relationships, ruined marriages, and ruined lives. As Deitz has written,

> Pornography is a medical and public health problem because so much of it teaches false, misleading, and even dangerous information about human sexuality.... A person who learned about human sexuality in the "adults only" outlets of America would be a person who had never conceived of a man and a woman marrying or even falling in love before having intercourse, who had never conceived of tender foreplay, and who had never conceived of procreation as a purpose for sexual union. Instead, such a person would be one who had learned that sex at most meant sex with one's children, stepchildren, parents, siblings, pets and with neighbors, plumbers, salesmen, burglars and peepers.[66]

On would think that with the abundant evidence to the contrary about the value of pornography for *anyone*, banning it on the Web would be easy. Unfortunately, for too many people, keeping the First Amendment absolute (when no such thing was even intended) is more important. Compare this with the approach many of these same individuals take with respect to the Second Amendment, where making the sale of *any* kind of gun illegal, not just semi-automatics, would be preferred. Indeed, many of these same individuals would think nothing about rescinding the Second Amendment.

Even those who remain diffident about filters see the need for a better policy. They understand that the "First Amendment is not ... absolute [or] that it requires an anything-goes attitude by the government and its personnel."[67] Indeed, as pointed out in this chapter more than once, the exceptions to free speech remain under the headings of libel, obscenity, fighting words (those which when uttered inflict injury "or incite an immediate breach of the peace") and child pornography.[68] While no one would argue that nudity *per se* falls into this category, surely no one would argue that nude women engaged in various forms of sexual intercourse (with men, other women, animals or children) does not. Even the Supreme Court has found, as we have seen in the various laws mentioned above, that child pornography, and more, can be restricted. That it has not been restricted on the Web attests first to the cleverness of pornographers in making sheer volume a deterrent against prosecution, and second to a weakness among good men and women to do nothing.

But isn't there something vulgar, something altogether untoward — a tergiversation really — about a librarian writing a book about the glorious values of full service libraries campaigning not only for filters but also for what can only be seen as a breach of the First Amendment, and the librarian's sacred vow to protect against censorship? Only First Amendment absolutists would respond positively. Not all library professionals are First Amendment absolutists, but most are. For most of my professional career I have encountered only First Amendment absolutists, or those who think the First Amendment prohibits censorship of any kind, *but especially speech some would find offensive.*

Treason of the Clerks ... Maybe

A curious thing happened on the way to bringing libraries cunnilingus and fellatio at a whim at every turn in the library. Many librarians discovered that supervising porn is not what they signed up for. The history of librarianship supports these librarians, for the history of this profession has never endorsed anything remotely pornographic, that is until the modern age, beginning roughly 1960. For example, "Most recent scholarship [in librarianship] suggests the reality of a democratic contradiction for these early 'apostles of culture' and their 'library hostesses.' [The excesses of] circumspection and conformity were really indicative of an initial professional commitment to censorship."[69] To characterize it as a "commitment to censorship" is silly but it does reflect this profession's allegiance to selection in libraries of only the best humankind has to offer. Just because early librarians made a distinction between schlock and good writing, decided their libraries would collect literature for the ages rather than scribblings for the moment, does not make them part of a conspiracy of censorship. In many ways they have proven themselves faithful to the profession for anyone can do this job if she allows everything for fear of censoring anything. Further, it is ludicrous to argue that more recent librarians "have held the belief that maximum access to public information sources and channels of communication is necessary for political, economic, and social participation in a vigorous democracy."[70] Parents have little help in this regard since even innocent searches for entertainment figures popular with children (e.g. Britney Spears) yield pornographic images.[71]

If "maximum access" is the ideal of librarianship, it is one we have *never* fulfilled. As pointed out earlier, libraries have practiced censorship at every level in the profession. The only difference is that we call it "selection" when we do it. But selecting some things and not selecting others is as it should be. For if we care about the quality of life, we have to favor some disagreeable level of censorship. Indeed, we do already, whether we are willing to admit it or not.

Further, the founders who wrote the First Amendment, as we have shown, never intended that it should be taken as absolute. Before the ink was dry, the Constitution foreclosed upon speech that was libelous, upon speech that incited fighting, upon speech that was meant to harm or to cause ill, or speech that was obscene. To argue at this late date that the Web must remain unfettered in all its inglorious offerings in order to maintain democracy is preposterous in the extreme. Rather, like Livy, "We can neither endure our vices nor face the remedies needed to cure them." And like Livy, to refuse those remedies — cures by the way which are easily implemented — we will witness our own, and richly deserved, ignominious end. No good awaits a country so awash in graphic depictions of sexual malversations that even its youth cannot avoid viewing them. Because we are unwilling to curtail pornography on the Web, we make certain our children will be the future's unwitting victims of it.

4

Footnotes? Who Needs Them!

"You may observe," said Sir Arthur in Sir Walter Scott's *The Antiquary*, "that he never has any advantage of me in dispute, unless when he avails himself of a sort of pettifogging intimacy with dates, names, and trifling matters of fact — a tiresome and frivolous accuracy of memory, which is entirely owing to his mechanical descent."

"He must find it convenient in historical investigation, I should think, sir?" said the young lady.[1]

Devilish Details

"Pettifogging intimacy with dates, names, and trifling matters of fact" may well describe what has become of footnotes — or footnoting — in this our brave, new cyberworld. While footnotes have grown from the nonexistent to the pedestrian, if Grafton's entertaining and enthralling history is even only half right, they still remain to most scholars the lifeblood of scholarship.[2] Present day publishing forces upon most writers only the most Spartan of footnotes, leaving behind Edward Gibbon's expansive and, oftentimes, sardonic approach.[3] Footnotes have become "Just the facts, ma'am," as Sergeant Friday often said in his signature deadpan voice on the 1950s television show "Dragnet." Today, even in print, footnotes are the merest of fact-checking, a will-o'-the-wisp substantiation of a claim. In our cyberworld, however, they may well have become even less than that.

We can't blame the slow decline of footnotes to cyberspace exclusively. Indeed, most publishers, at least most commercial publishers, have resorted to the most annoying form of the endnote, one that references a series of pages (e.g. 123–145); the needles of reference to the haystacks of claims. But even this use is important to scholars, for without footnotes of some kind, we could not check one another's claims.

Fun with Footnotes

Footnotes are no guarantee of the claims made, of course. They can be payback, as Grafton reminds. "Unlike other types of credentials," writes Grafton, "...footnotes sometime afford entertainment — normally in the form of daggers stuck in the backs of the author's colleagues."[4] Or they can come, he reminds, in the form of the *damnatio memoriae*, a claim made by one author against another's failure to cite, especially the whining author. They can also lay claim to reference where none has been made, or rather where something akin to the opposite claim has been made, what might be called a footnote of velleity. The poor reader must ferret though the reference hoping to find the ghost-like substantiation. It does not matter. What matters is that footnotes are to scholarship in many ways what shoes are to feet: while you do not need them every time and in every situation, if you appear once without them when required, you look foolish to say the least.

Now surely we cannot transfer the gripes we may have about the Web to footnotes, can we? While the chapters so far may be said to make a compelling case against the Web as a record of permanence, and against it as source for always reliable information, surely to complain about a lack of footnotes is taking it too far. Isn't the Web really just a copy of what has already been done? If it did not appear in the original, we can hardly blame the Web! Indeed, the Web is barely a record of the now, so quickly does its past fade. But footnotes? How can this be a problem?

Easily. The Web, *per se*, is guilty of lagging, missing, omitting or ignoring footnotes altogether. But the complaint in this chapter is of a far more serious kind. While the dot-coms and the dot-nets are certainly the most egregious offenders when it comes to vanishing footnotes, even the electronic proprietary databases — databases like *Lexis-Nexis*, *Academic Search Premier*, *InfoTrac* and so on — offend insensibly and unnecessarily. Not only must librarians worry about the retention of electronic titles in aggregate databases, they must also fret over whether to keep both print and electronic collections.[5] Now, while wringing hands over what to do about lost titles within database collections, they must also worry about a new phenomenon: link rot. Link rot, or what some refer to as the half-life phenomenon, has become an increasing worry since the late nineties, when it was first noticed. The Web had not been around long enough before then to notice the growing problem. Moreover, no one perhaps gave it any real thought.

Digital Storage May Hold Virtually Nothing

But first, a sidebar on digital storage. Nothing could have been easier than digital storage, though many had warned of the Web's impermanence before its maturity to centerstage, or so we thought. The former storage form, CD-ROMs, proved a most aggravating medium. Not only did libraries discover that CD-ROMs pressed in 1990 often did not work on *machines* they bought in 1995, they also found, much to their dismay, that CD-ROMs pressed in 1995 might well be unusable by 1998 owing to ink or some other form of data inquination.

After the ubiquity of the Web, however, many thought all had been solved though no evidence appeared that it had. Without notice, however, librarians and users discovered that "old" for the Web meant about a decade. Many aggregate databases took it as biblical authority that after a decade, every time you added a new year, you dropped the earliest one. Soon, libraries that had prided themselves on having long runs of periodicals so that history might be preserved, found that for Web-based sources two presidential elections were about as long as one could hope for. If that were not enough, some vendors took to purging articles from databases, in some cases very quietly.[6] Still other periodical titles disappeared from vendors because individual agreements failed or because publishers wished to pull their titles and make them available themselves.[7] The problem of missing journals and articles in the Web-based world became so serious that one company, JSTOR, carved out a niche by promising to deliver electronic versions of volume 1, number 1, in perpetuity. For libraries, there is no replacing JSTOR, but it serves as only the drop in the proverbial bucket. Its "vast" e-collections that no library wants to be without scarcely add up to 2,000 total titles, the size of small academic collections.

The Link Rot Pandemic

But I digress. The Web, as mentioned earlier, has infected us with yet another disease in link rot. The question is, is link rot a problem, and is it sufficient enough to warrant a screed against it? Research specifically aimed at the level of severity of link rot with respect to footnotes indicates that the problem is not only of critical importance, but it is also growing, and by leaps and bounds.

In a study of some 416 citations over four years, researchers Bugeja and Dimitrova found that only 61 percent of them were still accessible.[8] Moreover, 19 percent contained an error in the URL while 63 percent did not cite the date they were accessed. This is an unprecedented turn of events, especially when one considers that only a decade and half ago, such careless scholarship would have been unthinkable and unacceptable. While it is not a matter that is slipping by unnoticed, it is worse: it is slipping by with the full knowledge of many scholars.[9] One might excuse it were the journals in question what might be considered in the academic world (it is silly to say it) to be "back-ups" or "second string" sources, assuming there is such a thing. But the sad state of affairs is that the journals in question are among the most prestigious in a specific discipline. Given that the academic discipline is one wherein we teach others the importance of scholarly honesty and integrity, it is most odd to find that we, too, when pushed, simply accept the state of digital life in which we now find ourselves. We accept, like so many baa-ing sheep, that this is the state of progressive affairs, and so we must learn to accept and adapt to it. Many already have. Baby-boomers once chanted that no one would push them around; GenXers pride themselves on being independent, solitary. Yet when it comes to Web-based information, *both* groups take their marching orders from the Internet.

But the link rot story worsens. When researchers studied citations moving from

PDF formatting to HTML, a 17 percent failure was noted.[10] This means, at its simplest level, that not only is it likely that citations only four years old may not be on the Web at all (there is 39 percent chance they will be gone) but that common formatting changes will increase the likelihood of disappearing citations. What does this mean for Google's grand plans to digitize some 15 million volumes? Will these volumes (assuming — and this is a grand assumption — Google can surmount the copyright challenges) be complete texts, or texts with vanishing footnotes? Yes, of course, these will be mere images of pages, or so we are assured. But is the mass digitization plan accounting for changes in the Web over time so that these materials are here year-after-year? Moreover, it is common knowledge (or at least it once was) that re-mastering of digitized texts must take place at least twice a decade.[11] If footnotes are vanishing, and original texts are lost or discarded, what about the future re-digitizing of these texts? Will it be possible to create a stable text, much less a definitive one? And while the subject of definitive texts is on the table for discussion, what about them? With this state of affairs can *any* digitized text be considered definitive?

Footnotes, Smootnotes: Who Cares?

Some reading these words will argue that these comments are the hysteria of academics alone, and that people in the real world do not really care about such things as footnotes. Certainly this is true to some extent, but it also touches the searching environment of general users. For if some Web sites appear one day and are gone the next, even general users are going to find the most elementary research difficult. Furthermore, what of medical papers, advice or other information that people — scholars and layperson — must rely upon? With this level of fugacity, it does not seem possible that we can ever rely even tangentially on digitized texts beyond mere indication of citation. It points to a new kind of *quellenforschung*, a new source-hunting that directs us to the existence of information but requires us to find a more stable media to which to refer, the equivalent of a scholarly version of "Go fish." It is simply an impossible information calculus to demand that we accept verification that is, in some ways, written in vanishing ink. Is it possible that this is just one of the many reasons why the famed "paperless society" is the *ignis fatuus* it has so far remained?[12]

Some of the blame for link rot must be laid at the feet of the publishing world. Profiteering is at the heart of democratic capitalism, and that is as it should be. Democratic capitalism has proven to everyone (save a few political science professors working at American universities) to be the best form of economic government. But needless profiteering, or Enron-like profiteering, is no more a part of that cherished tradition than are political roorbacks, common though they are. Serial publishers, especially the scientific, medical and technological ones, have always pressed the limits of profiteering and, sad to say, have largely gotten away with it. The effort has been to make profits soar while corners are cut, and footnotes (not to mention graphs, charts and other graphic-intensive digital additions) get left on the cutting room floor.

Libraries, until recently, have simply anted-up to the next level when serial costs sky-rocketed from 30 percent increases annually to, in some cases, 150 percent or more.[13] Meanwhile, every publisher in the book publishing business is moving toward e-Books, some to compete, others to turn a new profit, though making e-books profitable has so far been elusive (for more on e-Books, see chapter 6). Still, with everyone in publishing moving in a general e-direction, link rot had better rise to the level of the academic radar screen before citation back-tracking is a lost art entirely.[14]

The good news is that technology has not driven library construction underground, or rather, in the ground.[15] Buildings are still required because books still need housing. This is not contradictory as it might seem at first blush. Book publishing remains robust, even when it comes to small, scholarly publishers.[16] Search engines notwithstanding, it is unlikely that this will change. Since 1972, about 50,000 titles have been published annually, and the vast majority are found not on the Web but in libraries. Companies like Questia and netLibrary have found that readers are just not ready to read on long texts computer screens.[17] The academic press at Duke University (as well as those at Cambridge and Oxford), for example, published, at the close of the millennium, three times the number of texts they were publishing in the eighties.[18] But as more publishers turn to e-texts, link rot should — rather, must — become a major issue. It will not serve academe well that e-texts become some inferior simulacra of the printed texts they hope — or intend — to replace. For most readers wanting access to large number of books, only libraries will satisfy. Imagine what would happen if the only available texts were inferior electronic ones, filled with either dead links to notes, or no notes at all?

This good news about library construction should not, however, make librarians, or anyone else, complacent. As mentioned in the first chapter, *even* librarians are pushing for an e-text world, perhaps not exclusively, but certainly as a rival to print. Ditto our scholarly counterparts. For example, some professors claim that today's students learn differently and so look to the "new" library filled with computers and computer banks, instead of vast libraries filled with books (see the introduction). Says one professor, "[P]eople are reading the things they really rely on for information online. So to pretend that we're living in yesterday isn't helpful."[19] But this is just the sort of mentality librarians should being trying to dispel so long as the present state of affairs persists. So long as e-texts cannot be counted as stable, they should be ignored as a record of permanence. To some, a fully electronic-only pedagogy has great appeal because it appears to reduce costs (it really doesn't). As matters remain today, however, even a partially electronic pedagogy cannot begin to replace a full service library.

Online Library: May Be Everywhere and Nowhere

Unfortunately, we may already be too late. Students, and faculty members, are only too ready to make research an online venture exclusively.[20] Even though these same students and faculty members view print as a more trustworthy medium, most are ready to make print, and therefore libraries, a thing of the past.[21] If this continues to be true, and link rot continues apace, they will base future research on unverifiable information.

Indeed, they may be basing forthcoming research on completely *unreliable* information. While studies show that electronic resources are far more popular (88 percent), e-books still remain a least favorite source (18 percent).[22] What is disconcerting is that the more popular 88 percent is just where link rot is most likely to be found.

It's no secret that libraries hold vast numbers of books that go unused. For years, librarians have been aware of the 80/20 rule: Twenty percent of their collections will supply 80 percent of their use. But this is no reason to throw the remaining 80 percent out, or replace it with a much smaller percentage of books that have no footnotes, or footnotes that lead to dead ends. We cannot say now, for example, how an over-reliance upon technology will affect today's students' education, to say nothing of their literacy (see chapter 8 for a hint). Again, we saw in an earlier chapter how an over-reliance on technology already resulted in the formation of a poor drug protocol that led to the death of a young woman. It would be silly to argue that this will become commonplace, or that more and more electronic-only research will lead to poor research methodology. But it would be equally ludicrous to argue that it will have no effect at all. Numerous studies have shown the value of serendipity in research, the finding of a fact accidentally, while searching for something else, or being pointed in a new direction where one would not otherwise have thought to look merely by browsing huge ranges of books. While such serendipity is not impossible in an electronic-only research world, it will certainly be harder. If that electronic-only world is filled with texts that are infected with link rot, the resulting serendipity may well be one that leads researchers, not to mention students, in precisely the wrong direction, or no direction at all.

But are buildings still required? Can't we blend printed books and electronic materials to create smaller and smaller physical locations by using automation to its fullest extent? Perhaps all this will be possible in the distant future but for now, no. For only the richest libraries can afford, for example, to ship all their books to small compact areas and retrieve them when required, using automated retrieval systems. Automated retrieval allows libraries to warehouse the vast majority of their collections — for the sake of argument, let's say that 80 percent — in places other than the library, and retrieve them via robotics when needed. When a student or researcher finds the needed books, they request them automatically. The bin the books reside in is retrieved and someone (most likely a library worker) fishes through it for the specified materials. But these systems are extremely expensive, in the millions of dollars.

Bricks and Mortar May Be Cheaper

Some might argue that even at that steep price, it would still be cheaper than more library buildings. Again, perhaps, in time. For now, however, the cut off for such systems to be cost effective is about a million volumes. This relegates their use to only the largest of libraries. For smaller collections, only bricks and mortar will do.

It is a strange state of academic affairs, when one thinks about it. Students and faculty are pressing for more electronic resources. They both turn to electronic sources first. Both argue that place no longer matters and that only cyberspace has any meaning. Yet faculty tenure and promotion committees still look to the print medium as the verifiable means of granting either.[23] While we hear much about online publishing, blogs and the like, so far promotion and tenure committees are not yet ready to make any of them equal to their print counterparts. So, what are we to believe about these electronic resources? If electronic access is the preferred means and libraries move in that direction, how will untenured faculty members find career longevity?

So far, however, most case studies cited surveyed link rot in only a handful of journals (the one above, a few communications journals). If this is the only evidence to the contrary about link rot, it is admittedly not much evidence. If this was the only complaint to be lodged, the only example to cite for link rot, it would be sufficiently alarming to raise it, but hardly one to argue for a rethinking of the electronic world. Would that it were so. Electronic law journals and medical journals are also coming to the foreground as link rot infested information resources. "Over the past decade," writes one researcher, "the use of Internet citations in the footnotes of law review articles has grown from a trickle to a flood. But it is well documented that Uniform Resource Locators (URLs) experience link rot, that is, over time, the URL is more and more likely to become a dead link, making footnote citations worthless or nearly so."[24] In a discipline where footnotes are, in large part, the "meat" of the article (law) this becomes much more a serious matter than just a handful of journals in an esoteric discipline. According to Lyons, there were four instances of Web citations in three law reviews in the early nineties. By 2003 there more than 96,000.[25] This would not be a concern if these citations could be relied upon for a reasonable period of time, but they cannot.

Footnotes: Virtually Gone

According to Lyons and others, within one year, almost 18 percent of Web sites and nearly 32 percent of Web pages had disappeared. In one study cited by Lyons of 31 academic titles, almost half the links were dead at the end of a three year period. In a study by *JAMA*, also cited by Lyons, of 515 scientific links, nearly 28 percent were useless after only twenty-four months.[26] What is perhaps most disconcerting is that law review journals have a standard — the *Bluebook* (Rule 18.2) — that specifically discourages the use of Internet-only citations. While proprietary databases do fare better, they are not immune to link rot. This is because even proprietary databases like *Lexis-Nexis*, *InfoTrac* and *Academic Source Premier* do not maintain the same core journals from year to year. Sometimes this is because publishers of those journals pull them. At other times, the vendor decides, for whatever reason, to replace that journal with another more frequently used or cited one. And so the link rot saga continues, in law, in medicine, in academic journals and in science journals.

Whatever the reasons for it, or the disciplines in which it occurs, the end result is the same, electronic journals are here one day and gone the next, and now, of those that remain, their footnotes are vanishing.[27] While solutions are available such as citations to documents with persistent identifiers (not to some Web location), they are not being widely adopted. Until they are, link rot will remain a significant problem. Meanwhile

URLs have won out over the more stable means of identifying documents. The name itself—locator—was meant to serve as a warning of the ephemeral nature of the medium.[28] But the effect has been that URLs *are* the location rather than a means of locating where, at the time of citing, the document was found. This has given rise to citations, including some in this book, that identify a month and a year when the document was viewed.[29] But how many readers actually know that the month and year provided in these citations is a means of saying to the reader, "It was here during this month but may not be there when you go to examine it"? In many ways, it is a citation writ on water, in vanishing ink.

The problem is especially critical when citing documents in the dot-com domain names. Every user of the Web has experienced vanishing resources at one time or another. It happens like this: research reveals an interesting article. The scholar cites it and later goes back to recheck it. For up to thirty-six months—a generous amount of time—readers may find the citation working. But as each month inches closer to that thirty-six month threshold, the likelihood that e-citation remains at that URL grows smaller and smaller. The domain names of dot-org and dot-edu fare better but again are not immune to link rot. Even though organizations, universities, colleges and other groups have every reason to maintain Web sites with important information, there is no guarantee, no industry-wide agreement about maintaining them, or in what form, and no certainty they will remain where they were first discovered. In the case of medical and scientific papers or academic works of substance, this could result in an information-cesspool of dead links or no links at all. In the end, we may well have an information superhighway that leads to nowhere.

Librarians reading this text will likely think of a solution they know: PURLs, Persistent Uniform Resource Locators, created by OCLC, the national bibliographic database of materials, in the mid–1990s.[30] Aren't PURLs a workable solution for the problem of link rot?

String of PURLs

The idea behind PURLs is to establish a means whereby libraries can "catalog" Web sites for their online catalogs using MARC records, the electronic version of the old card catalog card. MARC records use tags for every piece of data of the bibliographic entry: author, title, imprint, pagination and so on. Each of the fields has a corresponding numbered tag. Thus, the author tag or field is 110, the title, 245, and so on. The 856 field was set aside to be used to record hyperlinks in an early effort to forestall link rot, provide for a stable locator and make the inclusion of Web sites in an online catalog possible and permanent. Obviously it would be useless to catalog important Web sites (e.g. Breastcancer.com) if the hyperlink changed frequently, or proved a dead end in a few years. The PURL functions as a better-than-URL, pointing not to an address where the resource may be temporarily, but to an intermediate resolution service which holds the actual URL, whatever it is, and returns it when requested.[31] While this is a solution that many libraries are using, it is a very high-maintenance, labor-intensive solution that must be checked and maintained regularly. PURL reports are generally created in the library's automated system's report file and can be checked for broken links, dead or changed links.[32] Someone must then put the changes in operation and remove bad or dead links. PURLs work because while changes often occur in what the PURL points to, the PURL itself cannot be changed.[33]

But PURLs are not a complete solution. Anyone who has ever tried to use GPO electronic documents, currently the number one user of PURLs, knows this to be true. PURLs work but not always as well as they should, or exactly how they should. Many GPO documents are ephemeral yet contain very valuable information. While PURL work is progressing, it is far from a fully satisfactory solution now. "Standardization," writes Shafer, "is necessarily slow and deliberate. Putting all the pieces in place will require consensus."[34] But it is just this consensus that may not be forthcoming in quick fashion, for the very online community which is best served by this remains perfervid in its independence.

While PURLs and other solutions — Lyons cites URNs, Uniform Resource Names, a more stable identifier — all are in development, link rot still happens. As many know who work in this area, compatibility from one format to another continues to be an ongoing problem. The likely result is that link rot will not only continue at a rapid pace but worsen over time before a satisfactory, low-maintenance solution can be found.[35]

"I'm looking at a world," says Grafton, "in which documentation and verification melt into air. My students come to college less and less able to negotiate a book landscape and more and more adept at negotiating the Web."[36] While Grafton is almost completely right, his assertion about students and their adeptness at surfing the Web gives them too much credit. As we have seen, students *think* they are adept because they have been around the Web for so long. Like their parents before them who grew up with libraries but did not know how to use them until trained, GenXers and all the rest "know" the Web but do not know its limitations and defects. Today's students are novices at both reading and research, and so their education will remain only elementary at best, quite lacking at worst. Meanwhile, scholarship, as most plus-forty individuals know, melts into thin air, as Grafton rightly concludes.

The situation is serious enough for all to be alarmed. Are we constructing the academic version of the South Sea Bubble, creating a false sense of security in an e-world only to wake up to information–Armageddon?[37] It would seem so. As more and more scholars accept electronic documents as a standard — and they do — the larger the problem with link rot becomes.[38] There can be no doubting that electronic access provides researchers and information seekers with a quick way for eventually locating reliable information. But what cannot be lost in the discussion is at what cost we make this access the preferred form. Surely when Gutenberg's press appeared, many an amanuensis worried about the future, and rightly so as it turned out. While the ubiquity of the book in the hands of many is a decided advantage over their scarcity in the hands of a few, one cannot dismiss the idea that the beginning of the decline of the art of bookmaking began with Gutenberg's 42-lines. But the manifest benefits far outweighed the losses. Our bookmaking may not be much to look at but the information is everywhere.

This is not the case, however, in cyberspace. Even as electronic journals become the preferred method of access, increasingly high failure rates are being noted in either broken links or the infamous "HTML 404 — Page Not Found" error.[39]

The proliferation of electronic access does not hold the same promise as making the book ubiquitous did. It is not the difference between having access and not having it. On the contrary, much has been written about the haves and the have-nots with respect to technology. Rather the contrast is one of degree: having the information tomorrow or the next day versus having it right now. We have become an impatient culture, so the latter triumphs now at the expense of the erosion of the former. If electronic texts are faulty, what good does it do to have it now or in the next fifteen minutes? It would be far better to have them *right* at whatever expense of time is required. My fear is not that this chapter is the voice of one crying in the wilderness, but the voice of one crying to a culture that is no longer capable of hearing. As noted scholar Carol Tenopir puts it, "In the rush to a digital information world we rarely pause to consider the long-term effects on libraries, scholars, and students. Even more rarely considered are the long-term effects that changes in the media of scholarly communication may have on learning and understanding of content."[40] This chapter might be considered our collective pause.

What every reference and bibliographic instruction librarian knows is the simple fact that entering college students are over-reliant on Web-based information. Moreover, they do not distinguish between sources that may have been put up by a clever 9th grader and those put up by scholars in the field. Finally, as search engines gain ascendancy, it became increasingly hard to teach students that "Googling" a subject may not only be a sorry way to do research but also among the worst approaches. The very idea that research may take more than ten minutes, and may require one to look beyond a search engine's returns, is simply incomprehensible to many students, not matter how old they are. Incomprehensible, that is, until those same students are faced with their first college paper, and the prospect of weeding through the proverbial 5,345,678 hits in .0234 seconds, the first *ten* screens of which are at best unhelpful. Only then do they run frantically to the reference librarian in an effort to find a more effective solution. Only then do they find that searching is really more an art than a science.[41]

Doorbells and Lovemaking

Losing footnotes may be considered by some not so much of a loss. After all, it is to some, as Noël Coward is alleged to have said, "answering the doorbell while making love." But what about lost content? Some researchers argue that full-text databases do not allow for the complex interaction of the eye and the brain, resulting in a loss of both content and context.[42] Any user of full-text, online databases knows this intuitively. The on-screen text is broken up, fragmented, and disconnected. Reading it becomes increasingly hard the longer the article is. One is always amazed at how much one misses reading online versus reading in print. Perhaps this explains our subconscious "finger-jerk" reaction to hit the print key after if the article we're trying to read exceeds three pages. Is our subconscious telling us, "You're not getting this. Put it in a medium I'm familiar with"? Perhaps. It is hard to argue with 500+ years of our culture's physiological reading history. We may well teach old dogs new tricks but only after a long, a very long, learning curve while surfing. Meanwhile, how do we deal with the information content "wipeouts"? (For more on reading, the Web and literacy, see chapter 8.)

While technology has eroded footnotes, it has also eroded library budgets. From about 1940 to 1965, library materials budgets were run on the proverbial shoestring but run quite well. But in 1965 and beyond, as automation advanced in business and in libraries, the latter saw more than sufficient materials budgets go from largess, to large, to lacking.[43] During one stretch in the nineties, for example, periodicals inflation sky-rocketed 145 percent in a short ten years. To put this in perspective, that exceeded every other putative out-of-control cost, *including health care.* But that was only the beginning. Also during that decade, electronic journals took off, moving from cumbersome CD-ROMs to Web-based texts. Libraries were faced not with one out-of-control cost, but three: the cost of print periodicals, books, and periodicals delivered electronically. To discover at this late date that those exorbitant electronic texts may be somewhat inferior is disconcerting to say the least.

Footnotes, content and context, cost. Is there more? Unfortunately, yes. Now we discover the commonplace habit of some periodical and serial publishers to publish special issues that may be impossible to locate after they appear electronically.[44] In an examination of five common science databases, researchers found that finding the so-called but often extremely content-important "special issue" proved difficult. What researchers found was alarming. Searching by topic or title did not retrieve all of them, even when searching for them in online catalogs in their favorite libraries. Searching by "special issues" found most but the results were generally uninformative, requiring an examination of the actual paper issue to find what was required. Tables of contents could not be found in any of those searched. While the research done is now five years old and improvements have been made in searching specificity, special issue topics remain a problem, mainly because search terms in databases are inconsistent. Even in most online databases, finding special issues of journals can be problematic.

If all of these were not enough to give one pause, another must be added, alluded to earlier: embargoes.[45] The open Internet does not, of course, have embargoes but numerous aggregate databases do. As librarians know only too well, embargoes are pre-determined publication delays of electronic journals that can range anywhere from three months to three years. These delays represent a certain time period between the time the paper version appears and the time the electronic version is available. Embargoes allow the publisher to preserve print subscriptions. Stated in a more jaundiced way, embargoes allow publishers of journals to double dip, profiting in the print version and again in the electronic subscription world. It's hard not to be jaundiced about it as many publishers embargo for no other reason than to prevent libraries from subscribing to electronic journals only.

Embargoes

If, for example, there is a 12- or 24-month "delay" before the appearance of the electronic version appears in a database, librarians must determine if that embargo is worth spending several hundreds (or even thousands) of scarce dollars to avoid. It generally comes down to how many patrons use it versus how much it will cost per use to keep. In practice, however, rarely do libraries subscribe to both as to do so would be so costly as to forestall spending on anything else. While it's true that aggregate databases do increase the pool of information by making heretofore unavailable journals available, their policies, like embargoes, have a chilling effect on that pool.[46] While many tell librarians to "get with the new program," few are willing to tell publishers that the days of 100 percent (or more) mark-ups on serials are over.

Whatever the reason for embargoes, this fact of electronic life serves to illustrate yet another hurdle in the race on the information superhighway. And embargoes are only one of the many frustrating cul-de-sacs. Also included under this rubric are "unnaturally halted" journals, or journals where the publisher or the aggregator pulls a title for whatever reason. It's true that the total percentage of embargoed journals may be very small compared to all that is available, but it is never small when it's the journal wanted *now*. Embargoes are generally known at the time of the purchase of the database, but embargos are never static once the database has been purchased. Some can become embargoed that were not at the time of purchase; others can have embargoes shortened or lengthened during the subscription year. While users may think they are immune to these difficulties, they learn only too soon they are not. A scholar may see a notice in a journal about a subject area she's investigating. She rushes online, sees the journal in her library's database and begins her search. Only then does she discover that she cannot get access to it. Regardless of the explanation given, most scholars go away thinking that librarians are dunces, that they have been duped or both. It is just one more maddening ring in this electronic inferno.

Finally, in the case of electronic access, more questions remain: Is the text version identical to the paper version, are all graphs and charts present in the electronic version, and can all of the electronic article be printed or downloaded? This is particularly important in graphic-intensive disciplines like art, technology or mathematicals. If the art reprinted is in color, can it be viewed well enough for students to observe nuances, brush strokes and the like? What makes sources such as ARTStor so valuable are features that allow for such close examination. ARTStor allows close examination of color, clarity and robustness, as well as printing and downloading.[47] But this is not the case in many other disciplines. All too often, patrons discover these important features are lacking in a database only *after* they have printed and discovered a blank space in the text.[48]

The picture painted in this chapter is a bleak one, but it would be wrong to think these matters are not being addressed at all. JSTOR has already been mentioned as one electronic source that attempts to preserve *everything* about the printed page. Other efforts are underway, for example, LOCKSS, where an attempt to create a viable archiving solution is underway.[49] It would be wrong for readers to get the impression that there is no hope. But it would be equally wrong to hold to the impression already held by most: that electronic access has replaced paper without as much as a hiccup. I would be the last person ever to argue for a return to journals in paper access only. As this book bears testimony, I use electronic resources frequently and expect this to become the standard *in the future*. It makes sense in so many ways, not the least of which is saving much needed space in libraries.

Electronic access is fraught with difficulties, some unforeseen, some anticipated and some ignored. The former group cannot be avoided with any new technology; and the technology should not be forestalled because of them, nor ignored simply to press ahead. The second group has been anticipated and to a larger extent, accommodated in some largely acceptable manner. But the last group, the ignored group, is the one group that troubles greatly. The ignored problems of electronic access remain and increase with no real foreseeable resolution. Meanwhile, information is being lost in cyberspace. Into this group fall link rot, embargoes, unprintable charts and graphs and more. If scholarship is to persist as the preferred means of communicating new ideas, we cannot allow the means of that communication to worsen over time. If it does, it will destroy the communication itself.

The theologian Origen once wrote, "It is mad idolatry to make service greater than the God." By this, Origen meant that one should not loose sight of the goal by making the means of getting there more important than the goal itself. "Getting there" cannot include overlooking obstacles to the goal, or making the process more important than the goal itself. We cannot allow the goal — the acquisition of knowledge — to fall victim to the process, the speed at which we can deliver information. To rephrase Origen in a more modern technological vernacular, in our rush to all things electronic we may *drown* the baby (knowledge) in the bathwater (access). Now that we hear its plaintive crying, it behooves us to rush to its defense.

5

Google *Über Alles*

Does anyone remember the world of research before the Web? Before Google? These are not impertinent questions, but poignant ones to remind us how quickly and how easily we became reliant, I daresay over-reliant, on two once nonexistent entities. Why, only a decade ago, Google was an embryo called BackRub, and the Web a vast uncataloged library of non sequiturs in a most cumbersome navigation medium.[1] In less time than it takes to reach puberty, both have arrogated to themselves the class of senior members of the world of research. Google *über alles*, we might say. And while the name Google refers to the company's commitment to "catalog" that vast "library" known as the Web (one perhaps of a jillion items), it could just as easily refer to the amount of money its founders, Larry Page and Sergey Brin, may one day (or already) possess.

Three Cheers for Democratic Capitalism

Three cheers for American entrepreneurialism, and I do *not* say that with tongue in cheek. Page and Brin took Google from a fledging idea and a half million hits a day to a giant worth multimillions, and more than 100 million inquiries daily.[2] We are a can-do country, and no task, not even the Web, is too great to withstand the power of democratic capitalism.[3] Surely there would be less factional nationalism and more global cooperation if the rest of the world would come to understand the equalizing power of our democratic capitalism.

But that's not to say that Webmania is without defects. Enter Google and its grand plan to digitize 10+ million unique titles from the so-called G5: the University of Michigan, Harvard University, Stanford University, Oxford University and the New York Public Library.[4] It seemed like a good, even a great idea.[5] These 10+ million unique titles were most likely not being read regularly, few people had access to them and no one had access to them all. What could possibly be wrong about it? When the news was announced in 2004, almost everyone jumped on board. The giant Google with its vast resources would undertake the project, the G5 libraries would partner with Google, little-read books would be showcased in those 100+ million daily hits, and everyone would be served. Or so we thought. Digital libraries did not appear all that difficult to build, would not require very many employees (easily the largest expenditure item in conventional libraries), and would be able to adapt quickly to market and technological demands. In the twilight of the first new digital day, everything appeared possible. Then the radar screen began blipping with numerous intruders threatening to spoil our mad rush to the mass digitization party. But the trouble began long before Google's plan. The symptoms were there, but few wanted to acknowledge them.

Promises, Promises

For example, the great promise of so-called open access did not pan out the way we hoped it would.[6] Digital libraries, we opined, would proliferate and free information would be shared routinely. And a law was made a distant moon ago that in Camelot, July and August cannot be too hot, while a legal limit to the snow was also set there. Open access has spread but not as widely or as comprehensively as imagined. It is also costing more than anyone ever dreamed. The reach of open access across disciplines has been a small one so far.

We have further found on the yellow-bricked digital road that the learning curve is much steeper than we thought; the decision tree, which we imagined looked pretty simple, now turns out to be as complex as Yggdrasil. Now we know that we have to look at the materials we want to digitize, determine why we want this one over that one (or why we can't do both of them now), figure out how access will be achieved, determine how images will be filed (using what format — for more on that see below) and on and on.[7]

Enter Google, and everyone wanted to party. But like a frat party that begins well enough only to end in too much drinking, the next day hangovers ensued. Some began to question how all of this would be done. Others asked about copyright. The French asked why the titles Google chose to digitize were all English ones. A few librarians began thinking seriously about the implications of a giant Google library. Some scholars wondered about how Google would be reimbursed (would Hamlet's soliloquy appear alongside an advertisement for Viagra?). Not a few publishers asked why they were not consulted, and by late 2005, the Google plan began to flag.

It's not likely it will fall to half staff forever. Google has always prided itself on "built-in innovation" and so will surely find ways to make something on this order (though, perhaps, not of this magnitude) eventuate. Still, it brings to mind an important question: is the rush to mass digitization the right approach right now? The short answer is no, and this chapter will explore some of the reasons.[8]

Make no mistake about it. None of the reasons given here should be understood to be reasons to stand athwart the digital divide and shout "Halt!"[9] But they are important enough to want to make us progress much more slowly than we are now. We need to be sure we are doing all our digital "stuff" correctly and are not, in our mad rush to make all things electronic, electrocuting, rather than improving, the research calculus.

Mass Digitalization: Problems and Prospects

A digital library (any digital library of any size) allows users to access required information electronically from virtually (no pun intended) anywhere.[10] Digitization, likewise, requires "acquiring, converting, storing and providing information in a computer format that is standardized, organized and available on demand from common systems."[11] And therein lies the rub, and the rub isn't always a soothing backrub. It can well be an irritant. While digitization remains in its infancy, many are rushing to make it a senior partner. To borrow a line from Gertrude Stein, there may not be a substantial there, there, certainly not now, and maybe not ever. Cyberspace while being everywhere is nowhere. Suddenly, we are risking everything: text, images, music, audio, video and so on to a format we are only just beginning to understand and may not ever fully grasp in all its implications. This is not a reason to stop digitizing but it should be enough to give us pause. What we do know about digitization so far should give us plenty of reasons to "make haste slowly."

For example, we know that for now, digitization is costly (though as we shall see almost no one really knows how costly); it should *never* (at least for the foreseeable future) be used as a preservation medium, and formidable obstacles such as intellectual property and copyright threaten to undo it. Yet here we are, damning the torpedoes and shouting "Full steam ahead!"

No one likes naysayers, and I include myself in that group. But some reflection on so important a matter as where all this digitized material will be in, oh, five or ten years, should be important enough to make us reflect more rationally than we have so far. Librarians know only too well that funding for the duplication of materials is the first to go, if it ever remained long enough to notice. What we don't want to see in a decade *or less* is the sudden evanishment of the original digitized texts and no way to retrieve them because funding dries up. Is this hysterical?

Consider the Library of Congress's microfilming plan, made famously public by Nicholson Baker's infamous *Double Fold*. Microfilming is a much more reliable, well-known entity. It would appear to last for a considerable length of time (scores of years as opposed to a few) and is easily convertible from one machine to another. And yet that plan, eminently sensible as it must have seemed at the time, left an enormous volume of originals, mostly one-of-a-kind 100+ year old newspapers, discarded. While not many think this will be a problem for at least 50 or 100 years, some still wonder what will happen when those microfilms are broken, faded, or are otherwise damaged. They do not, even in that more stable medium, last forever. How can we go back? The matter has become slightly more important as microfilm slowly fades to the back burner of funding priorities. When they are gone, if only in part, how will they be retrieved *in any format* when the originals are no longer available?

Does Mass Digitization Look to the Future?

Fast forward to a scant twenty years from now.[12] Digitization funding has absorbed all monies, and the originals are not readily available. First generation digitized texts are in bad need of a new master. Will those masters be again available? Let's assume most probably will. Will there be capital to once again digitize all 10+ million unique titles? Five million? One hundred thousand? No one knows. And from reading the literature, not many seem to care to give it much more than a passing thought. Further, what about serendipity in research? Lesk gives an excellent example of the discovery of penicillin via serendipity that would likely have never come about through digitized text searching.[13] Indeed, even in our electronic world today, browsing is not possible. Are we sure, in our mad rush to mass digitization, that we are not replacing with a new method that is inferior to the old methods?

But let's not be futurists. Let's consider the present. Brin and Page had the idea to digitize all the world's books very early on, according to Susan Wojocicki, the company's vice president for product management. The garage the two young googlers inhabited, before the nondescript noun became a capitalized verb, doubled as their laboratory.[14] In fact, a giant digitized library was what they were trying to perfect when they invented the search engine that became known the world over as Google. Even as they became multi-millionaires overnight, they continued the idea of creating the world's largest digitized library, digitizing not some, but all, the books they could find. At the time they began, less than 1 percent of all books were accessible online. With this plan, it would be everything, only not really everything. Now Google is telling publishers they have to opt out, not opt in.[15] Of course Google's stated position is to stay within copyright law. But all of us who work with copyright have every intention of doing so. Publishers keep reminding Google that they own copyright. It does not appear to "click" with Google, shall we say. Now for some foreboding. After the plan is in effect, will Google give new meaning to the phrase "pay-per-view"? No one knows, and Google isn't saying anything that would cause furrowed brows to, well, unfurrow.[16]

Digitization of texts is by far the easiest to accomplish (as opposed to, say, images, audio or video) but it is not without its looming potholes. All such formats, we are assured, will be easier in the future. But the process of digitization, occurring now without much standardization, results in some loss of data.[17] No one knows for certain how much, or whether it will be a problem, but everyone agrees there is data loss through either the lack of standardization (there is none) or the failure to follow those few standards that have been agreed upon. The present argument is muddied because proponents of digitization *über alles* minimize the data loss, while opponents of digitization maximize it. Still, both agree loss is present to a certain extent.

Anyone who has scanned a page from a book using even a very elementary scanning process knows about this data loss. Shouldn't we be more certain that standardization is consistent and thorough before we get too far along this unknown trail?

Already some are arguing that our "rush to large-scale digitization may be creating a Tower of Babel, with too many individual and unique projects that have no way to communicate or search among them."[18] Shouldn't we be leaving bread crumbs along the way so we can find our way back? Current practice is to dismiss such questions as Luddite-seeming. Let's hope current practice is right!

Once Bitten Twice Shy, Except with the Web

Do we have any insights from our present technology that might guide us in this consideration? Consider for a moment the CD-ROM era that occurred only a handful of years ago. CD-ROMs, we were told, held the promise for eternal preservation. They would last a minimum of 500 years, and some specially made ones would surpass the 1,000 year mark. It seemed like a small number to me, given that some *paper* texts in our possession now have surpassed the 5,000 year mark, but let that go for now. So for a short time, everything went CD-ROM. All sorts of "shoebox" size library predictions appeared: the Bible on a disk; Shakespeare's complete works on a handheld that includes commentary from a half dozen experts included. And so it went.

About five years into the CD-ROM-mania, we discovered a curious thing. Some first-generation CDs could not be read on new machines. Other CDs could not be read on machines they had been read on only a year ago. Soon we discovered that the ink from the printing titles on CDs inquinated the data of some, making them impossible to read. While we hated to admit it, CDs were not the panacea we thought. Did the CD-ROM South Sea Bubble burst because it would not work or because another, superior technological invention appeared in time to replace it? Perhaps, yet here we are again, putting blind faith in yet another new technology before we work all the kinks out.

While standardization is not entirely consistent, different kinds of standardization with respect to digitization have emerged. Various file formats are known to most who undertake the digitization process. For example, text files may be in either electronic text files or image files.[19] There are image formats, tagged image file formats (TIFF), joint photographic experts group format (JPEG), graphic interchange format (GIF) or portable network graphics (PNG). Unfortunately, as in most things in life, there is no "one best way" or one best format, so all are being used. The formats depend upon what one is digitizing, and why.

For example, TIFFs are excellent for creating a file with the maximum information captured, say for master files. This is mainly because TIFFs are not compressed (lossless) in any way (more on compression below). TIFFs will create an image that is both sharp in resolution and of the utmost quality. So why aren't TIFFs the standard of choice? Because they are large, they are next to impossible to transfer over a network, save for those high-speed networks developed just for that purpose. Moreover, a small-scale digitization project that saved everything in TIFFs would likely run out of server space far more quickly than if using another format.[20]

Many Formats, Many Problems

So, what are the other formats? JPEGs are mainly used because they are com-pressed files that are easily delivered over local networks, and over the Internet. So why not use this format instead? JPEGs, by virtue of being easily delivered over networks, use *lossy* compression, meaning that while most likely losing some of the original infor-mation, they still deliver a "reasonable" facsimile. Ah, but there's the rub. Reasonable to whom? To a scholar? Certainly not. Reasonable to a regular but disinterested viewer? Possibly. Reasonable to anyone else not an expert or a scholar, but to one wanting to see the as-close-to-the-original as possible? Nope. You'd never want to save a master file as a JPEG, and you should not really save images in JPEG simply because the res-olution is of a much lower quality. Those wishing to study the technique, say, of a painter would not be able to do so with a lossy-compressed file.[21]

Little has been said about the most obvious file format, PDF, and for good rea-son. PDFs are fine for text. They print on run-on-the-mill printers as well as very expensive ones, but quality is lost in both cases.[22] Though they are often used for mul-timedia files, they are not nearly as good in these cases. While they allow for the famous thumbnails, the quality is merely a facsimile and not necessarily a good one, or one that would satisfy those beyond a mere "voyeuristic" look. Further, they allow for pro-hibiting certain kinds of actions (such as printing, by using a password to protect the content). But these all depend on the expertise of the person who created the file.

This is what troubles some about the rush to digitization. We don't know who is making decisions about what formats to use, what types of materials are being chosen, how they are being saved (as text, images, graphic-intensive files, audio, video, etc.) and whether enough information is being left behind to tell others years from now how they created the files and whether any data loss occurred. We have no assurances so far that anyone is recoding all this information consistently on every project.

Take for example the local group with rare papers of some local celebrity. The deci-sion is made to digitize, but those making the decision think that buying any scanner and scanning away in JPEGs is "good enough." But good enough by what definitions? And what happens when funding runs out, or parts of this collection are not chosen for digitization (known as cherry picking, about which more below)? Will the part of the collection not chosen be cared for in the same way even though it is not part of the glamorous digitization project? This may seem far-fetched, but consider a parallel sit-uation.

When the Human Genome Project (HGP) got underway and billions were spent in its direction, many scientists worried over the funding drain this would cause for other equally important but far less glamorous projects.[23] Money, some worried, for HGP would siphon off funding for other projects. Scientists already knew that when fund-ing broke for a particular area, researchers would follow it. Sure enough, they did. More seriously, however, was the passage by some states of funds for genetic research and the refusal of others to do so. When California announced over $300 billion for stem cell research, states around the country reported a sudden loss of researchers who rushed after the funding.

NCLB: No Copy Left Behind

A similar thing may occur with digitization projects. The "noise" (archive artifacts) that is chosen for digitization receives all the attention and funding. Meanwhile, the lesser noise left behind is, literally, left behind. (Perhaps we need an NNLB Act, a No Noise Left Behind Act). It isn't, of course, left in the dustbin, but it may as well be. Does anyone ever go back to it? We don't know yet because enough time hasn't passed. We do know, however, that there are no plans for materials not yet chosen.

What about GIFs? GIFs have a similar inefficiency about them as JPEGs, but because they are easily transportable over local networks and the Internet, they also have become a widely chosen format. They should not be masters and also have compression problems which make information loss a near certainty. Are we digitizing material in GIFs that we shouldn't?

This leaves PNGs. Most PNGs are not supported by the newest Web browser versions, hence the format may not be as familiar. They do have a more efficient compression system but are, because of that, much larger files than either GIFs or JPEGs. This leads the same problem mentioned with TIFFs: they take up too much space. Some might argue that with memory at rock-bottom prices, who should care? It should matter to those of us charged with saving historical records, records of research and the trail that leads from start to finish. One need not be too concerned with those large organizations flush with cash. They will likely — for now anyway, but see the end of this chapter — save in the best formats possible. What should worry us more, however, are those hundreds or thousands of smaller digitization projects all over the globe that may be discarding the originals or placing them in harm's way because funding does not allow them to do anything else. *In other words, digitization has given us a false sense of preservation security, and it should not, must not be allowed to do so.* Preservation should never be a reason for digitizing anything.[24]

If digitization is so complicated, so complex, why is anyone digitizing? Because digitization opens up access, something librarians, especially, cannot resist. Access is for librarians what the Babylonian whore is to the Apocalypse: that enticing, irresistible miscreant that leads to destruction.

Digitization *does* lead to greater access. Look at the dynamics: a collection that is 150 years old has not been looked at by anyone in 100 years, parts of it are too fragile for anyone to examine, and it takes up valuable shelf space. What to do? Digitize the collection or, what is far more probable, digitize *parts* of it and, presto! Hundreds of thousands, possibly millions now can view what no one even knew existed. Once online, who needs those sprawling, space-hungry originals? The collection is "saved," space is freed up and everyone is happy at having "solved" the problem. Not only can everyone in the propinquity of the collection visit it online, but so can those from the four corners of the globe. Suddenly, Podunk University is now "international."

Such projects are commonplace now and there is no way to know how many are being undertaken, or at what expense to the original collection. Few take into consideration the necessity of planning the project from the beginning.[25] They do not assess goals, do not set achievable ones, think about the purposes of the collection only after the fact, and may not even know about copyright issues, preservation issues, or the future security of the digitized materials.

Virtual Cherry-Picking

Selection of materials to be digitized is often *ad hoc*, what can be done now and by present staffing.[26] This leads to cherry-picking of the collection, alluded to earlier. Cherry-picking refers to taking those choice or best items and forgetting about the rest. Or, selection can go the other way, and lead to what is sometimes referred to as "low-hanging fruit," to maintain the fruit metaphor.[27] This refers to that part of the collection which can be done now and without difficulty. Google has been guilty of this, choosing what is already in public domain without regard to whether it is the best or the most worthy to be digitized first. Imagine what academic collections would look like today if, fifty years ago, what was chosen to be in collections was that which was ready available, not what was needed to support curricula offerings. No librarian in the country would have agreed to such a scheme, and yet nearly all of us have accepted this as a standard selection procedure for digitized collections.

But the fun is only beginning. Color in images is one of the most persistently neglected yet one of the most critical when it comes to digitization.[28] Color in digitized files is represented, as are most things computerized, mathematically. Color space (the limits of the file's color), color profile (how the hardware "reads" the numbers) and gamma (the black and white range) are but a few of the issues to be resolved. One doesn't have to become an expert in these matters, of course, but they certainly must be thought about and set beforehand. Finally, calibration (setting the hardware limits according to profile) is also very important. While these things may not be noticeable at first, they will become so as the image ages. While hardware costs have come down and now $500 scanners scan as accurately as $15,000 scanners did only a decade ago, knowledge of the hardware limits needs to be known and factored in, *before the project begins.*

Outsourcing May Mean Left Out

Can't all of this be left to outsourcing? Not only can it be but it often is, without the requisite discussions that make the outsourcer aware of what is wanted and needed. As with any project, there are pros and cons to outsourcing.[29] Often the results are better but the costs are much higher, making many pass on outsourcing altogether. Today, funds are readily available for digitization, and so outsourcing is more easily in reach. But if those heading up the discussion are not aware of these requirements, what one pays for outsourcing (and dearly so, in many cases) may not in five years be what anyone wants, or, far more importantly, anyone can use. Think of the fuss made over acid-free paper only a few years back and what bedevilment ensued when we discovered yellowing and brittle paper long before we thought it possible. Now we know what to ask for in that regard and the standard is universal. We need the same sort of discussion to occur, and the same sort of standards to ensue, with respect to digitization.

Not many think about stakeholders, either, when it come to digitization, at least beyond a very narrowly defined limit. But if digitization is going to replace paper — and clearly many want it to — we need to define stakeholders beyond a narrow audience before it's done, and before originals are lost, misplaced or discarded and re-digitization cannot be done. All of these things make the cost of any digitization project increase.[30] Calculating the number of images that can be scanned per day in addition to the number of hours it will take to digitize the entire project will also aid in predicting the required number of personnel, the kinds of scanners required and so forth. Very soon, a project of, say, 50,000 images explodes to a cost of more than $200,000.[31]

Fewer still take into consideration the required digitization expertise, the cost (which is always more than budgeted), the instability, if not of the Internet then of your local Internet service provider, and the amount of time required to superintend the digital collection.[32] By superintend, I mean the number of individuals who will call in to complain that they cannot see the online collection. Someone with more than a modicum of computer expertise will be required to walk them through the myriad of interconnectivity issues that surround digital collections: browser issues, computer resolutions, display issues on a PC versus a Mac, why PDF files do not print and the like. Will Rogers once said that revolutions are like cocktails; they merely organize you for the next one. If so, these are some of the morning-after hangover factors we need to consider in our digital revolution.

Some reading to this point may begin to wonder: has he heard about OCR? Of course optical character recognition is available with the most rudimentary of scanners. But as any who have used it know, it isn't the first pass that's hard. "[I]t is one of the truisms of OCRing that first pass   the capturing — is relatively cheap, but the second pass, in which the tidying up of the material is done, is always more expensive."[33] This is why many large projects bypass this step and accept mistakes as they appear, capturing the material as an image (in, say, a PDF file) and correcting only the most egregious mistakes ... when they are discovered, if at all. But this is no way to build a library for future generations. Some may argue that print has had its own morbid history of mistakes, and that cannot be gainsaid. Moreover, in these tight financial times, only the largest of publishers engage fact-checkers, and only for their most revered clients (as witness the James Frey episode mentioned in an earlier chapter). But the number of mistakes per page in print is far less than what one finds on the Web *daily*. It would be hyperbole to say that the Web is a cesspool of errors of fact, simulacra and misinformation. But it is equally hyperbolic to say that the Web is equal to what we have in print, by and large error-free. Digitization projects, a subset of that whole, contain some of the most glaring examples of scanning fiascos.

Anybody Here Ever Heard of Copyright?

While copyright has been alluded to in these pages, it deserves, perhaps most of all, some further ventilation here.[34] Copyright has sunk more than one grand plan, even when no real grand plan was thought to exist.[35] While Google might not ever admit it, either its underestimation of copyright, or its benign neglect of it, has certainly slowed down its 10+ million books plan. A review of the Tasani case would help Google and all others in this regard.[36] At any rate, digitizing *cannot* be undertaken *without* a firm grasp of copyright, something no one on earth, not even attorneys, really has. If material is in copyright — and that is the first plan of attack of any digitization project — it *cannot* be digitized without some sort of permission, usually written, or else some fees paid to someone. For the vast majority of those digitizing it rules out using that material.

But the matter doesn't end there, either. Public domain material may seem straightforward, and it usually is, but it is not without is own kinks. One may have material in hand that antedates the 1924 cutoff for materials in public domain. So far so good. But is the material one intends to use a modern translation or paraphrase that falls after 1924? If so, it may not be in public domain. Were the rights reassigned by another? Has a family member or relative come forward to stymie fair use (see for example the current controversy on James Joyce's materials)? Fair use, itself a complicated and complex construct, may well be the most abused ideal among academics. Too many think fair use means if I am an academic and I want to use it, it's fair use. Nothing could be further from the truth.

True, copyright holders can be found, but that search is costly both in terms of dollars and time. Finding a copyright holder in a "simple" search may take the person assigned the task two or more weeks. Even then, the search may prove futile. Here's a personal example. For a book I was doing some years ago I found on the Web the perfect illustration. I e-mailed the Web site manager, who referred me to the parties responsible. No, they didn't have permission but had gotten it from X, a major university in the North America. I called that place and no, they had gotten it from Y, a department in the university, and, no, they did not have permission. I called them and they referred me to another (they did not have permission), who referred me to yet another place entirely. To make a very long story short, about a half dozen sites had "borrowed" the image from another, none, it seemed, with permission. After about three weeks, I finally found the copyright holder of the image. No, he said categorically, the image could not be used in my book, even for a fee. All too often, copyright searches end this unhappily. Violations abound, especially on the Web, and finding an image there does not mean it is being used legitimately.[37]

Mass Digitization at the Expense of Staff

If we're honest, many digitization projects are undertaken without much thought about staff development.[38] While much is available in this regard, the rush to mass digitization often means some unsuspecting staff member will be given a new "duties as assigned" role. If digitization is to be done right, however, some money is going to have to be set aside to bring staff up to speed, even those staff who are newly minted professionals. Even if library staff do not undertake the project originally, they are likely to be called upon for expert consultation. Sound improbable? How many librarians were trained to become the resident experts in their institutions for copyright law that they are today? Much can be learned in workshops in online training, of course, but not if these costs are not part of the funding mechanisms from the beginning. The best approach would be for staff involved in the digitization project to receive coursework ahead of time.[39]

Another would-be hangover is the necessity for quality control, not much of which is apparent save in extremely large undertakings.[40] It's not clear that even in the largest of undertakings that the *best* controls for quality are being met. For example, automated checks used by the Digital Media and Image Center (DMIC) at Indiana University use a Perl script for automated checks according to project specifications for the structure of the file name, correct file format, compression, byte order, image resolution bit depth, photometric interpretation (e.g. grayscale or RGB), and more.[41] But how many small to medium size projects either know about such checks or have the funding to do them? And what happens in three, five or seven years if these controls have not been put into place? Will the image be rescanned? Can it be? Will the same loose oversight be reapplied? And what of the original? Will it still be available?

While some projects might allow for a few of these controls, how many are saving metadata and how much is being saved?[42] Metadata is data about data. It outlines what was captured and how, much in the manner the old card catalog card was used to capture particulars about the book being cataloged. While few paid much attention to those cards, for librarians they represented the "ID" of each book. The rule of thumb in digital collections is this: one can never save too much metadata. But how many such projects are undertaken with this in mind? With the old card catalog, only one group created such data, often to the ridicule of those who did not understand its purpose.

Today, however, *anyone* can digitize, and many are. The question remains, what are they doing, how are they doing it, and are they doing it in such a way that others can come back years later and reconstruct its creation history for any required reason? Even with automated metadata extraction programs available, we have no clear picture who is doing what and how. We need to raise these questions now rather than later, when it will be too late to recover what has been lost.

Sound too hysterical? Too anal retentive? Perhaps, but consider the scholar who wants to learn everything there is to know biographically about a subject. Perhaps some famous writer marks his places in a manuscript with a crayon, or makes what appears to the uninitiated as stray pencil markings. Are these removed or erased when scanning? James Joyce, it is said, edited his famous *Ulysses* with multiple colored pencils, signifying changes made and when. If the scanning is done in black and white, how will future scholars know?

Conversely, some scanning being done ramps up the text a notch, shall we say.

What then? The book, once a somewhat impersonal entity, may now be transformed. Its opening page may introduce a character who leads the "reader" (really now a spectator) upon a journey. Color may be added that was not present in the original. Sound may be added. The letters may move and turn. The book is now more a spectator's experiences rather than a reader's intellectual encounter.[43]

For those who wish to scream, "Luddite!" at this point, let me hasten to add that my contention here is not that such things are wrong or inherently bad. Rather, they have significantly changed the experience with the book that others who did not experience the digital encounter could not have. Are these changes better? Do they enhance the experience of the book, or do they rather lead the "reader" to a certain, specific kind of experience with the book? We do not now know and perhaps never will, but it should make us at least pause to consider if all these changes are uniformly good.

Shadowboxing in Digital Light

Take another example. In high school too many years ago to remember, football players (among whom I was a terrible one) were often asked to play "donkey basketball." I chose not to but many of my friends did. They would attempt to get the donkey to move about the court and make shots. The resulting chaos was funny, inhumane, if not harmful to the animals, and the very least an idiotic pastime. No one present, however, would argue that the "game" was really a game of basketball. Everything had been changed and though the number of players on both teams remained the same, they wore jerseys, they played on a court and used a basketball, it remained a very different game, and a very different experience.

Likewise I wonder about our rush to mass digitization. It appears to be the same experience but it is decidedly not. Of course not all such projects turn out to be as extreme as donkey basketball. But there can be no doubt that many mass digitization projects change the nature of the reading calculus. Whether they have changed the reading calculus for the better remains to be seen. Even if we can dismiss projects that use color, sound, odd little assistants and moving letters as constituting an infinitesimally small number of projects, we must still worry about the number of projects with little or no quality control, with limited funding, or that have mistakenly used digitization for preservation, or quasi-preservation purposes.

If quality control is not a concern, certainly the care and preservation of the original scanned materials must be. Obviously, there are quite a few scanning projects that use individuals to turn pages of books or manuscripts. But such a process would be unthinkable for, say, Google's 10+ million-plus-book project. For that project, and others like it, there are robots, some the size of sports utility vehicles, that turn pages and can scan up to 1,000 pages an hour.[44] If the robot turns more than one page at a time, a puff of compressed air separates them and scanning begins again. But—let's call the robot "Hal"—does Hal know when to begin again, and does he begin at the right place?

Digital Delirium

The delirium of such technology, particularly for Americans, is palpable. We can digitize hundreds of thousands of books and the kid in Brooklyn who has never been to a library, and the kid in the darkest part of the African Amazon will now have access. Every child is a winner, as educators are wont to say. This assumes that the kid in Brooklyn and the kid in the deepest dark of the Amazon have a laptop and an Internet provider, but let's move on. It also assumes they know how to read and want to, but let's not quibble over details. It's the robot and the books we're concerned with. Are the books being cared for?

More or less. Occasionally books have to be rebound from mass digitization projects. Some may even be too far gone to rebind. Are these replaced or simply thrown out? The cost of mass digitization can run anywhere from $1 a book to $500. The difference is only in quality. For example, some claims are made that in India or the Philippines, books can be digitized for between $1 and $4 each.[45] This is significantly cheaper than original estimates. Trouble is, everyone understands that there will also be a loss of quality, but no one knows how much or how significant that loss will be. Moreover, we also know that the real costs of digitization can be four times as much as is reported.[46] Who finds out which books are lost to slipshod digitization? Who rescans?[47] What happens to the poor-quality images? Do the kids in Brooklyn and the darkest part of the Amazon get the cheaper scans because they have little or no political clout?

Unseen or hidden costs mount up. For example, in a recent study of eighteen ARL libraries over the last five years, researchers found that "digitization has had a rapid and significant impact on existing reformatting workloads of preservation departments."[48] What cannot be ascertained is whether the process of photocopying damaged pages for preservation purposes is being replaced by digitized alternatives. While staffs have remained the same, increases (by ten percent) in digitization tasks have taken over or replaced traditional preservation activities.[49] It's unlikely that any of these libraries are using digitization as a replacement for traditional preservation practices ("it is clear that digitization has not replaced traditional preservation strategies"); they are, rather, taking on more digitization tasks instead.[50] This becomes a hidden cost on two counts. First, we do not yet know what this is costing in dollars now. Second, we haven't any idea what this will cost in preservation needs in the future when we discover that traditional preservation tasks should have been done but were not. It is simply to say that staffs need to be increased. As anyone who has ever worked in a library knows, however, increasing staff is easily the most difficult, the most costly, endeavor that can be incurred.[51]

Digitization Dollar Diving

Needless to say, digitization costs are formidable. We can surely agree that there are no "short-term cost savings to be realized by digitizing collections."[52] If the cost of digitizing doesn't send the cost projections to redline, then certainly the almost ephemeral life cycle of hardware will. As has been pointed out repeatedly in this chapter, we do not know how images created today will "play" on machines created ten years from now, or even five years from now. Too many pundits try to downplay this factor, making non-sequitur comparisons between Gutenberg and monks transcribing manuscripts. But the differences are far more dramatic than that, and far more different. While access issues may be similar, it's not an industry we may be losing owing to digitization; it may be all the information so far digitized. We may lose more than a sense of proportion: we may lose everything about the text. As John Updike pointed out recently, we may well be losing the soul of what we have come to know as information delivery because "books are intrinsic to our human identity."[53] We may well lose it, too, to nothing more than the titillation of the neoteric.[54]

All of this has been presented without reference to digitization failures: Questia, netLibrary, Gutenberg, Xanadu and Fathom.com.[55] Sure, some of these can be "victims" of a new technology, or the dot-com bubble burst. Call it what you will. It still represents significant failures of the very type we are now encouraged to embrace without question.[56] Some may wish to quibble that these are not *real* failures, or are not mass digitization projects failures, per se. They cannot say the same, however, for the mass digitization project undertaken by the British Broadcasting Company in 1986.[57] BBC spent more than $5 million to develop the Domesday Project, one that digitized materials relating to all aspects of British life to celebrate the 900th anniversary of the *Domesday Book*. In less than fifteen years, all that had been digitized—video texts, photographs, maps and the like—were obsolete. Granted, some of this has been recovered, but at an even greater cost than ever imagined. Other projects have not been so lucky. Those left holding the bag—including materials on punch cards—now have to be maintained by the parent project in order to save the data collected in that manner. These are the mass digitization projects we know about. What of those others that simply died an unnatural death because funding dried up and no one came back to revive them?

Funding models for mass digitization are all over the place: institutional funding, funding that comes from corporations or granting agencies, and free distribution (but of course it isn't really free—*someone* is paying for it).[58] Again, this does not mean mass digitization cannot be self-supporting; it does mean that for now no one model works best and that only the richest need apply.

So, is it all worth it?[59] As mentioned at the beginning of this chapter, it's too late to put the genie back in the bottle. The answer to the question is a qualified yes. Yes, if we can do it right, but no if it must come at the expense of proven practices. It cannot be done to preserve, to save space or to save money. Those doing it must be aware of the complexity of copyright, the preservation and conservation of the originals and the very complex nature of hardware changes that occur irrespective of what has been done heretofore. They also must be aware that failure of technology projects are common: 32 percent owing to inadequate project management and control, 20 percent from a lack of communication, 17 percent from ill-defined objectives, 17 percent from a lack of adequate knowledge of what was being undertaken and 14 percent due to the wrong technology used.[60] We cannot view digitization *über alles* when collections are failing, funding is drying up and staffs are shrinking. We cannot do it if it replaces everything else we are doing now. And we must *never* let digitization serve as a replacement for traditional preservation strategies unless and until it proves itself capable of serving as such. It sounds like a broken record, but mass digitization, at least as we know it in the first decade of the new millennium, is not even a bad substitute for anything other than access. This is not to say that in the next two or three decades everything will not change. But we cannot sacrifice everything now for the hope of some unspecified future. Or, to put another way, we cannot make service (digitization) greater than the god (information).

Damn the Torpedoes, Mr. Scott, Full Speed Ahead

One of the more distressing statements made about mass digitization projects comes from one within the ranks of librarianship. "We cannot slow down to make things perfect. The rising tide will lift all boats."[61] The image of a rising tide is a nice one. But an extreme rising tide, sometimes known as a tsunami, will lift all boats and even some not in the water, before burying them all under tons of sludge. The question is, what's our hurry? It isn't as if the process is such that if we do not do it now we will not get it done next year or even the next decade. It *is* a process whereby if we do it wrong, we can lose everything. In more than twenty-five years in this profession, I have not seen as a management rule of thumb, for any sort of long-lasting collection development or information stability, the idea of not trying to get things right. Oddly, the speaker, Karen Wittenborg of the University of Virginia, a woman greatly admired and rightly so, admitted to the pressure to rush digitization projects "before everything is perfected." Good enough, a phrase she uses to describe the goal, will be fine. We can only hope so.

Much of this chapter has been devoted to mass digitization developments in the United States with only a few mentioned elsewhere. But the problem is not a U.S. problem but a worldwide one. In England, libraries worry that mass digitization projects and digital publishing may make it harder (or even impossible) for some to access their collections in the future.[62] Many publishers there are putting restrictions on digital books and journals and specifying how they may be used. The British Library predicts that by 2020 90 percent of newly published works will be available in some digital form. Their copyright law clauses, "fair dealing" and "library privilege," may well be restricted in the coming years. The issue there as here comes back again to digital rights management (DRM) and whether the future will allow libraries to have as wide and as free a distribution of materials digitally as they have in print. Since digital distribution is, by definition, everywhere, the chances of some restrictions on digital materials appear to many to be very great. Proposed DRMs have the potential to allow rightsholders to override existing copyright exceptions.

No one doubts the need for digitization, or even to press on with mass digitization projects. Wiser men and women than I have pointed to this need and to the fact that Google and others will provide much needed funds for libraries that are always crying over the scarcity of same. This is true enough, so far as it goes. But are these funds the ones we want for the perceived need of, as one person put it, "instant gratification of one in a billion need"?[63] A question rarely asked is whether all this money is being put toward the right project at the right time. Certainly mass digitization projects are pushing libraries to rethink everything. The fear expressed here is that our "progress" may cause us, not to get the proverbial cart before the horse, but to leave the cart behind altogether.

For too long we have heard pronouncements about the dying book, not to mention the dying library.[64] With the advent of mass digitization some are even saying there is a good chance that publishing, especially small publishers, will eventual die off too as a result of mass digitization in general and Google's plan in specific.[65] Compared to the information superhighway, libraries are quaint antiquities, something to look upon nostalgically but nothing to become fixated upon in our high-powered cyberage. And yet, after all this time — now going on three decades of such pronouncements of the dead and dying book and library as artifact — we are not even marginally closer to the goal that ushers in everything paperless, everything online and everything at our fingertips (see chapter 7). Perhaps the time has come to look again with a fresh rather than a jaundiced eye and see libraries for what they are: the soul of the whole past time, the living memories of who we were, of who we are, and of who, with any luck, we can one day still become.

6

E-books to the Rescue!

E-books, or something very like them, will eventually become a common part of our reading history, much in the same way octavos replaced the once familiar folios. The question is not, therefore, if, but when? Yet other questions loom with respect to e-books, two of which are how many more years will it be before this happens, and what will e-books eventually look like? The question of how long before we see e-books (or their facsimile) edge out books is the easier of the two questions to answer. What they will eventually look like, present trends notwithstanding, is a much more difficult one. More about these questions momentarily.

The inevitability of e-books is a safe bet because so much time, effort and dollars have already been sunk in them although so little has been seen in return. E-books have, in one shape or another, been in the reading conversation for more than fifteen years.[1] In all that time, we are still far away from a consuetudinary acceptance of e-books. But their inevitability is secure because print materials are the new *bête noir*.[2]

E-books: Question of Maturity of Technology

The more difficult second question may be explained by this illustration. The now defunct "Malcolm in the Middle" sitcom aired an early episode during its first season in which the father made a call from a local bar on what was then called a "mobile phone," our now detested, loved, cursed, adored, ubiquitous, cellular phones. The phone looked to be about the size of two shoeboxes or a small valise. It also looked to weigh about 25 pounds. Looking at it in its infancy reminds one that the least likely attribute of the phone — its clunky mobility — became its epithet. At any rate, one of the lead characters made a call and literally screamed into the phone, but not because of the barroom noise. Rather, the phone's reception proved so primitive that hearing the conversation became the challenge. The conversation ran along the lines of two people trying to talk to each other over enormous distances without the benefit of amplification. Both kept repeating themselves while the other would say, "What?" and then begin with another line about how convenient such phones were, obviously neither hearing the other very well.

Of course the mobile phone evolved into the cell phone and is today one of life's most annoying modern conveniences. Everything changes while remaining the same: we can hear each other fine most of the time, when the calls aren't dropped. Nevertheless, the episode, whether intended to or not, served up what we have come to expect of technology. It may begin bad and even clunky, but it often ends convenient, sleek and sometimes even necessary.

E-books today are on the evolutionary chain's first link, at the point of that two-shoebox-size mobile phone: clunky, cumbersome, and frustrating yet with some promise. What makes them less hopeful than mobile-phones-turned-cellular is that they are not anywhere like an improvement over what they purport to replace, calling to mind Karl Kraus's definition of psychoanalysis, "the disease of which it purports to be the cure." In other words, e-books may be an example of what Edward Tenner called "the rearranging effect." That effect runs like this. Subways, because they are below ground, should be cool, yet during the summer they can be like blast furnaces. This is because subways come equipped with air-conditioners that blast out so much hot air from the cars that the subway tunnel itself is heated up and so needs to be air-conditioned.[3] The rearranging effect occurs when we create something that causes a change which requires us to create something else to accommodate what we did in the first place.

So, the cars need air-conditioning because the air-conditioners heated up the subways stations and made air-conditioning the cars a necessity. E-books may be necessary because we have created a culture that expects everything to be Web-based. We created computers and like to carry them around with us so we created computer books which require a computer to read them. It isn't entirely clear why we need e-books other than the fact that we have computers and need to make them more useful. Besides, print books work so positively well. No one thinks e-books have replaced their print counterparts, and no one really thinks they will replace them anytime soon.

Yet, we'll have e-books because someone out there wants us to have them, and, as said earlier, because paper is the new evil. It will take much longer than a few years to perfect the e-book (it's already taken four times longer than anyone thought and we're not there yet) because the technology is still clunky, the perceived need isn't real and because our current solution (print books) is so much better than any e-book iteration so far.

Moreover, most e-book companies are trying to make an electronic version of the book, not an entirely different mode of delivery from their printed counterparts. In early iterations, e-books even *smelled* like leather, and at least one iteration came equipped with a screen that mimicked the turning of a page.[4] This is the equivalent of creating an electronic version of scissors that looks exactly like real scissors but cut only virtual paper. At some point, someone is bound to ask, but why?

E-books Coming but Not Yet

Given present configurations, it's not likely that e-books will become a regular part of our reading history for the next 50 or 100 years. This is not because we do not have the technology or the ability to configure them to do so, but because we are too wedded to the current, excellent solution. Rather, it will take that long because those making these new widgets do not want an accessory to books, but a replacement for them. Not content with filling part of a market, however small (and right now the market of e-book readers appears to be less than 5 percent), they want all of it. This desire — or cupidity — will retard the growth of e-books because nothing on the horizon appears even to begin to replace print books. When we saw the mobile phone, we knew it had already solved a problem that standard phones could not: mobility, of course. We were (for some the reasoning appears inexplicable) willing to put up with some awkward facsimiles because the promise of mobile phones — talking anywhere, anytime, any place — seemed a worthwhile goal (something many will question when they hear a cell phone go off in a public restroom ... and *it is answered!*)

So e-books are coming, just not yet and, if present trends continue, likely not during the lifetimes of many who are reading this chapter. That makes the more difficult question of what e-books will eventually look like harder to answer, because it hinges on whether we are willing to take the future we have, or are willing to insist on waiting for the future we should have.[5] Thankfully, we are unwilling to take the e-book future we have so far, and so are forcing a potentially better e-book future later. It will have to be better because what we have so far seen is hardly good. We have rejected heavy, cumbersome e-books readers, and rejected e-book readers that only be read in the best possible lighting. We have also rejected e-book readers whose power source lasted a scant 60 minutes or so, before requiring a new charge. Some will wonder why all this isn't the most optimistic news so far regarding our cyberage. Make no mistake about it; it is it very good news. But the cynic in me says it's going to come all the same.

What some fear, however, is that we will become satisfied much too quickly with where we are and accept the inferior now for the potentially much better future. That worry remains because so many in this cyberage are happy with "good enough" (see the last chapter) and telling us not to "make perfection the enemy of the good." While that sentiment is understandable and predictable, there are cases in life when perfection really must be the enemy of the good, as for example when our cultural future is put at risk. Our attitude should not be, "e-books are inevitable." Rather it should be, "If e-books want to be in our reading future, they must present themselves as worthy candidates for that future." And in the short run, that's been the problem all along. E-books have not been worthy candidates. I use e-books here as the synecdoche for both the books themselves and the readers they must be read on.

This two-fold problem for e-books has been so far insurmountable. First, look at conventional books themselves. Books "are extremely durable information sources. They are stable and preserve relatively well. They are read in many contexts."[6] E-books, on the other hand, are not stable, they do not preserve well and they cannot be read in either many contexts or even under multiple conditions.[7] E-books (or their earlier incarnation as HTML books) are simply by and large inferior to print books. While we can argue that they are cheaper on the balance — but some doubt even this, owing to the numerous hidden and unaccounted for expenses in digitization — little more can be said for them. Even access to them is not an improvement over print books. But even these problems are not the whole story. More remains to be resolved.

E-books Adversely Change the Reading Experience

First, e-books change the entire reading experience. Hotlinks (to HTML books online) are often added as a putative value. Reading only one page of an e-book (especially in a "live" online environment) can lead one to read a dozen or more pages, often taking the reader so far afield, or filling the reader's mind with so much extraneous (though not necessarily bad) information, that the poor reader has often forgotten what took him on this information snipe hunt and must begin all over with the first page, even the first sentence. Reading is a discursive experience that should not be made to be any more discursive that already naturally is.

For example, a reader might begin a book by reading a first sentence: "Philosophers today are much engaged with questions about the essence and meaning of History."[8] An intelligent reader might process the sentence thinking about philosophers at the time the book in which this sentence appeared was published (the mid–1950s), as well as those in the field today, thinking that while things change, everything remains the same. She might be alerted to the choice of the word "essence" and recognize it as somehow philosophically important. The words "meaning" and "History" (especially its designation as a proper noun) will also likely intellectually arouse our erudite reader. These things will be quickly and readily processed in the mind of our hypothetical reader. If our reader is not quite as learned as the one we suggest, she might resort to a standard biographical dictionary to get Bultmann's dates and possibly his weltanschauung. Beyond all of this, nothing more. Even granting this, all of it occurs within the mind of each reader — with some readers, more; with others less, depending on the education brought to the reading experience. In the case of print books, only the author *suggests* and each individual reader *supplies* according to the education brought to the text.

An e-book, or HTML rendering of the same sentence, might have nearly every word hotlinked. For example, the word "philosopher" might be linked to a dozen names living at the time of the published book. "Today" might likewise be linked to the time of the book's birth. The phrase "much engaged" might lead a reader to several of Bultmann's controversies and his eventually falling out with the more orthodox of his faith. Further, a rather long runabout might be sent up over the word History, including both its use as a proper noun, and its uses in general. There might be several papers on the meaning of history over the past two or three decades. Finally, links galore might be attached to Bultmann's name, linking readers to everything he has written, as well as a few biographical essays, or even a few biographies. One hour or more later our erudite or even casual reader is exhausted with the runaround. The book has been put down as too formidable or too complex. Our fictive reader is spent after reading only one sentence in a short book.[9] After all is said and done, the reader has become a *spectator* to the information.

This does not begin to touch whatever else might happen in the e-book. It does not address the fact that the lines in the e-book, if on the Web, will be highlighted in black and blue at the very least, and possibly other colors. Pictures and or images of some kind, an audio clip, a video clip and more may also be supplied. There may even be a computer-generated character (see chapter 5) that leads the reader about as she reads from page to page. While most e-book readers may leave the text in its fairly innocuous state, all have added something, and most of what has been added is thought to be a value-added-something by someone, though not necessarily the reader.

But is it? Is it value-added to lead a reader on a wild-goose information chase? Is it value-added to say to a reader, in effect, do you know about this, this and this? Let's not make it negative but positive? Is it the place of a text to say to a reader, "Click here for more?" at nearly every conceivable juncture? Even the innocuous Amazon.com's persistence to remind users that they ordered such-and-so, and so might also be interested in such-and-such, leads the reader to more information not necessarily implied by the author. It is also a presumptuous persistence, too. Are the reader's reading habits something that can be quantified by what he or she has ordered in the past? Perhaps, but also perhaps not. Certainly some, even many, find this useful. Can a computer program really analyze tastes so well as to recommend usefully and consistently?[10] E-book publishers think the answer is yes, or the text would not come with so much supplied. But some readers surely find all that readymade content annoying. This has slowed the move toward a widespread acceptance of e-books.

E-book Content Lacking from All Vendors

Another more important reason e-books have not caught on is the content available in the electronic environment.[11] We are now more than a decade into the e-books venture and so far they have not delivered the world's literature as originally promised.[12] Indeed, this late in the game we do not even have a bad library of books, just a series of texts, for whatever they are worth, assembled willy-nilly for the putatively interested. Again, the point is not that e-books will not overtake print books, only that they have not done so in a widespread manner so far. But surely by this juncture in our e-book history we should not still be at the starting line, looking for a good beginning. At least at this point, shouldn't we know how to read an e-book, and more of us be doing it, something that the data indicates most are not?[13] In fact, for all e-books delivered on the Web, most of us print after the third page, if we wait that long. For e-books that must be read on a reader of some kind, not even 5 percent of us are reading them, if sales are any indication. Yet, why the persistence of e-books if not that publishers know a potential cash-cow when they see one, if they can only make that cow moo and give milk?

We have many examples of e-books and all of them suffer from the same set of problems. Take for example, Project Gutenberg, a great idea. Project Gutenberg is a content provider, so no reader is required. Project Gutenberg only offers what is already available in public domain. For classicists, this is a nice resource. Unfortunately for Project Gutenberg, there aren't that many great book readers left, and very few want to read for that long on a computer. No one doubts the *bona fide* of access. But the access is more for reference-finding than actual beginning-to-end reading. When we want to check a quote, find a citation or the like, Project Gutenberg is a grand resource and it's free. The same can be said about the Loeb Classics on MIT's Web site, mentioned earlier. The addition over the years of both the classic dictionaries (Lewis and Short for the Latin series, Scott and Lidell for the Greek) is a tremendous asset. Yet again, the same problem remains. Once one has found a specific quote, found the needed citation, most of us resort to the fabulous printed texts that nearly every library of any size has available.[14]

Questia, another major source (and another content provider) that claims to be the largest electronic academic library online, has similar e-problems.[15] When the pitch was first made, Questia proponents crowed about its $100 million in venture capital.[16] By 2005, the company had laid off more than half its force and had begun to refashion itself. While some of that force has been rehired, no one doubts that the venture as presented has not turned out as expected. The blame can be shared both by the dot-com bubble burst and by the fact that even $100 million proved insufficient to gain a foothold in the reader market. (What a conventional print-based academic library could have done with $100 million boggles the mind, but we'll let that pass for now.)

Questia still struggles and part of its problem may be that its success still relies on libraries holding many of its e-texts in print. That $100 million proved insufficient has still not dashed the hopes of many who seek an all e-book library. It remains most puzzling to many observers: some confused about why it has not worked as planned; others, that it still manages to attract so many dollars. Questia's search engine, a free service, is probably used by many who, once the searched-for citation is found, repair to a local academic library for the actual book. Questia's approach, to charge by the hour, the week, the month or the year, is reasonable enough. Still, that it continues to struggle for users should indicate just how far short we have fallen of the sought-for goal of a fully electronic library.[17]

Xanadu, a thirty-year enterprise, suffered from the same fate and, in the end, threw in the towel. No amount of funding could have changed the outcome for Xanadu. The company netLibrary discovered the same fate, falling into Chapter 11 before being rescued by OCLC. With about $80 million in venture capital, netLibrary found too few takers to make it financially successful. The library I now head subscribes to about 15,000 titles of netLibrary's collection. It remains the *least* used of our 100+ electronic resources.[18] Some could argue that it's because we do not have enough titles. On the other hand, nothing we have seen indicates to us we should send more of our scant resources its way. We subscribe to it through a consortium. Any one of the 55 subscribing libraries representing some 200,000 users may use it. But once *one of them* subscribes to a given title, that title remains locked until it is checked back in. This is of course the same way all our printed texts work, but our printed texts, about 500,000 of them, are only available to at most 6,000 users at any one time. E-books, to be successful, must be better than this, not worse. This does not begin to address the problems encountered by those potential 200,000 users of e-books who must first register before they can check out even one book.[19]

Registering before checking out an e-book is one of a number of problems facing e-books, whether from content providers or from those requiring a reader. Demand is driven by the distribution chain, not by the needs of those who use the e-books.[20] So far e-books come bundled, and while one may be able to buy one or 1,000, the titles have been pre-selected by someone else. Some may argue that any library is like this, but most libraries, even small ones, will have 100,000 or more volumes to choose from, and all have undergone a rigorous selection process, tailored to specific user needs. Moreover, most e-books tend to be only one type, mass trade. If one wishes to read something other than Dan Brown's *The DaVinci Code* and others like it, well, that's too bad. While Questia and netLibrary do offer a wider variety of many academic titles, netLibrary requires hoisting a wireless laptop about, and a service purchased either by a public or academic library.[21] Questia, meanwhile, mimics the gasoline pump with its running dollars every minute one spends reading, a point that does not encourage long stretches of reading and reflection.

Variety Not the Spice of E-books

E-book readers will free one from the laptop, of course, but so far there are more than a dozen to choose from and their costs run from about $350 to more than $1,000. Still, of all those who read e-books, dedicated e-book readers (or PDDs) are the most favored.[22] While advances are definitely being made in e-book readers (see below), many e-books cannot be read in direct sunlight. This attenuation of their utility is therefore obvious and certainly makes the conventional, very low-tech but highly portable book more highly desirable. The lack of standardization forces one to chose between e-book readers A, B or C. The choice of the e-reader determines what can be read since the formats are not interchangeable.

The lack of flexibility among a reader's choices further limits what a reader can choose. A reader may like the offerings of vendor A, but hate the reader required, or, conversely, like the reader but hate the pre-selected choices. Nothing so far is being done to change this or to make any one reader's format easily read on another. Ideally, there would be only one or two very fine, inexpensive readers that one could use to download whatever one found on the Web to read, or save and read later, in an iPod-like fashion.[23]

What has made the Web attractive to many is its ubiquity and variety. For many, Web users being able to find *something* they like *whenever* they want it makes them swear by it. E-books have so far not been able to mimic this in any satisfactory manner. PDAs that are Web-accessible are useful but not to eyes over forty. Trying to read e-mail on many PDAs is unwieldy if the e-mails are very long at all. Converting a book to fit those small screens is not practical now, and there does not seem to be any way around this technologically for the short-term future. Making screens large enough to read easily generally means making the hardware too cumbersome to carry around. It also makes carrying them about a financial burden. Dropping one from a height of more than a foot or two usually means having to buy another. Even at the low dollar end for e-book readers — $300 — this is not something many users can afford. Laptop technology has overcome *some* of this, but no one really wants to lug about a laptop instead of a book. As more options are presented, "retrieving relevant information has a become progressively more challenging and time consuming."[24]

By far the biggest advantage of e-books is the ability to search the contents of a given collection. As mentioned above, Questia's collection may be searched for free. The problem remains, however, that someone — the reader or a library — must make the full collection accessible. Although Questia pitches itself to students and offers them many options for payment, it also presents something of a financial commitment even though Questia's many payment options may be affordable to some. The contents of Questia and netLibrary can be viewed anywhere one can gain access to the Web: at home, in a dorm room, or wherever wireless access is available. Not many are willing to pay for full access individually, however. If libraries were to mimic these models, patrons would be charged per use, or even per page. In many ways the democratic nature of libraries to make available vast collections to its clientele without charge (or in the case of academic libraries, as part of the benefit of matriculation) has inadvertently cut a potential market out from under these providers.[25] Not many patrons would knowingly pay for what they can access for free. While there is no way to ascertain statistically how rampant the practice may be, many might well search a site that offers free searching, only to obtain the book in question from a local library.

E-books Not Ready for Prime Time

In short, e-books still have far to go. While there are many offerings in addition to those mentioned here, e-books still lag behind other digital technologies. Studies so far do not show widespread usage.[26] The problem appears not only merely to be educating users about their availability, but also getting them to repeat using them once they are well known. Libraries owning content, and publishers offering both content and readers and using multiple marketing strategies to make them well-known, have not been successful in shoring up e-book usage. The latest figures for e-book titles are closing in on 300,000.[27] This remains, however, a drop in the proverbial bucket as print books number many times more. Academic books alone number about 50,000 annually. Most e-book users still complain about the limited number of titles available, the limited coverage in various areas, or both. Even in high content areas, such as business and management, usage of e-books still lags well behind printed formats.[28] This may seem obvious to some, but with all the push, why have e-books not caught on? Given the very limited funding most libraries experience, is it any wonder that scare funds are not shifted in this direction?

One area where e-books have soared in both the number of titles and usage is in online reference materials. No one doubts, for example, that electronic access to journals represents one of the more grand "tipping points" in electronic access.[29] It makes sense in every mode of consideration: access, ease of distribution (no more claims madness) and ubiquity. Journal articles once placed on a library's reserve circulation function can now be linked to the database containing the article. Oversight is minimal, comparatively speaking — though those who make it available would contest the word "minimal" — and access is 24/7. Earlier chapters have pointed out some significant problems even with this, the poster-child of electronic access. The higher usage noted by industry experts even in this area is still referred to as "a measured [i.e., small] upturn."[30]

Many of the same attributes for electronic journals are also true of electronic reference books. "Reference materials (i.e., encyclopedias, dictionaries, indexes, etc.) are extremely useful in digital formats. Many of them are created, marketed and licensed to libraries as *separate* entities with their own unique interfaces."[31] No one should contest the utility of having access to large numbers of reference e-books. Most of the early renditions of reference electronic access have been solved. For example, the first electronic rendition of *Statistical Abstracts of the United States* was just short of a nightmare to use. Much of that has been corrected (though the Government Printing Office's outsourcing of electronic versions of its materials continues to be problematic) but the problem of standards remains.[32]

E-book Standards Still Undecided

For example, in 1998, a group publishers and techies promised to put together e-book standards that would "define an e-book format that could be used on any device; that would be interchangeable between e-book brands; and would make it easy for publishers to create e-books from the same data files that were used to derive the printing of the hard copy product."[33] By 1999, they developed the Open E-book Forum (now the International Digital Publishing Forum) and pushed for much needed standardization.[34] Needless to say, nearly ten years later, we are no closer than we were in 1998. The trouble is, no one but librarians seems to care that this chaos remains unresolved. This is not to dismiss what OpenReader is doing, a nonprofit organization that hopes to present an open standard based on XML by summer 2006.[35] The trouble is, it may be too little, too late.

Meanwhile, the distinction between e-books and reference materials in electronic format is important because reference materials, by definition, are not read as books are read and so mesh well with the bite-size (dare I say byte?) version of reading the Web encourages. If we include reference materials as e-books then the whole tenor of the discussion changes. It is, perhaps, no wonder that these are often a separate creation, a separate marketing strategy, and a separate interface. Publishers know these materials will sell, whereas the history of e-books sales *per se* remains low. Most publishers still offer only a very small percentage of their total published content in electronic format, ready for delivery.[36] This will change over time but the rush to place us at the mercy of this digitized format is much too premature, certainly too early before we have worked out all the kinks. One other matter needs to be addressed, however. For example, how much time is spent with e-books? One analysis suggests that the average time can be measured in minutes rather than hours, the unique pages viewed, never more than twenty.[37]

In order to make e-books work, publishers need to find out from users what they want and how they want it. They also need to make offerings easily interchangeable so that what one orders can be read on multiple e-book readers. Even on-demand titles would be a plus, if these titles were offered to users at a reasonable rate. While some publishers offer libraries access in digital or print format, offering them both at the same cost will likely result in libraries ordering only the print version of all but reference type materials since most library budgets are too small to afford both. Offering the electronic versions of print titles at a nominal cost when the print version is purchased may help increase usage.[38] Still, users are likely to request the print format when available if the text must be read cover-to-cover. Even the multiple formats offered (e.g., increased font size, hotlinks, organizers, reading guides, note-taking features and more) often do not make e-books any more attractive for the reasons mentioned above. The many free e-book content converters (such as saving texts as a text file, using Adobe Acrobat's converter, FrontPage Express or MS Reader, to name a few) do not solve usage issues or the other problems mentioned above.[39]

Mass Digitization Project: Where Fools Rush In

The rush (mad rush, really) to digitization via e-books troubles many library professionals, especially with respect to school libraries. Mention has been made of the threat to school libraries of mass digitization projects in earlier chapters but it should be highlighted here, too. The change of school libraries to media centers some fifteen years ago has not helped the school library's identity, and it has certainly hurried the push to eliminate print books in their midst. Because schools suffer from funding difficulties like all of education, placing a golden apple of deceit in their midst only exacerbates the problem.

Administrators, who often believe everything they read about the Web, become impatient with librarians or media specialists (as they are often called in K–12 schools) who are slow to move everything they offer to some sort of electronic format. Only our students — really your children and mine — suffer as a result. They cannot get the materials they need and so are often forced to use whatever is made electronically available. Having access to only one kind of electronic format only serves to accelerate the widening gap between the haves (those with high speed Internet access at home or those who can afford e-book readers), and the have-nots (those with either dial-up access only, or, as is more often the case, no access at all).[40] Even narrowing the gap between the haves and the have-nots does not address special-needs students, especially those visually challenged.[41] Even if we are not to make electronic access the only access but merely the preferred access, we still have a long way to go to make sure we do not leave the impaired without comparable access *when they require it.*

As alluded to earlier, e-book standards are a paramount need. "A more advanced publication structure would facilitate the long term archiving of digital texts so that back list books could be republished ... long after the hardware and software of the proprietary formats have become technological dinosaurs."[42] Having 100,000 e-book titles today would not help their distribution and commonplace appearance in libraries or among users if their hardware and software formats quickly become obsolete, or their access becomes difficult. Further, being able to add e-book content by discipline, or even *partial* e-book content, would be especially useful.[43] Making such a requirement possible would make e-books far more useful and far more highly desirable. College and university bookstores might find e-books a valued source if the content were made much more readily available by being more easily accessible, and the formats to read them on interchangeable.

The development of standards industry-wide is a necessity. Doubtless it will be expensive to develop, complex to work out, and have devilish compatibility issues to resolve.[44] But much of the R & D would be recovered by having one system that would run all e-books, no matter how delivered. Standardization would mean that any company could make its materials available, and any user could access them on any machine, whether from a laptop, a Palm-device or an e-book reader. It would be much like the delivery of multiple videos and DVDs is today. Anyone can play videos or DVDs offered by any company on a wide variety of players. E-books must mimic this somehow to become more user-friendly. Imagine having to match up DVDs or videotapes with a dozen or so machines, or being able to see some only on lap- or desktops, others only on device A, device B and so on, the way one finds e-books today. It's no wonder that e-books cannot find their niche! Right now they are trying to fill several instead on only one. Perhaps this is why some reports indicate that less than 50,000 have purchased e-book devices.[45]

Copyright and Digital Rights Problems Loom Large

Copyright, too, must change. While the current copyright law remains a mystery even to copyright attorneys, it simply has not kept pace with the digital environment. My call to ease copyright is not an argument for the wholesale opt-out feature demanded by Google; it is a call for a more reasonable digital copyright policy. So far, digital copyright, even in its iteration as the Digital Millennium Copyright Act (DMCA), not only does not answer these needs, but it also has, in some ways, made it far worse. While some may not agree with so bald-faced an assessment, no one believes that current copyright policy with respect to digital materials, or materials delivered digitally, works well. If anyone thinks this is as easy matter to fix, let him review the work on CONFU, the Conference on Fair Use. After working for months during the Clinton administration, the committee could not come to a conclusion. In the end, it issued only guidelines that are not legally binding and, if followed precisely, do not give those following them any assurance they will not remain liable.[46]

All of these obstacles represent a major drawback to e-books and will be difficult to resolve in the coming years. For now, people use e-books to solve special problems, check a fact or a quote, and find some specific reference. What they are not doing is reading e-books from cover-to-cover.[47] Whether all or most of these problems can be resolved to the satisfaction of users remains to be seen. Still, getting users to read e-books as they do printed books is another matter altogether. Some of this has as much to do with the physiology of reading (the light over the shoulder versus one directly in the eye) as it does with anything technology can solve. The familiar saccade of reading (the movements of the eye when reading) may only be possible when the eye is scanning a printed page.

A new generation of readers may have to evolve who are more used to this form of reading. Since humans have been reading with the light over the shoulder for hundreds of years, it's hard to say whether this is merely a facility we have become accustomed to, or a requirement of the reading calculus. It may be impossible to wean readers from this habit, or to wean them from it in order to really read an e-book from virtual cover to virtual cover. Perhaps the only niche for e-books is the quick access to facts, quotes and special problems, and therefore they will not ever replace print books but only make the pursuit of reference information easier. Certainly no one would argue that trying to find specific facts via a paper index (only to discover the term isn't listed) is easier than finding them using a digital search tool.

Finally, e-book devices themselves must change. Most of the first generation readers are either obsolete or the companies producing them no longer in business. Of the companies remaining, many are pushing altogether different products. Early iterations were clunky, did not read well, cost too much (remember, users purchase only the book when reading printed texts) and were useless in the sunlight. Newer e-book reader models have made great progress. The Sony Reader, for example, shows great promise.[48] Touting the E-Ink screen technology, the Sony Reader promises a reading experience not unlike that of reading a book on paper — which may cause the jaundiced among us to ask, why not read the book in paper? — but we'll ignore the impulse to question. E-Ink technology may solve the problem of backlight or light in the eyes mentioned above. Moreover, the Sony Reader does not need to be refreshed regularly and it features a much longer battery life. The Sony Corporation claims one can "turn" 7,500 pages on a single charge.[49] The new Sony device weighs less than 10 ounces, has a 6 inch screen display, and measures about the size of a paperback, again leading the ... oh, never mind. Sony claims the reader can hold 80 books The E-book Reader retailed in late spring 2006 for about $350.

Sony also plans to open what it calls the "Content Store" and will offer books based on the model that Apple iPod and iTunes store made famous. Titles from the Content Store will cost about 60 percent less than their print counterparts in bookstores.[50] What has made industry experts claim the Sony Reader is a breakthrough is the fact that this e-book Reader can do more than read e-books. It will also read other file types, such as PDFs, digital pictures, music files, news, blogs and RSS feeds. In other words, it can capture Internet content and download it for later use. While Sony has made the claim that this reader will do for e-books what iPods have done for music, most experts thinks this is a stretch. Many do feel that while it will not be a major breakthrough, it will make e-books look more attractive to some serious readers. But it hasn't so far.

Other new devices are presenting themselves, such as Panasonic's R3, FlyBook, OQO, and Sony's Vaio.[51] All offer a variety of access and convenience: Wi-Fi, audio and video capabilities, Bluetooth and so on. But these are basically laptops masquerading in one feature as an e-book reader. All come with a hefty price tag to boot, making their attractiveness less and less like Cinderella, and more and more like one of her sisters. ETI-2 (aka, e-bookwise 1150) may well be the least expensive dedicated e-book reader. At right at $100, it proffers itself as one of the more promising readers with updated (but not fancy) software. It only holds about one fourth the number of books as the Sony but also costs only about one-third as much.[52] In the Sony category of e-book sophistication comes iRex's Iliad ER100. It sports a touchscreen, uses built-in Wi-Fi and supports HTML.[53] The list could easily be expanded but these are enough to illustrate the old, the current and the soon-to-be.

Perhaps all of this will come to pass just as Sony (and other companies) hopes but let's not forget the colossal failure in 2005 of Librie. Several things continue to militate against this hopeful scenario. As late as May 2006, publishers, experts and others at the International Digital Publishing Forum: Connect and Mobile 2006 admitted that e-books "are still struggling to find a niche."[54] Lack of content, too many platforms and no settled standards made experts doubtful about the future of e-books. The content issue continues to loom large because there are not enough customers. Most agree that the scarcity of customers is the result of too little content. Publishers are reluctant to convert many books to e-book formats without the customer support; consequently, the circle is a vicious one that causes e-book popularity to wax and wane, the wane side of the equation far out stripping the heretofore noted gains. Even participants at this conference did not think the Sony Reader would make *that* much difference.

Amid Numerous E-book Failures Hope Springs Eternal

Some at this conference did think cell phones might hold some hope for the future. Indeed, it isn't just cell phones either, but PodReader, Sony's PlayStation Portable, and Nintendo's Gameboy. All are making claims to be the new e-book reader.[55] But anyone who has tried to read e-mail on a BlackBerry or a Palm device knows that trying to read even a simple but long message is more than a little problematic. Imagine trying to wade through one of Marcel Proust's long, very complex (yet beautiful) sentences! A reader could not get through even the first set of dependent clauses without having to backtrack repeatedly to get the gist of the sentence, a self-defeating purpose when reading Proust's sinfully beautiful *A La Recherché du Temps Perdu*. Experts also echoed a claim made earlier: most everyone reading a digital text prints out anything over "three or four pages."[56]

Again, perhaps it's too early to argue that a built-in human reading requirement will sink e-book content forever, but for the short term it does leave their potential longevity in serious doubt. Indeed, most experts agree that we are in the "Tower of eBabel" where too many options are presented on too many different machines for too few users.[57] The idea that cell phones or Blackberrys might be able to solve the e-book

difficulty does not bode well for the literacy of future generations who might be dependent on electronic access exclusively. The claim of some at the meeting that free e-books
should come with all new devices will not guarantee the future of e-books among serious readers.[58]

Part of what hinders this daunting effort to push digital readers beyond the Google-
mania that so many digital champions applaud is their lack of information about what
is in traditional libraries. While more than 50 percent of users believe that Google offers
very good information, less that 35 percent understand that even better content is available via the databases that most libraries (public and academic) offer to patrons who
come though their doors.[59] This is of course a perennial problem with libraries. Those
of us who work in them simply have not made the content we offer more widely known.
Even among academic libraries where our constituency is almost captive, many of our
patrons do not have a full knowledge of all that we offer.

Most academic library directors or deans have certainly experienced this commonplace conundrum: a faculty member e-mails or calls over about a "great, new" database
the library "must buy immediately" only to discover that said database has been available
for the last three, five or even ten years. Libraries — especially academic ones — are simply
not ready or able, nor do they even know how, to market what they have. We often make
the erroneous assumption that our clientele will know what we have because it's in their
best interest to know. No amount of special pleading or wishing will make this so. We
simply have to do a better job of making what we have much more widely known.

In 2005, we set making our resources more widely known as a goal for our public services unit at Winthrop University. After some study, we determined that text e-
mails had not and would not work well for this task. Our students and faculty received
far too many e-mails and ignored most of them. Those who did not ignore them often
did not access their e-mail regularly. Although we had placed on our library home page
a "new" button that anyone could click on, we still felt what we had for use in all our
disciplines did not come readily to mind to those who needed them. We came up with
the idea of using postcards to make what we have better known.

The results have been both staggering and impressive.[60] It seems almost too simple to think this would work, but what is known is not always obvious, and what is
obvious is not always known.[61] Of course this is not the only marketing strategy that
will be required of us, but it does point to a very inexpensive and easy to implement
plan that has better promulgated the 100+ databases we have ready for use. We have
targeted various ones to both faculty and students over the past year and have seen an
amazing increase in databases we thought would be "obvious" to anyone wanting information in those areas.

All of which serves to underscore the problems inherent in the digital enterprise.
Too much of what goes on in cyberspace strikes one as so much bric-a-brac in the digital curiosity shop.[62] These digital exercises provide a flash in the digital pan and make
for fun reading (usually in a printed format) for some who mistakenly see them as
breakthrough potentials. After a few weeks or months, everyone goes back to the status quo, as for example Rice University's plan to begin an all digital university press
while using the same paper-based peer review and editing processes.[63]

Some will doubtless argue that such "flashes" are required with new technology in order to provide others with vision for a better iteration later. Perhaps they are right. What troubles others, however, is that it will seem to the less informed that these have, or will, replace what has served for so long and so well: paper-based scholarship. The doubtful will perhaps be more swayed when e-publishing is accepted alongside conventional publishing for tenure and promotion. But tenure and promotion cannot enter that arena until changes have been made to prevent the widespread abuses common to the electronic format.

"A digital repository of books and journal articles" writes Steven Bell, "is not any more an academic library than a digital collection of syllabi, lecture notes, and reading lists is an institution of higher education."[64] This may seem harsh to digital minions who want a paperless society *today*. But it is the fact of academic life in which we now live. If we do not heed the potential dangers, we may find we have lost much more than information. "Hence, perpetually and essentially," writes Jacques Derrida in "Plato's Pharmacy," "texts run the risk of becoming definitively lost. Who will ever know of such disappearances?" And Derrida did not have in mind texts lost in, to, or because of, cyberspace.

7

The Paperless Revolution
Is Complete!

The din of grand claims about the Web often drowns out some of its inglorious failures. Some of the more far-reaching failures have been rehearsed in these pages; but none is more colossal or more inglorious than the paperless society hailed for the last thirty years as the coming brave, new world. In fact, everything about the Web, the Prime Mover of the paperless world, screams "Ultimate Significance," when we cannot possibly know at this early stage. "The Internet is too young," writes Robert J. Samuelson, "for anyone to foretell its ultimate significance.... But some present claims aren't true."[1] Samuelson goes on to point out that it did *not* spread faster than any other innovation, that it *is* a work in progress and that many other innovations have far outstripped it in seismic afterclap (take indoor plumbing, for example, or electricity). We forget that we are, as Robert Burton reminds us in the *Anatomy of Melancholy*, dwarves sitting on the shoulders of giants.[2] We moderns hate the thought that, not only did many things and many greater people come before us, but also that they invented many things far better than even the Web.

Where Is the Paperless Society?

At any rate, of all the grand claims of the electronic age, none has been more bold than that of a coming paperless society. And none has been more wrong. Normally this would have put an end to the matter. No so for the motherboard mavens. The great fear now is not that the paperless society will fail (in most respects it already has), but that amid its stunning failures so far, we'll get it anyway, ready or not. We *will* be without paper and therefore books, so live with it! This insistence is all the more puzzling given a recent survey of about two dozen modern so-called luxuries: iPods, cellphones, television, CDs and so on. Books, that droll invention now closing in on Methuselah's age, outstrips them all in popularity.[3]

Over the last twenty-five years, automation's prognosticators made increasingly bold claims abut the coming paperless age. Offices, businesses, industries, libraries and universities would eventually all become paperless and the New Jerusalem would be ours at last. Some made changes by redefining the library as no longer a single entity but "a range of services" that would be (somehow) seamlessly connected and would reach beyond any one campus or laboratory.[4] Others suggested that the library would be freed, as if once a slave, from paper and occupy "infinite space" and be "interconnected in a transparent way."[5] (All predictions must apparently include either the word "seamless" or "transparent.") The library as a place would disappear; it would be replaced by a network of every imaginable file or database, there would be no walls, buildings would vanish, communities of every size would provide their citizens laptops, and electronic files would never ever be lost.[6] Of course, there would have to be paradigm shifts, for where would we be without them? Librarians and users would have to learn to accept those changeling paradigms or be lost in the dust of the parabolic arch, or some such matrix-like vacuum. But wait, it gets better.

In the library of the future, scryers promised that the digital medium would replace everything, not just paper but analog, hand drawing and even handwriting.[7] Who knows? Maybe even people. By the end of the nineties, we were told, a scientific library without paper would be possible because *all* science and engineering publications would be available, as if wishing made it so.[8] In our new age we would have cuddly e-Books, while all, or nearly all, computer screens would posses resolutions that matched paper, and cataloging would become obsolete.[9] In short, there would be nothing, nothing at all that the computer could not do. While computers may not be able to brush one's teeth, why, give them a year or two and they'll make teeth démodé. Some few Cassandras worried over silly things like standards and even a few dared call it treason. But by and large, most were on the peace train headed to the promised land of new libraries, new services and a brave, new world. Since all of these prognostications were pontificated in the late eighties or the early nineties, we are at a perfect coign-of-vantage to see what happened.

Paperless Society Memo E-Mailed: Deleted as Spam?

A funny thing happened on the way to the new paperless world: society didn't get the memo, maybe because it was e-mailed, and we all deleted it as spam. Somewhere along the way the New Paperless Jerusalem ended in the pages of Samuel Butler's old *Erewhon*. The only paperless society so far successful occurs in the heady environment inhabited by George Jetson, his wife Jane, his daughter Judy, his boy Elroy — well, you get the picture. The paperless society expired even before that new world began. We are no closer to the paperless world than we were thirty-five years ago when it was touted as the next new thing. Surely this helps explain why in the last ten years almost no one has been talking about it, *but that has not stopped the forcible move in its direction.* What is disturbing to some is the continued march, lockstep really, toward this goal, although most if not all the predictions of the coming paperless society ended early, or simply failed outright.

Not only has the paperless anything not found us, we are awash in paper more than ever before. Paper usage has increased, not decreased, and much of the reason why resides in the very culprit putatively responsible for its replacement: electronic delivery of materials. Still the madness continues unabated. It is as if some are demanding this paperless revolution whether we can achieve it or not. Further, and this is most lamentable, it appears they *will* have it, regardless of what we must lose to get there.

"We are drowning in information," writes John Naisbitt, "but starved for knowledge."[10] Naisbitt hits upon the very reason for this embarrassing failure. Along the way to paper-freedom, someone forgot to distinguish between an answer and the right answer, between information and the right information, between facts and data, and knowledge. As one wag put it, "Information doubles while knowledge halves and wisdom quarters."[11] In other words, having an ocean of fish doesn't mean you've caught anything yet, and weltering in information does not mean you're awash in wisdom. Paper has allowed us to tame the information revolution that threatens to undo us. No one seemed to notice that having an industry — computers — that could churn out with lightning quick speed disorganized morasses of data did not mean we would be any better off than when we had to distill it into wisdom as we once slowly ferreted it out on paper. Take, for example, the new datum that 75 percent of all e-mails today are spam.[12] This grand new resource threatens to drown us in "Maybe You're a Winner!" notices.

Apart from being spammed to death, the electronic cesspool overlooks another important fact. Although we can send all of the *Britannica* across the oceans and to the darkest recesses of Africa, people on *both ends* of the computer calculus have to be able to read, have to want to read, have to understand what it is they have read, and have to be able to fashion it in to something other than a string of factoids that by themselves are more meaningful than a roomful of ones and zeros. Oh yes, and both transmitting and receiving ends must have a computer! What computers are able to easily generate — information — also happens to be the least useful commodity until someone turns it into knowledge.[13]

Random Data, Not Information

In our rush to the paperless society, we forgot that along the way all this information had to be turned into something readable, something comprehensible to others. "Bogota," "3.14," "5,280 feet" and the like are nothing but random facts. Putting random facts into a digestible form for others to use is what reading is all about. It is how we acquire knowledge, and how information is transformed into wisdom. Paper has been that form of distributing knowledge to others for the better part of our intellectual history. Yet here we are, with no better indication of the success of our electronic venture, rushing about, trying to eliminate all things paper, perhaps for no better reason than it *appears* as if we can. Discarding paper before we have a *better* replacement is the height of stupidity. Once again, because this has been delivered to us by the new Delphi Oracle, the Web, we have closed our eyes, to say nothing of our minds, and forbade the paperless society cant to fall where it should forever remain until its replacement is found: the dustbin of history.

Almost no one talks about the paperless society now that we know we cannot get along without paper. Yet this has slowed neither our mad dash to make everything electronic, nor our seemingly mad rush to do away with books. We rush, like mad dipsomaniacs behind the wheel of a runaway car headlong down the information highway to nowhere. Perhaps it is for the coming illiterate generation that the paperless society is being created: they won't be able to read anyway, so there will be, *ipso facto*, no reason for having paper.

One of the more amusing stories about thoughtless progress came across my desk a few years ago. An aboriginal tribe in a remote part of the world had an astonishingly high birth rate. The United Nations in its infinite wisdom sent in a horde of well-intentioned meddlers to "correct" the problem. Sociologists, psychologists and an army of PhDs descended upon the unsuspecting tribe. Its chief and his fertile followers received first-hand instruction on the practice of safe sex. Language barriers proved as much a problem for middling meddlers as for Margaret Mead in *Coming of Age in Samoa*.[14] Trying to overcome the language barrier, our impavid and inventive progressives took the men to a place outside the tribe proper to demonstrate the preferred application of condoms using the tribes' spears. Everyone nodded in agreement. The booty for the conquering tribe came in form of scores of cases of condoms airlifted in. Weeks passed into months, and the months into years. Oddly, not even a statistically insignificant downtick could be observed in the rate of live births. How could this be?

Back flew the well-intentioned but now brow-furrowed progressives. After much gesticulation and many hand signals, the tribe understood what the progressives wanted to know, and took them to a place just outside the tribe proper. Arrayed in perfect symmetry stood, as far as the eye could see, hundreds of spears, each with its perfectly applied talisman-like condom well-secured onto the blunt end of hundreds of spears.

Paperless Society Perfect for the Age of Illiteracy

In many ways, this story could be changed a bit and applied to our current dilemma of a plethora of paper in a society in which many thought none would now be in use. Someone forgot to communicate just how this would be done. To replace a much-valued commodity requires a superior substitution. A paperless society cannot be the goal of a culture that values knowledge and still distinguishes (however more dimly) between knowledge and information. We appear unable at this junction to be able to read for long on computer screens. Eliminate paper and we're all at the mercy of the vanishing returns of memory. Striving for a paperless society in a culture awash in data without meaning is, well, a meaningless endeavor. It should surprise no one that thirty-five years later we are no closer to that dubious goal than when it was first proclaimed.

Reading is best accomplished in a medium that the eye can, literally, behold. If all we ever hoped to accomplish were disparate glances at random facts, then perhaps we would already be well on the way to a world without paper. But reading disjointed facts has not, until recently, been defined *as* reading. Reading is still best accomplished on paper, a medium that the eye can see and the mind can comprehend.[15] Reading requires time, effort, and great mental agility, something that does not lend itself well to the flickering of so many computer screens. The best computer screens provide resolution four or five times lower than that of the paper in this book you are now reading. Typical computer screens, even the best ones, put out words at resolutions of far less magnitude than even the poorest paper in books.[16] This means that even the briefest kind of communication — say an e-mail — requires much greater effort on the part of the mind to comprehend. It's no wonder then that tackling even a short book online becomes too difficult for even the savviest geek.

As mentioned in the previous chapter, e-books have been a noted failure, perhaps because to read them online requires a paperless mentality, something we haven't been able to invent as easily as we have pretenders to the paperless throne. Worthy of a bumper sticker: In the paperless society, toilet paper will come in plastic. To predict the words of some old sage, "Ouch!"

Even Project Gutenberg, for all its grand protestations to the contrary, is only *making available* texts online. This is not the same thing as handing 300 million people 300,000 books. In order to have access, a number of things must obtain: computers, wired or wireless access, a stable Internet provider, and so on. Newt Gingrich's plan to distribute laptops to the homeless to the contrary, not everyone has access. Of those who do, fewer still have *high speed* Internet access. *War and Peace* is hard enough to plow through on paper, harder still online; *impossible* on dial-up. Project Xanadu, mentioned earlier, is another free-text service that's already belly-up. "[The paperless society] is an incredible and diversionary nightmare," writes one observer.[17] We do not tend to think in these terms when it comes to the dizzying, intoxicating promise of the paperless society. It's only the next morning, when the hangover wears off that we finally come to our senses once again.

The Web: New Age of Democracy or Crackpot Heaven?

Perhaps we need to think again, heaven forbid. When the Internet burst upon the scene, even in its Pine-mad, WAIS-infested, Gopher-chained infancy, only grand promises spewed forth. Democracy would come of age; townhalls, not the ones in local communities where people saw one another face to face and discussed relevant issues, but worldwide chat rooms where all could participate, would proliferate. At that stage, only the elect few could figure it out well enough to use it; and so it proved not only a new but a very valuable commodity, as the Department of Defense had known all along. After the creation of HTML and domain names, however, the elect were shoved aside for the benefit of all, or so we thought. Today, we know differently. Now, every Einstein, every Oppenheimer and *also every Unabomer*, every skinhead, every hate group organizer can have his or her say. In fact, so bad has all of this become that the vocational world I inhabit, academe, known for its near eleutheromania for all, is crying for an Internet II, a dedicated (and pricey) line that will allow professors, scientists, and medical specialists to exchange information without pop-ups, Viagra commercials and crackpots. Well, okay, there will still be crackpots, but the gist is the same.

The Internet today has the opportunity for the best minds to express themselves; it also provides an open forum for the emergence of a dominating kakistocracy instead of a democracy, the rule of the worst over the rule of the governed. "The Internet is a populist, anarchistic, quirky intellectual playground," writes one critic, "in which ideas, data, insults, comments, drafts, comments on drafts, and on and on are exchanged at a rate that defies rational use."[18] I would add that the cranks and the crackpot outnumber by a huge ratio the rational comments of the rational few. All of this comes about with the idea that if everything — videos, images, documents, books — you name it — is available to everyone all at once, all will be well. Have we forgotten that for any of this to be of any value, it still must be read *one word at a time*?

I am reminded of a book I used to read to my children years ago, a classic book titled *Petunia, the Silly Goose*. Petunia thought it would make her appear wise to carry about a book, and for a while, it did. That is, until she had to live up to her fame. She had not actually read the book because *she did not know how to read*. Has the Internet become, or is it becoming, the modern age equivalent to the Victorian practice of having huge library facades, wooden blocks painted to appear as books? It would appear so, since to get at the heart of the Web, one must wade through the electronic version of a human cesspool of ideas to find its useful information.

Knowledge versus Information

This is why libraries have always, until recently, been about providing access to knowledge over information. Bibliographies identify documents, locate where they are and describe them, and provide access to the physical documents.[19] It does not do much good to point to a building and say, "there's your answer," any more than it does to point a user to tens of thousands of mostly useless documents in answer to a request for information, much less knowledge.

Why does so much of the world remain agog over the putative but little seen "vast" resources of the Web? Sure, eight billion pages is vast. But when two-thirds or more are the equivalent of a crank phone call, vast suddenly seems much smaller. Yet in our rush to electronic everything, we are called upon to ignore most of these crank phone calls and stand amazed in the presence of emoticons, video clips of stupid animal tricks, Internet solitaire, and a cesspool of pornography, all for the grand benefit of getting tomorrow's weather forecast today, or being able to e-mail the latest puns to your best friend, who happens to work down the hall. But such talk will only land us in the Office of Anti-Luddites. We must face up to the fact that the paperless society is winning even when it's losing. Sadly, many of its wins come largely for those in my own profession.

The modern version of this "treason of the clerks" goes like this. Recently OCLC, the national database of library-owned materials, released a report that proves the treasonous clerks are not only winning battles, they may have already won the war.[20] Not all the news is bad. Students are using libraries, have library cards, and have used a library Web site.[21] But students go on to point out that library usage in the future will remain flat, that the Web is outvying libraries for "information," and that search engines are the preferred approach to research.[22] Moreover, almost 70 percent are more likely to begin (and usually end) with Google, regardless of the fact that vast sums of money are being spent by libraries on proprietary databases.[23]

My own experience confirms this. When I pose the question to students I teach (as many as several hundred a year in research classes), only 1 percent admit to going beyond the *first screen* of returned results from Google. What's wrong with this picture? Recall that relevancy ranking often determines what appears first on a screen of returned results. Any astute user of the Web knows that these resources are not the best, and may not even be any good. The *first* choice of students (*college* students, mind you) is a search engine (Google, Yahoo, Ask.com, MSN Search, etc.)—72 percent—over a physical library (14 percent). In other words, they are choosing search engines over libraries five times as often.[24]

But that's not all. When asked where they find "worthwhile" information, students who claimed to have used both, found that Google (61 percent) provides it over the academic library's Web site listing those proprietary databases (41 percent).[25] What is most puzzling is the admission of many college students that the library has more "trustworthy or credible" and even more accurate resources than search engines, but search engines are more reliable, more cost-effective, much easier to use, faster and far more convenient.[26] Even when users know the library's information is more trustworthy, those users still choose what is faster and more convenient over what is right and more reliable. Further, when librarians are compared to search engines and the satisfaction received, librarians match search engines in every category measured: information provided, quantity of information, speed, and overall experience.[27] In fact, some now argue that the "most reliable" search tool may be the *librarian*. Many have now come to realize that in order to cross the sulfurous river Styx of the Web, the librarian may be the only Virgil one can lean on to make that safe passage to good, unimpeachable sources.[28] The snatch and grab mentality the Web encourages is so persuasive that rising generations of students prefer the easy over the accurate.

Odd, isn't it? On the one hand, libraries have better and more valuable information. It is more reliable and more credible. Librarians are better at finding information than even search engines. Yet the students whom they serve jettison all of this for faster, more convenient, easier to use information. It doesn't matter to students if the information they are getting from the open Web is only half as good. What matters is that it's fast, quick, easy. (Perhaps libraries should cancel all those expensive databases and see what happens then.) Meanwhile, librarians and library organizations that should be touting their value and usefulness routinely shoot themselves in the foot before shooting themselves in the head. Think back to the introduction, where the argument lodged there claimed that the generation that built libraries is leaving them to one that underappreciates them. Libraries may well have become the mom and pop information store to Google's Wal-Mart. Obviously the important distinction between information and knowledge is being lost, or is lost already, on the rising generations.

Reliable Information and Disparate Facts

But the matter is more serious than choosing something faster and cheaper over something better and more trustworthy. The clearly inferior information on the Web is easily outdistancing better researched, more reliable, but more costly and harder to use information. While some will only dismiss this argument by shaking their heads at this author's presumed Luddite tendencies, others may realize that it will not take long before college administrators simply capitulate to search engines since that's obviously what students want. And who can blame them with the grand claims made? What cost-cutting administrator will accept as a legitimate argument the expense of tens of thousands of dollars (in our case, a modest size library, of several hundred thousand dollars) over the so-called "free" Web, regardless of what it has to offer? This is not good news, but it serves to help explain why academic libraries are jettisoning books and offering more computers. Give them what they want, even if it's not what they need.

It gets even worse. When asked to rank the library, students ranked *studying* there as the top activity. One does not have to be a bean-counter to look at what this means. New libraries are a very costly venture. Depending on where in the country one is located, the average cost per square foot is about $200.[29] A modest building will require 140,000 square feet, even utilizing high density compact shelving. With new library buildings costing of tens of *millions* of dollars, what administrator will choose that over a much less costly space with easy chairs, ambient lighting and five dozen computers hooked up to the Web?

Yet, this is not as it should be, unless we are ready to short-change all succeeding generations by claiming the paperless society is a done deal and simply declaring that, henceforth, libraries are no longer needed. Hysterical? Consider that some legislators already believe this is possible, that we can move to a fully paperless library and let students fend for themselves. In an earlier chapter I mentioned Questia's invitation to school-aged children to use its services at a greatly reduced cost. How long will it be before administrators think that a fee could be added for Questia (or some reasonable facsimile) for all matriculating college-aged students? Libraries will vanish, and students will be forced online to find whatever they can, wherever they can. Questia (and all other providers) is not a useless resource. But as a substitute for a full-service library, it is a phantasmagoria! Yet to cut expenses, to eliminate the necessity of a new building, to curtail completely the costs of personnel for a library, is very much like Atalanta's Golden Apple of Deceit. Recall the story.[30]

Atalanta had been warned by the god Apollo that she would lose herself if ever she married, so she determined not to. Living in woodlands and hilly places enabled her to train and become not just the fastest woman, but the fastest *human* to have ever lived. She offered her hand in marriage to any man who could best her in a footrace. If he lost the race, however, he would also lose his life. Hippomenes at first scoffed, but when he saw her, he too fell star-struck even after witnessing the defeat, and death, of those foolish enough to challenge her. Atalanta felt moved by the young man's appearance herself but refused to give in. He, on the other hand, cried out to the goddess Cythera, who lent him three golden apples. As they raced, Atalanta began to catch him.

He tossed a golden apple to one side, and she ran after the gleaming apple (perhaps the first such woman to fall victim to the glittering of gold), and fell behind. Soon she caught up and passed Hippomenes. Three times she did this, and three times he tossed a golden apple to one side, diverting her with each one's shining brightness. Each time, and to her dismay, she fell behind only to lose the race, tricked by the seeming-gold. When Hippomenes won the race, only then did Atalanta realize what she had given up — her freedom — for ormolu, the pinchbeck of golden apples. How long will we run our Web-race, mesmerized by its gleaming Wow-ism, before we realize that what we have lost can never be replaced? Will we lose our intellectual freedoms to this fool's gold, learning only too late that we cannot recover them?

We have already seen a decline in libraries in K–12 schools. Public libraries throughout the country suffer from a lack of funding and some, albeit only a few so far, have been forced to close, or severely curtail hours. Now we see a decline in popularity among college users for whom libraries in those locations were specifically designed. This is graffiti even Belshazzar could read and understand. Only a hardened cynic would argue that the mad rush to digitization and electronic access had the library's ultimate demise in mind. Yet the turn of the screw, so to say, is coming to pass as if it were so.

Taciturn Technicians in Hair Buns

As mentioned before, librarians are as much to blame as anyone. We have not done a very good job touting our services, living up to the hackneyed image of the taciturn technician complete with hair in bun. Patrons of whatever stripe need to know that they cannot live without libraries, and so we should not let them go. But they cannot know this unless librarians do a much better job of showcasing what libraries are about. Some will complain that the American Library Association designed the "@Your library" campaign to do just this. But I would argue it is accomplishing almost the exact opposite. For reasons that cannot be explained to me, ALA is somewhat diffident (or at the very least, chagrined-seeming) about the abundance of books in libraries. This is rather odd because when asked about the library's "brand," most respondents claim it is books.[31] ALA would much rather tout anything but paper in libraries, and so has helped create the assumption that those of us in librarianship fully endorse the paperless society. This is not to say that a full-service library is only about paper. But in most libraries, the vast majority of the square footage is clearly occupied by paper. The time has come to celebrate the portability of books and their unstinting service to mankind, along with the places that provide them with a lifetime of housing.[32]

ALA's seeming skittishness about books appears to be catching on. It is helped by the advent of the Internet. The Web's presence, many argue, means that libraries must change, not just from what they are, but to what the Web is. So now, libraries rush to empty their shelves of books.[33] While academic libraries jettison books and K–12 libraries become "media" centers, some high schools are rushing into the act by supplying textbooks exclusively online, creating the first textbook-free environment.[34] Of course, for many years students have worked out of a "textbook-free environment" in the sense that they never read them to begin with. But the new age has now made even the physical appearance of books (textbook or otherwise) no longer needed. At a public high school in Vail, Arizona, for example, students are now among the first to receive laptops instead of textbooks. Students do their reading and their homework online. In the new age, students will read and do homework because it's online, and July and August cannot be too hot!

Paperless Society Means Library-less Society

Some of these changes come without warning. At Cal Poly, for example, professors and librarians learned that the new renovation and addition will leave *less* space for paper.[35] Apparently the paperless society, though no one can see how it will work, will come nonetheless. Although library administrators and other university officials, caught off guard by the outcry, pointed out that the second phase of the renovation will "greatly expand" the facility shelf space, they forgot to budget for the expansion. The stopgap measure, though few users like it, will be to send hundreds of thousands of books to storage (285,000) where they will remain until called for.[36]

Now, some libraries store books and then permanently withdraw them after a few years of low or infrequent use. Because these storages are very expensive, withdrawn materials cannot be placed in any old empty building but one equipped with the proper heat, light, and humidity controls to preserve them, in other words, a library building. But the question becomes one of whether they are little used because they are not needed, or little used because few patrons will want to wait for delivery of materials to their location. In Cal Poly's case, the books are being sent to "inaccessible storage." In other words, they are being quietly discarded permanently. While they may be available in other nearby libraries, they will not be conveniently accessible to CalPoly users, and so those users will simply satisfy themselves by using whatever is available, inferior or not, much the same way they do when the Web returns tens of thousands of items in a single request. It will represent a new strategy in research: not finding what you want but finding whatever you can. One Cal Poly faculty member complained, "It seems to me that a modern university library should be more than a study hall and a computer lab. I think there's an agenda to get rid of print."[37] Precisely, for that is the single-minded agenda of the paperless society. To disfigure the familiar Carlyle quote, "The true university these days is a collection of ... URLs." Somehow that doesn't resonate quite in the same way as, "The true university these days is a collection of books."

For libraries of all sizes, space becomes, sooner or later (most often much sooner than anyone anticipates) a key and very costly matter. But until now, scholarly concerns always put a premium on providing spaces for books and journals, the lifeblood, the building blocks, of research. What has made space a paramount concern today, however, is that for journals, Web-based storage has provided some genuine relief, assuming the full backfiles are accessible via something like JSTOR.[38] The reasoning seems to be that if it worked for journals, it *must* be made to work for books. But this reasoning is like arguing that because camels can go for days without water, then so can dogs, cats or even people. The driving concern appears to be to provide, at the lowest possible cost, library support for research even if it means forcing the paperless society on all involved. Compare this with the same concern by administrators for the university's sports programs!

Some will argue that the paperless society is less an agenda than it is an attempt to bring the have-nots what the haves already possess.[39] For those countries that cannot afford access to full-service libraries, this may well be a good beginning. But nothing in the argument requires us to sacrifice what has already been built in those places that have full-serve readily available. Surely, developing countries will want to use the Web in the best and fullest possible way, not as a paradigm in which to straightjacket the rest of the developed world, but in an effort to overcome formidable obstacles. (Still, someone should run cost estimates on making a fully conventional library available versus a fully electronic one for all to use. My guess is that they are close in cost, if you add up everything required.)

To argue that making everything electronic is a good approach because not everyone can have paper (a suspect argument anyway) would be the same as arguing that we can solve the poverty question if we just make everyone poor. Redistribution of income is, of course, an argument made by some, but never with much effect in countries that value their freedom. Likewise, requiring libraries to be as lean and as nondescript as the Web solves nothing. Rather than bemoaning the cost of libraries (again, a cost not unlike that of a fully electronic one), we should be celebrating the value they add to the research environment. After all, it was they that enabled our intellectual history from the beginning. Are we positively certain it is now time to replace them with so weak an ersatz as the Web?

"Paperless Society" Originator Rues His Words

Some may be shaking their heads ruefully at this point. Poor fellow, the information highway built its right-of-way to zoom past his epigone library. He didn't adapt his "business" to the growing demands of the electronic world and his customers are leaving him.[40] This would resonate loudly if the inventor of the phase "the paperless society," F.W. Lancaster, were not himself having second thoughts.[41] Lancaster recalls when he coined the phrase at a conference in Finland as describing "a largely paperless, network-based communications system having many of the characteristics of today's Internet-based environment."[42] He saw the confluence of events moving us quickly along to a time when most everything would grow out of this electronic medium. "As the transition actually occurred, however, I became less enthusiastic about the developments and implications and, in the past few years, *downright hostile to them*."[43] But how can this be?

Lancaster cites dehumanization as much to blame, arguing that, at least in the Untied States, it has replaced the human element. But he goes on to blame librarians because they have become "completely uncritical of information technologies."[44] While this is largely true, it cannot be left unsaid that those of us who have been critical have been branded as Luddite or worse.[45] He also goes on to point out "wild assertions" about technology that cannot possibly be true, such as providing access to information anywhere, any time, any place, because they assume if it is in a database, it can be found easily, when "nothing could be further from the truth."[46] He argues that many scholars and experienced researchers were happy with results found *until they discovered how many important items they missed.* Individual librarians, as well as a team of librarians, missed fewer important citations but more than they should have.

This should come as no surprise. Not only are search engines inferior, but so also are proprietary databases, and for similar reasons. Online catalogs are beset with imperfections, as are most databases. Finding the right materials isn't easy. The difference is, however, that searching in an electronic medium often masks what cannot be seen. No effort to change this will make it much better than it is now. To base what is required in a modern research library, *even by experienced searchers,* will also leave stones unturned, so to speak. To remove what hasn't been found based on these results will likely remove very important but never-found resources. If catalogs, databases and other electronic resources are marred by construction owing to the electronic format — and repeated studies show that they are — then we *must* avoid making decisions based on what students like over what they actually need, if those decisions would jeopardize valuable resources. We must distinguish between finding resources, any resources, and finding the *best* resources for a given research problem. The electronic format, in addition to proving us with a false sense of security, also blinds us to making these important distinctions. To phase it another way, "not only [are we] losing [our] knowledge base, worse, we are losing the ethic of public service."[47]

Paperless Society Erodes Knowledge Base

Chasing the paperless society will further erode our knowledge base. Removing books from libraries because they are unused, or are not used as much as we think they should be, will put in jeopardy all that we have so far built up in those libraries. Only later, when we are madly trying to find what we know must be there, will we come to learn that we mistakenly eliminated what turns out to be the heart of what we have come to know. Like some mad surgeon, we will have mistakenly removed the brain, when we should have removed the infected appendix. Moreover, if we continue to attenuate that base, we will soon come to question the value, or worse, the need for human interaction in research. Librarians have for years worked with users to get at the heart of what it is they wished to find. At one time, we librarians were concerned about the reference interview in which a human interacted with another, and the two together strategized until the inquirer had made clear what she wanted, and the librarian produced the sought-for results. In an all-electronic format, we will lose this valuable and important step.

If we proceed along these lines, searching for materials to answer pertinent questions of inquiry will be all too painfully familiar: "Press one if your answer is yes; press two, if you need more help. Press three if...." After a long line of such questions the poor user will be referred back to the menu, and the endless, useless loop will begin anew. And for what? For the paperless chase that leads to nowhere. We have arrived on the information superhighway, all right, but we are rushing all too fast to make libraries, and library service, its first roadkill.

8

A Mile Wide and
a Mind-Numbing Inch Deep

Over the course of this book, we have examined a number of practical cost-related disincentives *vis-à-vis* the Internet substituting for a library. Mention has been made of the costs relating to the Web in general, requiring cash outlays for a computer, an Internet provider, hardware, connections and so on (not to mention millions for accessing proprietary databases). We have examined issues relating to screen resolutions and how no computer today really matches the visual resolution of a page in a book in clarity, ease of reading, or comfort to the eyes. Intellectual property issues and copyright have both come up as considerable, though widely neglected, issues. We have also crossed paths with the lack of standards in mass digitization projects and how this not only increases an already costly proposition in digitization, but also threatens the future of those projects when hardware and software inevitably change.

Hidden Costs

Throughout this book we have examined hidden costs on the Web, such as its very content, or the lack thereof, and dispelled many myths regarding the size of the Web and its content that runs the gamut of useless nonsense to somewhat valuable information. We also addressed issues such as fraud, pornography, scams, hate sites, identity theft and the vast numbers of young people providing TMI — too much information — about themselves and others in places like MySpace.com and Facebook.com, without respect to future consequences (when did a library ever do this to anyone, much less young people?). While we have been quick to point out that any one of these obvious or hidden costs would hardly be enough by themselves to question the Web's utility, cumulatively they do present a strong argument against the Web's stance as a possible substitute for a full-service library. We have also pointed out that while it may not necessarily be the intent of the Web's proponents to make it a substitute library, the effect has been to compel many to treat it that way. We offer in this chapter one last reason that presents itself by implication and direct observation.

Suppose you present yourself to your physician who, after running a number of tests, discovers something amiss. He gives you several reasons for a possible diagnosis, along with a number of things to avoid, among them certain foods. Having pointed out the danger of the disease with respect to these foods, he lists, let us say, a number of foods, their only connection being their fat content. Avoid these, he says, but eat as much steak as you like because we don't really know yet what effect steak has on this disease. But, you argue, doesn't steak contain fat? Yes, he replies, but we haven't any real data about that kind of steak for now. Chances are you'd avoid it anyway, just to be on the safe side.

A New Cost of the Web: Reading Comprehension

Reading comprehension presents itself as a possible casualty of the Web.[1] We know for example that when we read on the Web we do not read in detail but in snatches (sometimes referred to as the "snatch and grab" process) and not in the same manner as we read books, cover to cover. Yet very few are examining this problem in great detail with an eye to possible contraindications. Even so, preliminary studies do not provide promising results for the future. Indeed, if anything, they point to just the opposite, that Web-based "reading" contributes to an even more cursory reading comprehension, along with a decline in literacy. Very little is being done to point out how this problem is a negative consequence of making all our access to information digital, or nearly so. The question remains for us whether we will discover some years hence that it is, indeed, a serious matter. As with most of the problems we have encountered in connection to the Web, our solution appears to be that we need more of the Web, not less; and if it turns out to be a bad thing, well, it will somehow manage to right itself in the long run.

Reading Redux

Part of the problem certainly exists in how we teach reading, a point touched upon in the Introduction to this book. We know, for example, that many young children today see reading as a much more difficult process than, say, generations prior to the Web found it to be. While it's true that this could turn out to be epiphenomenological, as scientists are wont to say — two things occur together while the one is not a cause, or even a causal agent, of the other — the early evidence points to the fact that Web-based reading is making reading difficulties worse, not better. It is as if the physician has passed judgment on one's condition but has argued that because the data is not entirely complete, we cannot say for sure, so do as you like even though it makes you feel worse.

One cannot dismiss out of hand the contribution that the way we teach reading adds to this problem, and remains a fundamental part of it. Reading wars are being fought even as I write this chapter, and Whole Language and Phonics, to name only two, are warriors. It is beyond the ken of this book to treat them here, or their contribution to the problem.[2] Suffice it to say that their contributions are significant but not exclusive. For now, we know that Web-based reading does not ameliorate the reading problem, and the early evidence points to it as being one of many culprits worsening the problem. Further, we have incontrovertible evidence (even beyond the obvious) that when reading is poorly taught, it plagues those who are the victims of it for all their lives, not just their academic careers.

Reading is a very complex process. The mind makes connections during the reading process that are not always neatly rule-based. How it works for some is not always how it works for others, and why the mind works the way it does during the reading process for some and not for others is not always clear.[3] Regardless of the many complexities in ascertaining reading inefficiencies, we do know that rising generations will not only find reading difficult, but as they progress in grades from the earliest to the latest, the gaps in their reading abilities increase as the reading material becomes more complex and sophisticated.

Online Dictionaries: Page Not Available?

One very obvious reading deficiency reveals itself in the small vocabularies of today's students. Even if all the evidence were only anecdotal (and it is not) we see at once that the paucity of what students read attenuates the size of their vocabularies.[4] Not only are young people having a difficult time naming books they have read, but so also are they slow in identifying what were once common vocabulary words among those who were students decades ago. Words that would have been seen as somewhat commonplace for the college age (for example "impetus," "ramshackle" and "lucid") are, it turns out, no longer common at all among today's students. Students may well have hundreds of digital dictionaries to look at online, but either they are not looking at them, or when they do, they do not care to learn from them. Moreover, it is clear they do not own or use print dictionaries much at all.

When I graduated from college, my oldest brother gave me a collegiate dictionary. Though held together with string, I still have and use it today, along with a dozen others. Such a gift given to a student today might well seem anachronistic at best, useless at worse. While I do not teach many classes at the university where I work, when I do, I am amazed at the number of students who do not bother to look up unfamiliar words. I have to remind them repeatedly that one of the fundamental processes of knowing what a text has to say is to begin with the words they do not know. Many of them receive this bit of knowledge as if it were some mystical insight. Twice now, when teaching *honors* students, I have been assailed for assigning as many as thirty pages a night as a reading assignment "with too many hard words." The "hard words" are words like "*sub rosa*, indict, cursory" and so on.[5] My students find "this much reading" an impossible task. They cannot read that many pages or understand anything about what they have read. My investigation has revealed that this is not an endemic problem to my university but a pandemic one among all college students.

Reading proficiency scores for students have been declining for a number of years, at least since 1990.[6] For example, reading proficiency for 9-year-olds from 1971 to 1999 has remained static, rising from 208 to 212 before dropping slightly and leveling off. The 212 level is barely above the "partial skills and understanding" level, and far removed from "learns from specialized reading materials," a level we hope they will achieve before entering college. Although the National Assessment of Educational Progress (NAEP) has been conducting reading studies for a number of years, some would argue that the proficiency levels noted there (in the low 200s) may not even rise to the level of what many would call literate. While these students may well be able to read, they still exhibit what is sometimes referred to as the "knowledge deficit." Such young people are unlikely to overcome this lost or weak ability once it is entrenched at the age of 9, the last age at which any positive gains in reading can be measured. It could be argued that the correspondence between stagnant levels of this proficiency and the rise of computers in the home and in the school is merely coincidental, but it strikes some as more than that. If the skills are weak to begin with, and activities and interests pull readers possessing those weak skills into yet other weakening activities, strengthening those reading skills will be highly unlikely.[7]

Reading Scores at Bare Minimums

Moreover, this report shows that the level possessed in 1971 is nearly identical to the skill level possessed in 1999.[8] In *more than twenty years,* the skill could not be improved, even marginally (this period, it should be pointed out, mimics the rise of the computer age). It appears as if literacy simply stopped growing in the early seventies. Furthermore, while the levels increase somewhat at age 13 (in the middle 250s, barely a literate reading ability), at age 17 these skills fail to achieve being able to understand complicated information. Again, in all three cases, the reading levels at each age do not improve over a twenty year period, so that the level of reading proficiency at ages 13 and 17 in students in 1971 is equal to those measured in students more than twenty years later, in 1999. In other words, today's students are no better than students nearly thirty years ago in spite of all the money, time, energy and programs (online and otherwise) we have applied to reading improvement.[9]

While about half of all nine-year-olds report "reading for fun" on a daily basis, only about one-third of 13- and 17-year-olds report the same.[10] While more females than males report reading for fun at the age of 9, about the *same* percentage of males and females (about 30 percent) report reading for fun on a daily basis at age 17. Somehow during the reporting period (1992–1999) 13- and 17-year-olds simply decided to quit reading altogether, or to read far less frequently than their much younger peers. This is not to imply that the Web is the new cause of everything. But neither should we conclude that it has no bearing at all. Ages thirteen and seventeen are, of course, prime puberty ages for many other distractions than just the Web. Still, a medium that encourages "snatch and grab" learning aids does not aid and abet reading skills and abilities.[11]

The Future of Reading Looks Bleak

Students show reading competencies in different ways, and this in no way discounts that fact. It is possible that "each student may have some reading skills and knowledge that reflect what is considered to be the proficient level, other skills and knowledge that are emerging, and other reading skills and knowledge that have not yet emerged."[12] But reading proficiency should require at a minimum some basic literacy, something these figures do not show. In fact, by 2009 students in grades 4, 8 and 12 must be able "to read both literary (fiction, nonfiction and poetry) and information texts (exposition, argumentation persuasive and procedural texts or documents)" in order to assessed as reading with proficiency.[13] Current scores indicate that we are light years from achieving that goal. Why would we, therefore, add *anything* to the mix that weakens their chances?

In other words, the abysmal scores previously reported will only grow worse as standards tighten. The 2009 NAEP standards define reading as "an active and complex process that involves understanding written text; developing and interpreting meaning; and using meaning as appropriate to type of text, purpose and situation."[14] If students are encouraged to "snatch and grab," if they are losing vocabulary, if they are rapidly declining in reading interests the older they get, the Web should be the last place we focus their attention. It behooves us all the more to make certain we are not saddling students with a skill acquisition (the digital context) that will only deepen the pool of potential illiterates. Perhaps this is why Google launched in October 2006 a literacy Web site, suspecting its own contribution to the problem.[15] Educators appear to rejoice at the prospect of students, even elementary students, seeing the Web as something they can contribute to, whether or not what they contribute will even skirt literacy. The Web has us on a fast-track collision course with shared ignorance. The Web encourages *spectators* to knowledge, not active participants. Students view watching television or a computer screen as equivalent activities.

Students are already "plugged in" to the Web. We who work with them must repeatedly remind them that "a Web search is insufficient for serious scholarly research."[16] It does little good because students naturally opt for an easier way. What they do not see immediately is that searching the Web is often one of the least successful ways to build a research paper, but they come to that understanding soon enough after spending hours in front of it and having nothing to show for the search. But, say critics, with the advent of plans like Google's Library Project, this will no longer be the case. Students will get plenty of scholarly materials, right?

Google Library Project to the Literacy Rescue?

Perhaps. As these pages have shown, neither Google Scholar nor Google's Library Project has worked out as planned. Google is still trying to get around the "little" issue of copyright, to say nothing of the digital rights management issue, but let's assume it can.[17, 18] For the sake of argument, let's assume that issues of privacy are also either brought under control or changed to make users more confident that their searches are not being "recorded."[19] Assuming that plan works as mapped out (though none have to date), it still will not prove the boon so many are hoping it will be, *including* many colleges and universities who have made their collections at the ready.[20] Let us assume that the Google Library Project eventually works better than the current Google Print, which to date does not allow printing and only allows one to view a few pages at a time.[21] Should the Google Library Project of fifteen-plus million volumes eventually be at every student's fingertips, won't that solve the problem?

Not really. Currently, so much online material has served only to increase plagiarism to epidemic proportions.[22] Having more of the same will unlikely decrease the offenses. Moreover, today's students do not read these texts, but merely snatch and grab what they want, not the best of scholarly practices. Having millions more books to pilfer does not seem like the best way of attenuating current literacy problems. It is not that students today are so much less virtuous than students of former years, but that having such an arsenal at one's fingertips only encourages more snatching and grabbing, more reading in bits and pieces, and more cutting and pasting. It is too risible to think that students will read these texts online from digital-cover to digital-cover when all evidence to date indicates they are spending *minutes* with online books, not hours, as pointed out in a previous chapter.

New Web-Based Literacy Definitions Will Worsen Our Plight, Not Make It Better

Moreover, new definitions of literacy are changing to include the Web-based definitions of the same. "Today, the definition of literacy has expanded from traditional notions of reading and writing to include the ability to learn, comprehend, and interact with technology in a meaningful way."[23] On the surface, this only makes sense. As new demands are made on students (as well as the rest of us), requiring new cognitive skills to decode and understand, it only makes sense that *expanded* definitions will arise. But we need to make sure that they are, indeed, augmented ones, and not ersatz ones that replace traditional definitions with ones that describe technique over ability. A student may be able to surf the Web perfectly without knowing a thing he's read. We cannot allow any expansion of the meaning of literacy to mean something other than reading and writing in a literal sense, and not just one that describes one's ability to navigate the Web. But perhaps we'll soon know better how the Web has affected literacy. The MacArthur Foundation will invest $50 million in a five-year study of the impact of digital learning on youth.[24] When we aren't spending millions on electronic sources, we're spending them to study electronic sources. Better to spend funds on discovering what *might* work than on what we already know does not. Ostensibly, we want to find more ways, not fewer, for the Web to take over our lives, as the MacArthur funds will study video games and social communities that students fixate upon. (Common sense would imply that students go to these sites *because* they aren't educational; to make them so would likely cause them to flee.)[25]

Even with the new definitions, the question remains whether the Web really encourages *literacy*. "These shallow, random, and often passive interactions with text are in direct contrast to the active, strategic, and critical processes of constructing meaning now being proposed by 25 years of reading research."[26] This is precisely the point. We are now rushing without breath into a medium that encourages passivity, that lauds the stochastic, and that rewards the unexceptional. Somehow we believe that this will *not* decrease literacy, and, astonishingly enough, that it will actually *increase* reading proficiency. Just how all of this is to come to pass is anyone's guess. If we were proposing that from now on we fly planes upside down to conserve energy or improve arrival and departure times, the hue and cry would be deafening. If we were to argue that because we cannot be sure when we arrest one individual that he or she is surely guilty, we will no longer arrest anyone, almost everyone would complain.[27] If our definition of a winning sports team were to change to include those teams that never won, or won rarely but still tried *very hard*, sports enthusiasts would laugh such plans into oblivion. Yet when one reading crackpot scheme after another presents itself to the education community, common sense is often the first casualty, and such plans are implemented, encouraged and eventually funded even, in the face of repeated failures. When it comes to some new education scheme, especially a reading scheme, virtually any solution is considered a good one. If readers think this more rant than reason, consider the Whole Language fiasco that left a generation of students unable to read. It took *fifteen years* of repeated failure before the question was finally called.[28]

In the end it may not matter about literacy. If the Web can change the definition of reading literacy while changing the definition of reading, it can also change the definition of schooling.[29] Online schools that spring up for various reasons allow parents to secure all their children's schooling online. While this will be cheered by many, such schools cannot exist without the printed materials of libraries. It also opens up questions about standards and who will oversee them. It will also redefine districts and allow long-distance oversight. While none of these things are by themselves inherently bad — and in many cases, if they challenge current abysmal K–12 education standards, a potential good — each one raises yet another flag of concern about quality, reliability, funding, oversight, accountability and so on.

The Myth of Transferable Skills

We believe that students *must* be learning better because the "text" in question not only has words, but also has pictures, sounds, video clips and more. We think that because students are forced to observe numerous other important and tangential concerns, the learning experience is thereby deeper and made more powerful. What we do not have to support these velleities is empirical data substantiating that these are transferable skills. We just assume it *must* be so, and that wishing will make it right. Even when we know that "many Web-based environments also introduce a new set of cognitive barriers *that can cause competent readers of conventional text to be cognitively overloaded and frustrated*," we damn those torpedoes and fund another round of mass digitization projects.[30] Of course, when we stack the reading deck in such a fashion that the only way to acquire this knowledge is in the digital environment, what choice do we have? No one wants to say, "We know this environment may not only be impossible for students, but it may well detract from the skills they have already learned." Instead, we devise whistling-in-the-dark strategies to help mask developments that reveal certain decline.

No one is forcing us into this impasse. No one *requires* that students *must* learn in this fashion. Rather, we have determined that this is the only environment in which they will be able to learn, and so we force them into a sink or swim scenario. We hide behind buzzwords like "teamwork" and "consensus building" because we are certain these are better attributes than those that taught older generations how to read and comprehend. In other words, we have declared the unbroken wheel broken, and so seek the only remedy we have at hand. We tell ourselves that because we know reading on the Internet is different, and that it is the manner in which future generation must learn to read, we should "envision new constructs of reading comprehension"[31] The question before us is whether we will develop new and better constructs of reading proficiency, or whether will we do what we have done so far, merely redefine it, making the new definition no longer mean proficiency but something much less. Chances are, we will have to compromise at best since more than 50 percent of all 12- to 17-year-olds have access to the Internet and prefer reading, if at all, in this environment.[32]

The Web's Sheer Volume Equals Frustration

In order to be successful on the Web, readers "must be able to handle the sheer volume of text, which can be described as massive."[33] If we were to assign a reader — any reader, even an adult one — the vast number of pages to read and comprehend required to follow all the links of a short *Wikipedia* article, most educators would realize it's not cognitively possible. Again, because it comes over the Web it must be right, and so we make these requirements. Imagine how an average or poor reader must feel. Faced with the daunting volume, many simply give up. At the same time, most Web users, when they cannot find what they want, or cannot comprehend it, feel they are to blame, not the infallible Web. When readers encounter a difficult printed text, on the other hand, they are generally quick to ask for help, even if they really want a quick fix. My own experience in helping college-aged users proves this true, if only anecdotally. Yet these same readers will spend hours, literally, surfing the Web because they feel they should somehow know how to find whatever it is they are seeking. When they do not, they automatically assume the deficiency is their own, and not anything inherent in the Web-based environment. Again, this does not mean we should (or even can at this late stage) jettison the Web. But it does underscore a significant problem presented by the Web. If even college-age students of above-average ability are not comfortable in an environment they have been subjected to since kindergarten, what hope is there for their future? Rather than make the Web an ancillary tool (which it incidentally serves as quite well), we have made it the only, the preferred, tool.

To ape the old song, if students cannot make it in Web, they will not likely make it anywhere. And yet Web-based learning does not reveal its deficiencies as readily as text-based learning. Just because readers are proficient with text does not automatically mean they will be proficient with Web-based reading, and vice-versa.[34] If we are to make this the only or preferred means, we will have to provide new strategies or else face a new generation of readers who do not like to read, not just on the Web, but at all. When a printed text presents itself to a reader, the boundaries are more or less closed. On the Web, however, with all its hyperlinks and multimedia presentations, readers must cope with a potentially limitless field to follow endless links of random information.

Navigation Skills Are Not the Same as Reading Skills

This argument does not dismiss the fact that above-average readers may be able to navigate well through such boundless media. But even these readers are not likely to follow every link, listen to every audio clip, or watch every video. Will what these readers miss be important? Will it leave gaps in their learning? Quite possibly. Even assuming it does not, it's very likely it will eventually weary them with information overload. Throughout this book every attempt has been made to distinguish between information random fact and disaggregated data — and knowledge, facts and data arranged in a way to tell a story, to explain a mystery, to solve a puzzle. The Web supplies information, while reading printed texts results in knowledge.

We should encourage the Web's use for a purpose that highlights its value. If, for example, we would use it much the way a handbook is used, or even a dictionary of unfamiliar words or phrases, we might well have a tool that would prove exceedingly valuable to readers. Its use is hard to beat for the stray fact, the random term that one cannot recall or has never encountered. But to require its use for long term study with a rich mix of hyperlinks, video and audio clips appears not only to defeat its purpose, but also to defeat its users. We seem to want it to be a panacea, a silver bullet, when no such thing can be devised.

The Web Makes the World More Flattened Than Flat

We often fret that rising generations are not prepared to meet educational and economic challenges posited by our so-called global market.[35] We believe that to meet such challenges we must have information of all kinds immediately available. The world is flat, we repeat, mantra-like, and so encourage the continued proliferation of information without regard to its delivery, its content, or its narrative. We have forgotten that the economic powerhouse that is America was not built in this fashion. Indeed, it has only very recently come to rely upon this immediacy of delivery. If what we build now in terms of Web-based delivery of information in fact retards the growth of literacy, we will not improve the education of rising generations, but impede it. If our rising generation cannot read, write, add or subtract, having every kind of data at their finger-tips will prove useless in the long run.[36] Somehow we have come to believe that because students had to master computer usage at home, they are now behind.[37] Our solution to this putative dilemma is to saddle schools with teaching computer usage, while those same schools are failing at teaching basic skills.

For most of our history, critics have complained it is because we do not spend enough on education. Yet today, the United States spends *more money on education than any other nation except Switzerland, averaging more than $8,700 per student* for elementary and secondary education.[38] For the last two decades we have been spending increasing dollars, and yet for the same two decades the National Assessment of Education Progress reading scores have remained flat, with less than one third of the nation's 4th graders scoring at or above "proficient" on assessments. For all those dollars, we have a rising generation that is *less* literate than their parents. In an effort to find a silver bullet, we rush forward once again with Web-based learning, hoping, perhaps even praying, that this will be the solution to our educational malaise. In other words, to solve this growing problem, we turn to an environment that may well make matters worse, not better.

A Bleak Picture Bleaker Still with Minorities

But this is only part of the bleak picture. More than 85 percent of African-Americans, Hispanics and Native Americans are not reading at the 4th grade level, according to NAEP data.[39] For mathematics, the figures are worse, with 90 percent unable to score at a proficient level. It's no secret that these same groups are much *less* likely to have computers at home. Our solution? Spend more dollars on an environment that has yet to show it will improve these abysmal numbers. And we are spending that money now. The so-called "Millennials'" use of information and communications technology is already reaching into the youngest of children. Surveys in 2000–2002 showed that the largest group of new users of the Internet was between the ages of 2 and 5. Moreover, we also know that 72 percent of all first graders used a home computer on a weekly basis during the summer, while 97 percent of all kindergartners had access to a home or school computer by 1999.[40] We also know that this rising generation of new learners believe that they are technologically savvy (How could they not? We tell them they are regularly), feel quite positive about technology and *"rely upon it as an essential and preferred component of every aspect of their lives."*[41]

Obviously we cannot now turn away from this precipice of new learning to bygone ways of knowing. We would not want to return to the old ways simply for the sake of the old ways, but we might want to if we knew the new ones weren't working. Knowing how students learn in Web-based environments *and whether what they learn is equal to or exceeds text-based learning* is critically important. Recall the condom story related in an earlier chapter. It is not so very important whether students use the Web, or whether they use it regularly. We know full well that they are, and we also know that they use it almost daily. What becomes of the utmost importance then is whether they are using it correctly. We have until now assumed that they are. But as studies come in, we find that they are not using it well or effectively, and that many express frustration using it. Not only that, but we are also discovering that they are not so very different from their predecessors.

Recall, for example, the new study that indicates students cannot multitask. While they may well be "ultra-communicators," they cannot read, study, use the cell phone, text message and listen to their iPods at the same time, though most try. We also know that they are rapidly growing allergic to text-based materials. One study quotes approvingly a student who complained that "We should not have to carry heavy books all day long and bring all our books home."[42] No previous generation of students has approached the chore of lugging about books with great glee, and the fact that many today are expressing this as a *bête noir* should not surprise us. But it *should* alarm us. We are at least two generations from a mostly independent text-based learning environment, and light-years from a fully independent one. Whether we like it or not, literacy is still measured largely by the written (i.e., printed) word.[43] It does not seem either right or wise that we should encourage students to become independent of text-based learning. Moreover, we should make absolutely certain that any Web-based learning is equivalent to text-based learning before we send a generation of students to their academic peril.

Edmund Burke may well have gotten it right when he warned that when it is not necessary to change, it is necessary not to change. We are not yet ready to dispense with text-based learning. While many more things are now Web-based than they were only ten years ago, most of the requirements in life demand a mastery of print-based reading. If we encourage students to leave print-based learning alone, if we encourage them to abandon acquiring the most requisite learning skill of all, reading and its mastery, for an environment that may well impede their academic futures, we will have committed the worst academic malpractice on a rising generation so far.

We Are Awash in Technology and Illiteracy

Consider that while we are awash in technology at its greatest "state-of-the-art" status, we have rising generations that do not read as well as their parents, cannot decipher texts as well as former generations, and show little desire to improve that status. How can any of this be termed progress, or be passed off as "proficiency"? It is an alarming turn of events, yet rather than worrying about the negative consequences already present, we merely push harder to make the state of affairs more the way it is. Rather than stopping to assess where we are, stopping to determine what we can do to improve matters and how we can prevent making matters worse, we press on to the electronic goal.

Path- and Link-Based Learning May Not Be the Right Answer

We must spend more time assessing path-based and hypertext learning to make certain that students, while navigating correctly and efficiency, are also mastering its content.[44] It is no secret that more complex texts require a greater reading sophistication and learning ability. Almost all Web-based reading requires these sophisticated skills, but it does not appear, despite efforts in this direction, that readers are able to cope with these needed skills when they have not mastered the process with the simplest of printed texts. NAEP scores mentioned above appear to show that the *majority* of students already cannot do this.

An unbiased reading of these scores would seem to indicate that an increasing number of students will struggle more and more with complex Web-based reading. They will not be able to navigate though the text, will not be able to understand what they read, and while they will be able to click on any number of links, will do them as if going through so many motions, understanding little of what appears before them. Meanwhile, their ability to read and understand printed texts will likewise decrease. This poses, and will pose, significant literacy problems for the future if this medium is to be the preferred means of communication. As we impose more path-based and even hyperlinked texts on students, "we also limit the ways our students can learn from and explore the materials we want them to read. The critical issue is whether what we now support helps or hinders learning."[45]

Whether we look at NAEP scores or any other measure of reading proficiency, it appears we are not doing much to support either Web-based or print-based reading. Further, it appears we want to push the technology envelope even further. Too often our studies merely bring to the fore the philosophy we claim to have derived from them.[46] Will we discover in five, ten or even twenty years, that our best-intentioned efforts have artificially increased illiteracy rates to ones even higher than today? While many have written about the technology "haves" versus the technology "have-nots," it appears few are worrying about the electronically unable. This does not refer to those who cannot master technology, but those who have it at their fingertips but cannot understand what is staring them in the face. While it's true that online technology is improving, especially path-based links, so that readers could be forced to the most useful links, all of this technology is predicated on readers who have mastered the basic art of reading, something reading proficiency scores indicate is hardly the case.

Text-Based Reading Second Nature; Web-Based Reading Must Be Acquired

Web-based learning requires more sophisticated and complex coding skills than printed text reading. Although readers are bound eventually to discover reading shortcuts for the Web, its use in learning remains in its infancy. Readers must work harder to glean even the simplest cognition from Web pages that would be second nature in print.[47] The table of contents, indexes and even footnotes are all second nature to us in print, and we have devised means for acquiring knowledge as we go through even difficult reading material. But on the Web none of these things is intuitive, and as we have seen, some things are left off or are vanishing altogether (such as omitted footnotes, pages disappearing information, longevity on the Web and so on). Even well-established readers have a hard time navigating a myriad of pages, do not always know if what they are reading is accurate or authoritative, cannot tell if the page is real or fake, see no discernible table of contents and worry if they take themselves several links away from the "home page" whether they will ever be able to find it again.

The Web is a gallimaufry of audio-visual text, popular and high culture, entertainment and good and bad information. None of these things are present in one printed text. Typically, readers who pick up a trade paperback know what awaits them, *The DaVinci Code* and Frey's *A Million Little Pieces* notwithstanding. Like online dating, when one does not really know who is on the other end of the line, there is no way of knowing about the contents of a given Web page whether it is by a recognized authority, or a clever rogue. As pointed out in an earlier chapter, thousands of students visit www.martinlutherking.org each year during Black History Month. Only a few of them know after reading a few screens into the site that it is prepared by white supremacists. For the unwary, who leads them through this maze? It's all well and good to argue that students will have teachers to help them while in school. But who helps them when they are doing their work in an Internet café or at home locked away in their rooms? Whatever a student has learned in reading print — and it does not appear many are learning much — most of that will not help them when faced with a new Web page.

Hovering in the background of Web-based learning are the hardware and software questions. Not everyone can run Active X on their computers, or make frames work the way they are supposed to work. Some will be able to navigate through the various kinds of software used for creating Web pages, while others will experience either broken images, unloaded pages and more. In a controlled environment, such a classroom, teachers may be able to pick and choose Web pages that will eliminate this difficulty. But they cannot, nor should they want to, do this all the time. For students with less than the optimum hardware and software, who will help them?

Some are doubtless thinking that this is a tempest in a teapot of worry, and that in five or ten years, everyone will have everything they need to navigate the Web in excellent fashion. But this is the same argument trotted out a decade ago, and it is no closer to being resolved today than it was then. An earlier chapter complained about the lack of standards for mass digitization projects, something that we knew about even before the first project had ever been mapped out. Yet here we are again, raising these same questions. Our "damn the torpedoes" approach has not resolved anything so far, and we are yet deeper into Web-based learning. It appears that our rush to move everything to this medium before we have ironed out many of its problems may well be dooming a generation of readers for future information pursuits. Furthermore, almost all the commands for the most popular programming languages are English-based and so easier for competent English speakers to know what commands might do.[48] Yet in our "world is flat" new age, English is not only no longer the dominate language, it is fast becoming a second language in our own nation of immigrants. Faced with such daunting obstacles, is it any wonder that less than average readers will give up easily or look elsewhere for their information, settling for not only inferior information, but also information that is defined only by its ease of use? We have created this state of affairs, are cognizant of it, but appear unready to do anything about it but add yet more technology making it more difficult to find workarounds.

The Lure of the Web

What has made the Web so attractive is its ability to do more than print text can. But as pointed out in an earlier chapter, these new conventions are very distracting to readers. Interactive sites that often have valuable information can easily lead readers astray, make the content too frustrating to use, or change the text so dramatically that readers either give up or become so fixated on the technology that they are distracted from the knowledge pursuit. It's no secret that elementary school children are fascinated by what they see on the Web, especially if pictures, video and audio clips are present. But if these readers become too distracted by the technology, are they still learning? If they watch a video clip, does a return to text become "boring" or so uncompelling that they no longer want to use it? While it cannot be denied that electronic access may be the only future for reading, what happens in the meantime, and what happens to a generation of readers who only want to "see" something instead of read about it? Learning is not always "fun," but if we create a generation of readers whose experience must also include an element of entertainment, what happens to them when they finally discover that not everything they must learn can be distilled to some level of titillation to make it attractive? Certainly watching a Shakespearian play deepens one's appreciation for the Bard more than never having seen one at all. But if one's experience is only this, or mostly this, how will those spectators ever appreciate his use of language? If, as experts tell us, "we are in the midst of a broad-based shift from Print to Digital-Electronics as the organizing content for literate-textual practice and for learning and teaching," doesn't it make sense that we get this right before proceeding too far afield?[49]

Transferable Skills Not Always Transferable

The so-called transferable skills do not appear to be as transferable as we once thought. Web-based learning not only proves to be more difficult, but also capturing all the right elements — hardware, software, analysis of contents and so on — is very elusive. Even on college campuses we find that a variety of approaches meant to meet the so-called various kinds of learning are just as likely to be "disempowering as empowering."[50] For every young person who feels emboldened to speak up in the anonymous context of Web-based or online environments, a dozen more are frustrated or annoyed by it. This should not come as any surprise to those who have tried to force audiovisual learning into the classroom. While it does not impede learning *per se*, many have found regardless of the approach used that such "teachable moments" turn quickly into disruptive ones and class management imbroglios. Remember how only a few years ago PowerPoint software rushed forward as the new media messiah that would revolutionize online learning? Just a few short years later, the only articles about using

PowerPoint in the classroom are the how-not-to-use-it kind. Like many would-be panaceas before it, PowerPoint can ostensibly be only misused in most classroom contexts. Web-based learning appears only to magnify these undesirable elements.

Because of the many different components of Web-based learning, it may be decades before we come to learn of its less salient features. So far, however, we do know that various Web-based modalities are proving disappointing. While most readers could easily point to success stories (for example Britain's Open University), we tend to turn our heads away from its failures, or simply ignore them. We are doing so at the potential loss of literacy. It may well be that "[n]ewer technologies ... are not necessarily better (or worse) for teaching or learning than older technologies.... The choice of technology should be driven by the needs of learners and the context in which we are all working, not by its novelty."[51] Unfortunately it is just this novelty that appears to be driving everything. We are fascinated more by the successes of technologies than we are by their failures. Indeed, we often ignore, or outright deny, the failures we encounter. Rather, we tend to attribute those failures to user error or hardware malfunctions, in short anything but the possibility that our pursuit of electronic everythingism is a fool's-gold, gold-rush.

Myths abound about Web-based learning and these contribute to our misuse of it and our potential failure to see its defects. Not only are schools driven to use it, but so are businesses, with estimates running close to 90 percent of the latter using some form of e-learning over conventional strategies. Web-based learning is not cheaper if all the necessary materials are in place: sound hardware and software, ample bandwidth, competent instructors who know how to use the technology well and who know what to do when it *doesn't work*.[52] To accomplish this makes it often far *more* expensive than traditional learning strategies, and this is often the reason we tend to fall back on them. The question that arises now is why we keep trying to replace successful strategies in the first place. Apparently we feel an overwhelming need to justify continued costly electronic expenditures.

We also know that what can be taught, as well as what can be learned in the Web-based environment, is limited by that environment itself. For example, simple lists might work well on a screen but a complicated theorem will require a very knowledgeable instructor to teach it successfully. Seeing the Web as the "silver bullet" to everything cognitive, however, we rush to teach everything we can in this environment, ignorant about what may be missed. We also under-emphasize what I refer to as the "imperfectability of mankind." For example, while we often look down our noses at the medievals, they understood better than do we both the value of a book's content and the imperfectability of man by creating the first book detection system: chained books.[53] Without assignments and deadlines, without a "day of doom," most students, even adult ones, are not likely to learn what is required of them. Web-based learning cannot provide these "drop dead" dates, and so students go on clicking endlessly into cyberspace.

The mind is more easily led by the eye than by the ear but that isn't always a good thing. *Watching* something isn't the same thing as learning it, and no one would call watching television "active learning." Yet when it comes to the Web, we are quick to forget these insights and assume that because students are fixated upon a screen, they must be learning something. Subjecting would-be learners to a constant barrage of on-screen items may only mean learners have *seen* a lot, not that they have learned anything. Furthermore, as any college campus administrator knows only too well, if the technology isn't constantly updated, what gains have been made will be quickly lost. For example, if we do not update the 100+ computers in our building every three years, students complain quickly and loudly. And they should, because old technology means slower, lethargic, and at times stagnant access. Yet it further underscores why this medium may easily not be ready to be the solution for every learning calculus!

One more telling story about computers and learning had to do with an elementary school that had equipped every classroom with computers for the teacher and every student. Astoundingly, a few years later studies revealed that computer literacy had not increased one bit. Impossible! Reinvestigations revealed one small detail: none of the computers had been plugged in. In other words, just because something is there does not mean it will be used or used correctly. For most Web-based learning, we can rest assured it is not being used effectively or well, and we have the literacy scores to prove it, though not the ones we like to talk about.

Large scale studies on technology report the same findings.[54] Technology immersion now being funded by Title II grants provides some insight on early results, and they do not look very promising. In Texas, where $14 million of Title II Part D monies went to fund a wireless learning environment for high-need middle schools, the early results are disappointing. The grants required six components, including a wireless mobile computing device for everyone at the school, production, communication and presentation software to be used as a learning tool, online instruction resources in reading, writing and arithmetic so to say, online assessment tools to track students' weaknesses, professional development for teachers and ongoing technical support, at least initially.[55] Reading scores remained either slightly below in technology immersed schools or statistically no different from any other schools. While technology immersed schools saw substantially improved school culture factors (e.g., leadership, satisfaction, innovation, collaboration), what some might call "feel-good" benefits, teacher lessons at technology immersed schools "lack[ed] intellectual challenge."[56] Teachers also reported "major challenges" in learning how to use the technology well and effectively even with ongoing technical support.[57] Moreover, while students at technology immersed campuses are more highly engaged and end up using technology with greater confidence, no effect on student self-direction, reading proficiency scores or mathematics achievement could be found.[58] Since the latter two, math and reading improvements, were the grant's main goal, one could say the experiment failed. It's too early to say whether this experiment left its subjects with any permanent damage. The study should be done again in five years, when all that technology must be replaced, not with grant funding, which will have run out, but by district funding, already in short supply.

Although some evidence of the growing failure in reading is anecdotal, the majority is not. ACT discovered in the spring of 2006 that half the students who do graduate from high school cannot read at the level required by freshmen college texts.[59] To assume that college freshmen will be able to read only 25 pages between classes is a quantum-leap assumption. Most of the students I've met over the years are bright and eager to learn. But many do not want to undertake the effort required to achieve that learning, especially if it means struggling with hard-to-read texts. They often see technology, George Jetson–like, as a shortcut, whether it really is or not. Given the workloads required in the majority of American high schools, this should surprise exactly no one. Indeed, as the workloads drop even further, out comes yet another report questioning the value of homework. With teacher unions micromanaging what teachers can and cannot do, how much work they are allowed to do outside the classroom, and so on, teaching will soon be an 8 to 3 job with no take-home work, literally.[60] Meanwhile, young people will continue to fall farther and farther behind in the educational basics, the 3 Rs. While all of this devolves ever downward, the value of libraries continues to be called into question.

Conclusion

Twenty years from now the Web is likely to be the cynosure of all our vocational and avocational activities, even more so than it is today. "The more autonomous agents," writes Rob Atkinson of the Progressive Policy Institute, "the better. The steeper the 'J curve' the better. Automation, including through autonomous agents will help boost standards of living, freeing us from drudgery." Even when virtual reality may become more reality than virtual, Barry Chudakov of the Chudakov Company sees this addition "as [a] ... phenomenon that will likely inspire us to understand the unexplored dimensions of being human."[61] Some even go so far as to say that, while we indulge in addictions and fantasies, reverting into subcultures of factionalism, in the future "only in the online world will they participate in any form of human interaction."[62] In other words, the Web will make everything better. Even as reading and writing literacy trends downward, most blithely push even harder for more of the same because the Web makes all things right. Whatever our trends tell us now about information literacy and reading proficiencies, many earnestly believe declines will cease, crops will grow, and all will be well. Would that wishing would make it so. We have an eternal optimism about the Web, and even when it may be responsible for bad news, we embrace it even more. Even when experts, such as Chris Sherman of SearchEngineWatch.com, warn, "There is a problem with information literacy among people. People find information online and don't question whether it's valid or not," we do not seem to care. When experts tell us that most people do not look beyond the first page or evaluate what they have, it doesn't matter. When we are told that while you can type in "Thomas Jefferson" in any search engine and get hundreds of hits, you cannot tell which is fact which is fiction, and which is personal opinion, it doesn't matter.[63] It's the Web and that's all that matters. We do not stop to think that we have *never* accepted this sort of slipshod, scatter gun approach to anything. Yet we not only accept it from the Web, we dare anyone to criticize the Web even over a matter as important as the nation's literacy. At the risk of the obvious, let me hasten to point out that our form of government is predicated on a *literate* plebiscite.

As the computer age began some thirty years ago, a library in Kentucky created a makeshift box and asked students to place whatever research questions they had into it. No one could see inside the box, and no one knew, because computers were still in their infancy, that waiting 24 hours for an answer was not unusual. Beside the contraption sat a librarian who would answer *immediately* any question anyone had if only they asked.

Almost no one wanted to ask the librarian any questions. Even though students had to wait for an answer, they wanted the machine to do the answering. To make the matter even more interesting, librarians began having the "machine" give out wrong answers. The students still kept coming, even though the answers were increasingly and obviously wrong, and the librarian at the desk would answer any question immediately and correctly. It would be hard to invent a better cautionary morality tale.

Americans love machines and we love what they can do. Even when they fail us, we are ever at their beck and call. The Web is not any different. It has acquired an almost messiah-like quality. We want it to work, and any critics, like those who might criticize our families, must be dealt with quickly. While all of this is understandable, it is not acceptable. We are progressing too rapidly down a descent from which we may never recover. When young people are poorly educated, they spend a lifetime regretting it. So, too, does the society which allows it to happen. The hour is late and the time is short. We cannot let our enthusiasm for an invention blind us to its nocent effects. Inventions often outrun our ability to keep up. As the "can-do" nation, we are slow to admit defeat about any invention but especially about one that appears as successful to us as the Web. We cannot turn a blind eye to its defects. Mary Shelley's *Frankenstein* began innocently enough. We need not let our modern-day Frankenstein's Monster, the Web, end with the same fate as hers.

9

The Endgame: *Quo Vadis?*

It's debatable whether we are a nation with the soul of a church, as G.K. Chesterton once quipped. But we surely are a nation with a short memory. When it comes to technology, we are patients suffering from incurable amnesia: Did that gizmo fail? Did that whirligig collapse? What do you mean it can't work? In some ways we are the most successful nation on earth when it comes to technology: we won't take no for an answer. But it is also why we sometimes bring greater tragedies on ourselves. If Hal went haywire in *2001: A Space Odyssey,* it wasn't because the technology was wrong: some stupid human pushed the wrong button. Technology is what has made all our lives better, and it's what will make all our lives perfect. The Jetsons may well have been a cartoon, but embedded deep within our American consciousness is a longing for a world just like that. We have been touting a push-button-everything world for at least the last fifty years. If you doubt technology, well, you're some sort of crackpot along the lines of the Unabomber.

Our Short Memories

Take, for example, the dot-com bubble. Few but the portfolio victims remember the millions lost when all those over-inflated stocks burst. Trouble is, even now we have a hard time thinking it was the technology that went wrong. For every Google or Gates story, a score of dot-com bursting bubbles are waiting to be uncovered. The millions of dollars lost, we are told, were merely a "market correction" that surely will be reestablished in a way that will make the run-up to the bursting dot-com bubble look as innocent as a Mr. Bubbles commercial — or so we tell ourselves. It can't bomb again, we say reassuringly.

We often forget just how narrow and short our Tower of Google really is. Proclaiming that it reaches beyond the stars (*ad astra per aspera?*), we discover it is merely stars that we're seeing. Most of the grand claims we made for the Web in the early nineties have never materialized. It should be a morality tale for the rest of our technological prognostications, but that's unlikely. For example, less than 20 percent of the world's population is even connected to the Internet.[1] Indeed, with the exception of the United States, where the Internet is used by nearly 70 percent of the population, no other country comes close. The world is flat all right, it's just more mountainous everywhere outside the U.S. In Africa, almost 97 percent of the population remains (blissfully?) unaware of the Web.[2] In Asia, just under 90 percent. Our European neighbors come close with almost 40 percent population penetration, and Oceania/Australia creeps closer to the U.S. with just over 50 percent. The remaining parts of the world barely reach 25 percent.

It seems, odd, doesn't it, that we have this world-is-flat notion when over 80 percent of the world doesn't know what we're talking about, and *cannot* know what we're talking about because they've never experienced it firsthand.[3] So are we saying to this 80 percent, get connected or else? Do we ignore the fact that much of this 80 percent suffers under monstrous regimes and cannot hope for a change? Talk about American arrogance! Apparently when we make such sweeping claims about the world, we're only going to talk about American economic and technological flatness. The rest of the world can eat cake, if only they had some, or watch it on television, if only they had one. Moreover, we tend to forget that about 80 percent of the world — in mostly what we call developing countries — doesn't even own a phone line.[4]

Digital Everythingism Is Premature

Is it possible that we're just a wee bit premature on the Internet making the traditional library obsolete, *even if we are talking only about America*? If most of the rest of the world doesn't know what we're talking about, and air-dropping four million laptops will not change anything other than clutter the landscape, could we be just a tad early on all electronic everythingism? The problem isn't only one thing about the Web, it's everything about it. It's *everything* about it: bandwidth, connectivity, Internet providers, hardware, software and so on and on. Even with ten million laptops to the remotest parts of the world, we would still have the problem of a disproportionately expensive connectivity problem, even by our own standards.[5] The problem for these underdeveloped countries is survival in its most primitive form: water, heating, cooling. Communication of any kind more sophisticated than carrier pigeons is out of the question. After all this is in place, we would still have training issues and language barriers, to name but a few, especially since most computers function on the assumption that English is the native tongue. Wouldn't libraries be easier, better, and much less expensive?

The answer in every case is, of course yes, but that's likely not to change current electronic trends. The have-nots of the world will have even less, because we, meaning Western civilization, have decided to move toward an exclusively digitized world. The rest of the world can eat our digital dust, or digital cake — whatever. This is a sad sate of affairs, and it will only get sadder the farther along we go. My point is not that we should curtail our efforts while the rest of the world catches up, but why we are pushing this hard and in *this* direction when better, more reasonable solutions are at our disposal?

For others, such as the 88 percent of all children of birth to nine years of age (or 1.2 billion children) living in underdeveloped countries according to UNICEF, they'll just have to wait.[6] What amazes about digital discussions is that this very poverty is often used as a *reason* they need the Web. They cannot get what they need in other ways, so we'll send them virtual food by making certain they have the Internet to access information. In other words, the Internet is going to be (if it isn't *de facto* already) the substitute for any sort of real library services that would offer the full panoply of literacy services.

Rushing toward mass digitization, as we are, and trying to make every library a digital one, makes no sense at all when issues of literacy for these countries — not to mention our own — are at stake and can be resolved by cheaper, time-tested and easier means. Why make the gap between the world's digital haves and have-nots wider than it already is when there is no real reason for doing so, other than that we can? It isn't as if we must prove that Western civilization is the best civilization in which humans flourish. The only people who do not know this are those teaching in American university political science departments.

Web Is No Panacea

We need not turn to developing countries, however, to see that the movement to all things digital is not a sound one. We see some negative evidence of this whirling dervish rush to make everything electronic right here at home. Many seniors in this country are getting connected, of course, but the majority of them either are not, or if they could afford it, cannot work the technology. The same is true of the underserved or the poor. While the poor in our country are far richer than the rest of the world's poor, that still doesn't get a digital book in their hands when their main concern is food, clothing, shelter, a better job or the safety of themselves and their children. The one respite many of these underserved individuals could count on was a library, a safe refuge that they could repair to with the dream of self-improvement. With the advent of the Web, we've made a good number of our public libraries havens for pedophiles. Are we simply to accept that this is the price progress pays to vice? Some reading this will no doubt roll their eyes, as if to say this isn't *much* of a problem. But pedophiles know it is because they know, as pointed out in these pages, that, after the home, libraries provide the single largest means of free online access, so there they troll there as often as they can.

As pointed out in the last chapter, printed materials still define the greatest part of our literacy. Our culture is built on books and their meaning and their value, still hold almost totemic sway in our culture, as well they should.[7] Words, and the fashioning of them into books, have always held a special place in our society. The book itself has often held a place of honor in our culture, as well as in many other cultures. We cannot discount these feelings any more than we can ignore the history. Truisms have, it has been said, a maddening quality of generally being true, and so it is about our love, regard and honor for books. But if the movement to an all digital world threatened only this, we would have to admit to being *laudatoris temporis acti*, praisers of the past because it is the past, and nothing more.

As we have seen, however, the potential losses in our mad rush to an all digital world, a world in which the Internet becomes not merely a substitute but a *replacement* for the library, are very significant ones indeed. As we saw in the last chapter, it isn't so much that this is a new kind of literacy we are creating with an all online world, but a potential universal illiteracy. If we are creating conditions that in three, five or ten years' time will result in most of the rising generation being unable to do even the simplest of literate tasks, then we are rushing to create the new Frankenstein's Monster without an amicable personality. As our enthusiasm for an all-online world forces us to buy more and more technology at the expense of traditional sources, we leave behind not only valuable sources, but many individuals who would otherwise be with us in a print domain.[8]

Money to Burn

At the risk of stating the obvious, consider that academic libraries (or any libraries for that matter) have *very* limited funds. For example, how does a library spend a materials budget of one million dollars? Traditional sources will consume all of this in a matter of hours, but that cannot happen because traditional sources have become so démodé. So, about *three-fourths* of it must be used for online sources, proprietary databases, and the like. With one fourth left, the money must be spent on printed sources, DVDs, serials that cannot be purchased online for whatever reason, and so on. While many argue that this new world is better for small libraries because they can get so much more for their money, all too often we discover that all our funds are so strained with non-traditional sources, we have little left for traditional ones. Meanwhile, those who cannot access online materials easily and readily are out of luck.

Contrary to popular belief, Web-based services are not free.[9] Everything about the Web costs money, as has been pointed out in previous chapters. But even the information presented online is costly to maintain. Some argue that because most text-based information is produced through word processing software, it can easily be converted to an online presence. But most who make this argument forget that this is only the first step. There are indexes to maintain, new technologies to acquire to be sure that information is not "overlooked" by new search engines, decisions to be made about where and how that information will appear in search engine returns, enormous labor-intensive costs to make certain the metadata is correct and someone in place to update the technology regularly. Sites that are not kept up to date are likely to fall into disuse more rapidly than remaindered books.

We remain goggled-eyed over Google even when it threatens reading literacy.[10] At the very least, an all online world forces us away from meditating over a text and into rushing to snatch and grab whatever we can. In the previous chapter mention was made about readers who have not had to read the printed page as much as their parents or their grandparents. But the threat is deeper even than this. The threat of an all-online world moves even sophisticated readers to read less carefully and more quickly. Our eyes and minds tire more easily from online reading than from reading print. The complicated nature of online reading requires a more sophisticated decoding skill than print does (or at least one more complex than we have developed so far). Faced with this new dilemma, most students will pick and choose, snatch and grab, getting from a text only what they must, not what they should.

What is most distressing is that we move in this direction not because we have proven to ourselves it is better, only that it is *ostensibly* better for publishers, better for libraries, and better for consumers. But as we have seen, even this dream is a fiction we have developed in obeisance to the ultimate online goal — or should that be god?— of an all Internet world. For, in our rush, we assume that everything required to run this brave new world will somehow be at the ready: hardware, software, Internet providers, content, connectivity, bandwidth and so on. We do not really know how all of this is to be, but we are certain that it will somehow appear, *deus ex machina.* While this list is merely the most basic of needs, we also assume other "perks" will be present, such as endless machine refreshments, interchangeable software, a continued decline in prices for everything associated with technology, and an unlimited supply of preserved originals or masters so that online texts can be regularly refreshed. We know this will happen, not because we planned it to, but because we are dealing in an online environment, and everything works out with online environments. The "better" we assume really only means quicker, easier, faster.

As literacy issues continue to mount, Internet access will continue to dumb-down children in desperate need of basic skills. By decisions we have made and are making, we have already determined that literacy will be measured by Internet access. As one writer put it, "Studies of children's information needs show that in many cases those needs are imposed upon children by adults rather than the needs felt by the children themselves."[11] It does not matter that reading abilities are greatly hampered by these decisions. We've already determined that this will be our future. When we discover that we have amputated yet another generation from reading literacy, what then? Develop yet *more* software programs to help them resume their study skills?

We like to think that every bit of data we need, every parcel of information, is only a click away when it comes to the Web. But many who use it regularly are beginning to see that this is not the case. Often that answer is buried amid a haystack of irrelevancies all neatly congregating in such a way as to hide our sought-for needle. Amid the flotsam and the jetsam of the Web (its "howling wastes") may well be our diamond in the rough. But it will not do us any good to have it "somewhere" when we cannot get there. The argument often made against traditional libraries is that while they may contain more information than the Web, there is no good index to get to them, beyond catalogs and indexes that are laboriously difficult to wade through. While I reject the description, just how much different is this than the Web whose sought-for needle is cleverly concealed under a thicket of bad information?

We Have No Choice — It's Inevitable

Some will argue that we must move in this direction because we have no other choice, for the "world" is moving in this direction and young people will not have it any other way. As we have seen, the world in this case is largely the U.S., and most other places, even our allies in the UK, are not as "connected" as are we. If this is the "world," it's a pretty small one. Moreover, while it's true that young people are more online than every before, we must look at what they are doing online.[12] The early evidence is not encouraging from an educational standpoint. Kids and young people are actively seeking YouTube and MySpace regularly, two sites that do not provide much hope for the future.[13] In the case of the former, a site recently purchased (October 2006) by Google for just over one billion dollars, a survey of offerings proved dissatisfying at best, mind-numbing at worst. Examining YouTube's top ten, its top 100 and its random categories, I was able to view a young teen "with large hooters," a young man setting his ass on fire as he tried to light his own flatulence, an enormous number of "jackass" stunts (appositely named), and about a dozen or more clips from various television programs, some of which I could view and others I could not because of my hardware.

MySpace offers a rash of sites where teens reveal everything about themselves: their favorite shows, television programs, music, likes and dislikes, and virtually a map to their homes — in short everything a predator would need to know to lure them to wherever he might want them to go. When young people were not doing this, they were engaged in exsufflicating, nauseating narcissism, what can only be described as "full disclosure."

But in case this might be considered a bad case of "cherry picking" that only the worst young people are surfing, the top ten as reported by Nielsen/NetRatings revealed little better: Originalicons.com, Blind Truth, Teen People, FireHotQuotes.com, Buddy4u.com, Bolt, Badass Buddy, Sparknotes.com, QuizYourFriends.com and Blurty.com. Some tout many of these sites as "elaborate social systems," but even if we grant this, these are only *virtual* ones. In other words, young people are withdrawing more and more because of the Web, revealing more and more *on* the Web, but having less and less real human contact owing to the Web. But the Web has so much to offer we accept whatever it brings regardless of what we sacrifice in the process.

The Best the Web Has to Offer: Teenagers

For example, curious about what 12- to 17-year-olds thought constituted a "top" or important website, I examined the top ten mentioned above, along with the next ten. Here's what I found.

Original Icons is a website devoted to various kinds of useless icons one can place on various electronic media. Blunt Truth is a site where users compose surveys and send them to friends who, if they answer incorrectly, will soon be enemies. This is billed as a site where you can "find out what your friends really think about you." Some content is an innocuous as those once familiar notes passed around in grade school: Do you like me, check yes, no. Other content is not in the least innocuous, and some quite troubling. Teen People is an electronic version of something like teen celebrity, where users can go to find whatever "inquiring minds" want to know about the latest heartthrob.

FireHotQuotes is a site devoted to quotes that users have written for others to see. Granted, the ages in question here are 12 to 17 and one must guess that the lower end predominates. Still, some of the quotes hardly give one hope for the future. All punctuation is as found at the site:

> guys are slinkies its always fun to watch them fall down the stairs.
>
> If ur nice, you can call me sweety. If ur sweet you can call me hunny. If ur hot you can call me tonight.
>
> A wise monkey never monkies with another monkey's monkey!
>
> A peach is a peach a plum is a plum a kiss isn't a kiss without some tongue
>
> GUYS ARE LIKE ROSES WATCH OUT FOR THE PRICKS
>
> If ur naughty go 2 ur room ... If u wanna be naughty, go 2 mine

Buddy4u and BadassBuddy are sites devoted to emoticons that reveal in a cartoon image what one may feel: anger, happiness, etc. Most are merely idiotic, but some raise alarms. One image depicts a smoking joint, while another shows a young man throwing up (titled "Drunk"). Another are two emoticons digging about in a mass of blood, searching for body parts. Sparknotes is the electronic version of the same, and, of course, had its birth in print with Cliff Notes and Masterplots. It proved to be the *only* remotely educational site in the top twenty, but not an educational site many teachers would approve. Quiz Your Friends is another site devoted to trying to find out what your friends really think of you. It's surely all in good fun, but the site featured one quiz testing whether users are good kissers, something inappropriate for 12 year olds (but of course unquestionably something they engage in — do they need more encouragement or less?).

Finally, Blurty proved to be the most disturbing of all the sites examined. Blurty pleads its case as "free online journals and communities for adults" but on the day visited (October 2006) no one pictured in the photographs appeared older than 16. Many middle and high school English teachers are enamored with journaling, perhaps the worst way possible for a young person to learn any usable writing skills, so it's hard to think of anyone over 17 *wanting* to use the site. Surely adults visit this site, but none of the viewed entries suggested any of the posters had made it out of their teen years.

The site features "most popular" communities, as determined by the number of viewed pages. The journal/blog titled "whycut" proved depressing. Cutting, marking or carving is common among middle school children and nothing viewed indicated otherwise. The journal is devoted to young people (all entries on the day viewed were self-reported to be under 17) who cut themselves for no reason in particular, "like" to cut themselves, or have serious suicidal tendencies. One girl admitted that she liked to "cut" herself and found that it "relieved" tensions. Another said she was happy that she had not cut herself in a while but recently had "fallen back into it." Another revealed a dialog between two people and how they hide their cuts from others. Both admitted that their significant others knew about their markings, "but were cool." Obviously this "adult" site is largely visited by young people in serious need of counseling. Some will argue that having this site is a "godsend" because these "young people need to know they are not alone." *Au contraire*, as fire here feeds fire. These young people need to be forced to see someone, their parents, a teacher, a minister, a counselor, but *someone* who could help them. As it is, the blind lead the blind on this site. What I read filled me with fear and loathing.

Also on this site in the "most popular" category was "yourstarvingme," a journal devoted to bulimia, anorexia, along with some (very few) healthy dieting tips. Most on the site were literally starving themselves, or trying to. The obsessive comments about food, the amount of calories and the sheer desperation of discovering "something else" they cannot eat, were enough to make one lose one's appetite.

"Sextips," another popular section on Blurty, again featured mostly middle and high school students. Of those pictured, not many looked to be over 16, but no photographs should have been allowed anyway. Coupled with their preferred sexual antics, and some information about where they lived, this site is a haven for a predator. The tips mixed incredible naïveté with unbridled promiscuity. One "hilarious" question asked by what appeared to be a girl not much older than 13 had to do with "sex near your period." She assured readers she "knew that sex close to your period" meant that the period would be delayed, but she wanted to know if it could be delayed several weeks. Many (at least 75 percent) of the tips focused on oral sex. One young *girl* asked about procedure, shall we say, while another asked about what to look for in case "something was wrong" with a given penis. No one expressed any inkling about morality, the wisdom of multiple partners, or the willingness to participate in the activity shortly after meeting someone. Still another provided several paragraphs on a part of that particular sex act too explicit to be revealed here. After reading more than two dozen tips, I could not bring myself to venture a peek at "artsfu*ks," a site whose name has been bowdlerized here.

Again, some will surely argue that these are only healthy young people investigating what makes them and their partners feel good. This is a suspect assessment even in our so-called enlightened times when referring to young people barely into their teens. Healthy sexual discussions are one thing; pornographic ones rivaling those found on hardcore sites, entirely another. But even granting this, can we really say that it's good for any discussion of this type to be carried out on online, complete with your picture and home state for everyone to see?

Readers at this point will complain that I have stacked the deck against the Web because these observations are taken from sites that 12 to 17-year-olds find useful. Some will argue that I purposefully chose sites by the very young that will appear stupid to adults. At their age, young people will inevitably choose many regrettable sites because that is after all what it means to be young. Readers are reminded that we continue to encourage young people to use the Web more and more. Readers are again reminded that many are making the Web an ostensible substitute for a library. And finally, it is with the Web that these same young people are now spending an additional 27 percent more time than they did a mere three years ago.[14] Readers are asked to couch this in the context that teens now spend an average of nearly 27 hours a month on the Web. Much of that time is spent surfing to these favored sites, so like it or not, these "best" sites have to be examined. None of the sites examined spoke in an encouraging fashion about the intellectual abilities of our future leaders. Much of what Web-based use studies tell us is that young people are not honing their intellectual skills online, but are in fact continuing the dumbing down that their elementary and secondary education began.

But suppose we look at what adults view as the best? Adults know what they are looking for and are a savvy users. Examining what adults view as the best will reveal the Web as sophisticated, intelligent, full of educational value, and providing at least minimal evidence that the Web can, indeed, replace the conventional library.

If wishes were horses.

Okay, the Best the Web Has to Offer: Adults

I looked at Yahoo's "100 Sites for Men That Won't Offend the Missus." Among the first ten sites were these: "80s Nostalgia," a site that "proves just about anything can be cool after 20 years," "Drinking Gadgets" will help turn your living room into a pub (one wonders which "missus" that would *not* offend). "MG Cars" gives surfers a look at "car porn" while "Attract Women" is "not porn" but the secrets of attracting women (which is a surefire way *not* to be successful). "Curry Wonderland," from the second ten, offer recipes for dishes using curry, while "Hangover Hell" (from the third ten) gives users, assuming they are upright enough to read, ways to cure hangovers. "Volcanoes" and "Fighter Planes" (from the fourth ten) did provide some valuable information about volcanoes and fighter planes, but clearly the sites were written for the under-30 group.

Obviously the trouble had to be that males cannot be trusted to look at anything of value that doesn't have a loud engine, encourage drinking or cure its aftereffects, so I visited Yahoo's "100 Sites for Women." Here the offerings ranged from "cutting edge" designed T-shirts, to sites with the "funky, stylish, elegant or more gorgeous," to sites on perfume, shoes, babies, a test for one's level of antisocial behavior, holistic medicine and celebrity gossip.

Best Sites? Compare to What?

Clearly my mistake had been aiming at too young an age group again, so I tried "100bestwebsites.org." This list is based on the opinions and reviews of a specialized Web-savvy group whose vocational life it is to know about these things. This is a portal "to the finest sites the Web has to offer!" The number one site is Yahoo!, which may or may not have anything to do with the association of those choosing the sites with the near-giant. Google came in second. Neither site points to information but to more sites, and both provide millions of hits in a matter of seconds. All you have to do is wade through them. Amazon.com came in third, the giant online book presence that merely lists books and is still trying to turn a profit. Number four on the list is About.com, a site that will "separate the wheat from the chaff," providing users are generous in their definition of the one, broadminded in their definition of the other. Google

Groups, Google News, CNN, eBay, and Download.com (for the software treasure hunter) round out the top ten. *Wikipedia* (about which much was made in the first chapter) is 13th on this list. The Weather Channel, Monster.com, Slate.com and Expedia.com made the top 20.

Next I tried *Time* magazine's best sites, though I must admit the title "50 Coolest Web sites 2005," followed by a category, did not fill me with either encouragement or enthusiasm. Some of the featured sites included Aardman Animation, an animation site about Wallace and Gromit, a cheese-loving inventor and his dog. The two had their first feature-length film, *The Curse of the Were-Rabbit*, in 2005. Opus 1 Classical is a resource for those "more into Handel than hip-hop," but I did not find anything that I did not already know from other sources. For those with larger travel budgets than my own, the site would be useful as it lists festivals, concerts and more, all over the globe. Somehow knowing what Prague had to offer during the week I viewed it did not make me feel any better about offerings within driving distance. Indeed, I felt envious rather than satiated, but those who can travel could not possibly have found out this information anywhere else, right?

Original.com offered dozens of free Web-based games, and Ze's Page, which debuted with "How to Dance Properly" just a few years ago, boasted millions of hits. While amusing, it struck me more as a joke one hears and not something one seeks to know. TV.com told me about shows I've never seen and gossip I did not care to know. Go Fug Yourself, also on the list, made fun of celebrity choices of attire. Shooting fish in a barrel to be sure, but even the writing's mean-spiritedness lacked something. Anonymous Lawyer is funny but entirely fictitious, stringing together most lawyer jokes one already heard in one form or another. Blinkx.tv did offer clips and "video bits" from major news sources and even ESPN and C-Span, but understanding why this would be a site revisited (assuming one fell into it by mistake) escaped me. Answers.com I thought would be right up my alley, as it is more or less a library reference desk online. Alas, many of the answers come from *Wikipedia*, a source that would have to corroborated (as *Wikipedia* itself points out) before it could be used.[15]

Outtah Site

Many good sites are on the Web, but all of the "best" lists examined did not reveal many that provide information one could not live without or not easily find elsewhere. Writing this in October 2006 it may have been too early for Google Earth to have made any of these lists, but certainly it is a powerful and intriguing site. The same could be said for MIT's Loeb Classics (in Greek and Latin with translations) mentioned in an earlier chapter. A good many of the Deep Web sites are also very useful, but in the dozen-plus "best" sites examined, none mentioned any of these. Although WebMD did not come up until I found (after several days of searching off and on) *PCMagazine*'s best Web sites, many alternative medicine sites did. But as pointed out in an earlier chapter, this has proven an approach-avoidance for many physicians and too many individuals use it instead of going to visit the doctor. Perhaps a physician would want to undertake "10 Reasons Why the Internet Is Not a Physician."

PCMagazine's list proved the best of the "best sites" lists I looked at, with at least *some* sites that would provide useful information. I understand that the definition of information I use throughout this book is not the one the Web uses. Finding random facts and tidbits are useless in my line of work. Finding answers to specific questions are. Even so, the best Web sites in the *PCMagazine* list were things like the IRS, the Library of Congress's Web site, Bplan.com (a source for would-be entrepreneurs), and OpenSecrets.org, a site that lets users know what their local politicians are up to by tracking where all the money goes and why.

The "Wow" Factor Does Not Equal Knowledge

The point of this exercise is not to prove that the Web is filled with junk. Anyone who has spent ten minutes on the Web knows that, as does even the most ardent Web aficionado. What it does show, however, is that even relying on the *best* the Web has to offer (as defined by various industry experts) provides users very little to work with, and less still that is not readily available in just about any library in every community the world over.

Too many of the lists are really lists of "wow" sites, more or less like going to the freak show at the fair, but electronically. Many such sites assume that users have the most up-to-date technology, ample bandwidth, and high speed access, an assumption that is simply wrong, not to mention wrong-headed. Too many using and touting the Web make this mistake. For example, much of what I do on the Web is made possible only because I work at an institution that has spent *millions* making it possible to do all that I do. If employed in almost any other profession, I could not begin to take advantage of even one-tenth of what the Web offers. I belabor this point because, in order for anyone to take full advantage, one has to have the full panoply of resources available, something no library requires of anyone. Library access only requires you to show up at the door. Those who assume the Web is "there" for everyone are often experts who remind me of a boss I had years ago. When I complained to him about our IT service and the limits it placed on the library and its users of online technology, he listened attentively.

"You know," he said to me, "I hear that from time to time, but I've never had any such experience. Whenever I call, they are here in ten minutes and fix whatever is broken immediately."

"Do you think," I replied, "that that's because you're the Provost and I'm the library director?" He did not. Likewise, those experts touting all that the Web can do may not be thinking through what this means for everyone *below* their status of Web access. At the library where I work, when we offer a new technology, we have to think of the least technologically able client we have and what unintended consequences our choice will have on them. For example, if our site won every award for technological wow-power at least half (or more) of our users could not access it from home. What would be the point?

At the risk of belaboring the obvious, let me point out yet again that libraries require nothing of users other than their minds. You don't have to have the latest anything, you don't need bandwidth, you do not need to inquire about an Internet service provider, you will not need to upgrade anything, and your speed is only determined by how quickly you can get to one. While some will be quick to point out, "Ah, but that's why the Web is better. I can work in my pajamas!," let me be the first to point out an additional advantage the conventional library provides: exercise!

Mental Junk Food

To argue that the Web can replace a conventional library with sites that offer the mental equivalent of junk food is not to make the world flat, but to the make the world fat-headed. My plea is not a *cri du coeur* from a purist (though some will doubtless complain that it is), but a plea that we not trivialize everything in our world, that we not turn everything we have into a ten second jackass clip. The Web wants everything at once and it encourages us to want the same. It feeds our sound bite mentality and we, especially we Americans, want anything that will allow us to know *something instantly and without effort*. But none of this helps us know more about our world, while it probably does speak volumes about ourselves. The Web will turn us into a nation of trivial people in search of trivia that masquerades as wisdom.

Knowledge Versus Information

Libraries and the millions that built them were not organized around such concepts but were, rather, organized around the search for wisdom, and, I dare to say it, even truth. The idea behind them was that if you spent hours within their walls using their resources you would come out a better man or woman. It is not only an old idea but even a conservative one that we have lost sight of. Libraries sought (and still seek) to make us an educated populace, and that is why, from the beginning of our country, they were seen as an essential and integral part of what made our nation the successful "experiment" it has become. The Web, inadvertently or not, seeks to undo all of this by making us go a-whoring after the latest gossip, the funniest (and stupidest) video, the most degrading sexual experiences imaginable (and many we cannot imagine), all mixed together with random helpful bits of information. While we are certainly entitled to entertain ourselves in whatever *legal* manner we choose, we cannot, we must not, let that ever be equated with knowledge.

Libraries in a Perilous Age

Whether we want to admit it or not, the Web is forcing libraries to a crossroads. Their future is by no means secure; if they try to become the Web, they will fail. They cannot possibly compete with its instant gratification (even if the gratification you get isn't what you asked for). If libraries refuse to be Web-like, we will eventually ignore them as being that old stodgy edifices that our grandparents used. Certainly, libraries cannot "wow" at all (at least not too many, and ostensibly, not too many who work in them) the way the Web does. Libraries will appear out of touch, not "with it" (whatever that means), and anachronistic. Anachronisms by definition go unfunded.

Jorge Luis Borges, in his short story "The Library of Babel," published in the early sixties, foresaw all of this, though he did not write about the Web.[16] He depicts a sprawling, nearly eternal library that has everything, information and disinformation. It contains "Everything: the minutely detailed history of the future, the archangels' autobiographies, the faithful catalogue of the Library, thousands and thousands of false catalogues, the demonstration of the fallacy of those catalogues, the demonstration of the fallacy of the true catalogue, the Gnostic gospel of Basilides, the commentary on that gospel, the commentary on the commentary on that gospel, the true story of your death, the translation of every book in all languages, the interpolations of every book in all books.... The Library exists *ab aeterno*.... [It] can only be the work of a god."[17] In many ways the description of this mythical library sounds like a Google business plan, and is not entirely unlike the Web, with the exception that the Web is everywhere, and this library was in one place. The followers eventually kill each other over what they can't find, or they are tossed aside after they die trying. In other words, it was information gone amok, not knowledge as once defined by the Western tradition. At one point, the narrator of the story remarks most poignantly, "Obviously no one expects to discover anything."[18] Borges depicts wanting to know for the sake of knowing without really wanting to learn. It is as Milton in *Paradise Lost* depicts the sin of Lucifer, as the first and only crime: the desire to be as God.

Our Information ... Swamp

The Web is to chaos what the library as originally conceived is to order. Being a swamp of facts is not the same as being surrounded by knowledge. We have forgotten that a swamp of facts is, for everything it might one day become, still a swamp. Today we have, it would appear, opted for the information swamp (as opposed to the information highway) over all else, and we are forcing everyone to jump in, like it or not. The metaphor is an apt one, for swamps contain just a little of everything but not exactly in the right proportions. The one ingredient missing is the necessary balance of oxygen, without which the pond becomes something not quite a cesspool and not quite a pond. The Web is very much like this. It contains a good bit of everything but in all the wrong proportions. For example, it has far too much junk, not nearly enough educational material, and does not distinguish between good and bad data, between information, misinformation, or disinformation. It has far too much pornography and not nearly enough useful knowledge. And whatever we would like to think, the Web has not much organization. Much like *Wikipedia*, anyone can add whatever he or she wants to add without regard to accuracy or expertise. Like amateur community theater, much of it is painfully bad. The biggest difference is that many will not know, or not be able to tell, the difference, much to their chagrin or even harm. Some of that content will be fine because some experts will in fact share their knowledge. Like a swamp, one doesn't want to get rid of it necessarily, but one does wish it would be something other than what it is.

Libraries: Treasure Troves of Wisdom

Contrast all of this with the way in which libraries have collected and arranged knowledge for years. Libraries, even very small, very local ones, did not collect whatever anyone in the community wrote, argued, invented or created. Rather, libraries have always sought the best that human kind has produced. Even when so-called screwball national groups sought to find a home in libraries (the John Birch material comes to mind), nearly all libraries rejected them. Obviously, readers can think of exceptions to this rule, but that is just the point. The fact that readers can think of a handful of exceptions only serves to underscore just how well developed this collection process has always been. When local collections did rise to the level of some sort of expertise, libraries collected them, but not without strict scrutiny. The Web on the other hand is the flotsam and jetsam of what *anyone* wants to share even if what they want to share is faulty, wrong, wrong-headed, hateful, spiteful, racist and so on. To argue that this is an improvement brings to mind what the Houyhnhnms said to Gulliver when he tried to explain English law to them: surely you are saying that which is not.

The Web's gold is pinchbeck or ormolu; it is all too often fool's gold.

Conclusion

So where does that leave libraries in the 21st century? It leaves them in a very precarious place. Libraries will remain flexible in response to publishing and technological advances.[19] They cannot remain so flexible that they lose the value for which they were created in the first place, as the only place to look to find the best that human knowledge has to offer. While some of what libraries do will change in the face of automation, for libraries to become more like the Web, or even more like Google (or any other search engine) will only cause them to fail even sooner than they already are because they cannot compete in that virtual arena. The "tones of flexibility" are critical.[20] If they become too much like the Web, the Web *will* supersede them; to little like the Web, and they will be ignored. The greatest danger to libraries now is that they seem so much like the Web that many will think, and rightly so, that the Web does a better job and so cease to fund them.

Libraries are costly operations, not because they are not delivered over the Internet (because much of what they offer can be, or already is), but because they collect not everything for its own sake, but because they attempt to collect, to use an old phrase, "the best and the brightest." Libraries have *always* been financial black holes, especially as the cost of materials began to rise (around 1970). Since then, everyone has sought ways to make them less expensive, but as Yeats once said, we often see the value of a thing in its passing. I only hope we see the value of libraries *as they are* before they pass away entirely. The start-up cost for them after they have all but disappeared would prohibit anything like their restoration.

Make no mistake about it. Libraries are beginning to vanish even now. The sentiment for their departure is everywhere apparent. Combine the decline in reading with the precipitous decline in literacy, and soon very few will be left around to remind us why we built these giant totems to the totality of knowledge. If we separate libraries from their *teaching* function and substitute only their *technological* function, the latter will be seen as served faster (and exclusively) by the Web.[21] The *raison d'être* of libraries has been the assumption of the role of helping those who come within their walls with skilled personnel who assist them in finding and interpreting information in such a way as to organize it into knowledge.[22]

Picture Perfect Participation

Libraries are the poster children of collaboration entities that so many state governments now declare that they seek. Libraries share resources, not only in the same region or the same state, but across the globe. Not only that, but libraries routinely share expertise with one another, share cataloging worldwide (via OCLC), and even share the purchase of materials. In the state where I work, South Carolina, we, like all other fifty states, share purchases throughout the state and even across state lines in order to bring costs down. Libraries share resources better than any other state agency one could name. They have been sharing for so long that they have become experts in participation and collaboration. Libraries are taking, and have always taken, great advantage of sharing not only knowledge but also dollars, whenever and wherever they can.[23]

The rush to mass digitization threatens, however, to spoil this collaboration and participation, as many libraries feel they must rush into this before standards are present, before preservation techniques are in place for digitized materials, and before they are ready to assume so many additional responsibilities with stagnating or falling budgets. Most have assumed these additional digitization tasks without the necessary funding simply because they do not want to appear as so many foot-dragging entities. My hope is that that they have not begun this process so prematurely that we have lost, or are losing, valuable knowledge.

The battle that has begun is over who — libraries or the Web — will "own and control the record of advances in knowledge in intellectual domains of critical importance."[24] Obviously I believe that bailiwick should remain where it has always remained, with libraries. This book has been a long argument about that. Yet I also fear that because the Web is ubiquitous, easy and convenient; that because our literacy is waning and so open to the quick and the comfortable; that because we as a nation always seek instant gratification, we will *mistakenly* place our hopes in this ready medium that cannot possibly do the job that libraries have always done in excellent fashion for so much of our intellectual history.

Libraries have done their jobs well because librarians know the importance of knowledge and its preservation, something the rush to mass digitization does not appear to understand at all.[25] Surely in ten or fifteen years, we all hope that digital preservation techniques will improve and that ways of holding on to all this digital swamp of information can somehow be made to last, not just for the next ten, but for the next one-thousand years. But as the past is sometimes a prelude to the future, we cannot approach this without fear and trembling. We have known about the inability of Web-based information to be preserved in anything approaching perdurability, and we have known that for the past twenty years. But knowing that has not caused us to slow down our rush to digitize everything. Indeed, if anything, it has accelerated our drive to have everything online, everything accessible in a matter of minutes. We have also known that some significant level of technological sophistication is required to access such material (something never before required by libraries), and yet we no longer seem to care, not just about the have-nots, but even the half-haves. The desire appears to be to get the best there is in technology and be ready, or be left out. Perhaps I should say, left behind.

This is not a plea to leave library buildings in the same architectural fashion they have always been, though I prefer their majestic beauty to their current plasticine contemporaneity. Space is not an issue. Spaces can change — and should — and those changes will not affect how those who use libraries will be able to use what is collected there. But access does change, and dramatically, not only how, but also *who,* can see and use that information. Moreover, how we fund libraries — or not — will dramatically change who gains access to the knowledge, and to what extent they can. Library buildings may well be able to become smaller, but they cannot become smaller until we have ironed out all the difficulties of preserving what is there now, and what will likely be there in the future. The question becomes one of whether we want to leave such decisions to the experts who have been making them for years, or take a chance on the virtual newcomers who may decide we only need more information *now;* tomorrow will take care of itself. Libraries have already transcended place, so that is not what is at issue here.[26] Rather it is more a question of who knows best how to gather, organize and make certain that knowledge acquired 100 years ago, and knowledge to be acquired 100 years hence, is always available. As one writer has put it, "The emphasis on quick search and the retrieval of nuggets of information defies the thoughtful process of the scholarly tradition and the libraries' role in preserving and providing access to the human record of recorded knowledge."[27]

If resources and energies are going to be required to fashion seamless systems for users to access information (and nothing so far appears to contradict this), then the ability of libraries to gather, organize and acquire knowledge in the manner that they have been doing so will be greatly comprised.[28] We are developing a "connected" generation that "expect[s] the information necessary for learning and research to be available when it [is] needed, regardless of time and location."[29] Few see this as anything but the natural evolution of user demand for new technologies as introduced into the old schema. But to manage these systems and to provide for this kind of access will require libraries to give up some of those things they have always done. Again, not many see this as the downside to a fully digital world. But in the process of making these demands, we have routinely reduced budgets and pulled personnel from other areas. Add to that the overall inability of more and more users to distinguish between good and bad information, not to mention knowledge, and disaster looms on the digital horizon. While users demand more virtual everything, and as the lines between work and play disappear (especially as the Web appears more and more like a large playground and less and less like a reliquary of knowledge), traditional library services will first gradually diminish, then ultimately disappear.[30] Indeed, some services already have. The morality tale is already being seen in the number of media centers that have closed and are closing in K–12 institutions and the astonishing number of public libraries that are fighting for their survival because they are poor business models in light of the Web's ubiquity.[31] Moreover, even in academic libraries many are predicting that reference services will soon be obsolete.[32] The Web has already satisfied many of us with its brummagem, often counterfeit information. Even though we know that more and more individuals cannot navigate the Web without some sort of expert assistance and analyses (Google's 50 million hits create a "wow" factor until one realizes that wading through them is step two), the appearance of ease of use will be all that most require. As more individuals see the Web's simulacra as an acceptable substitute for knowledge, they will wonder why we should continue to fund expensive operations like libraries.

Perhaps worse, however, is the trend (thankfully slowing) of merging libraries and information centers of IT operations.[33] Such mergers rarely work well, and all too often the end result is a continued diminishing of traditional library services. When these mergers and conflations are not at the heart of mischief, mergers of public and academic libraries are. To date, we have few examples of either working well, a number of examples of both working poorly, a realization that neither actually saved significant funds, and plenty of evidence that it hamstrung both operations to some degree. The failure of mergers could not be laid at the feet of either group resisting the change; rather it came about as the functions of both either interfered with or impeded the other. In many cases, these mergers occurred over the expressed disappointment of most involved. All of these examples strike me as but further evidence that the library is in a very perilous state; the disappearance of K–12 media centers, mergers of IT operations and libraries, and the blending of public and academic libraries all come out of a feeling that libraries are obsolete.

The rush to make everything digital, to continue to argue that the Web has or soon will make everything available, is based on false notions about the Web's abilities, ignores both financial and non-financial (e.g. copyright) barriers, mocks practical considerations and simply chooses not to acknowledge technological barriers that make such pronouncements impossible.[34] Even so, we will have it this way, or so we seem to be saying. It is a very odd state of affairs to have to argue what should be obvious. But as Samuel Johnson once said, what is obvious is not always known, and what is known is not always obvious.

The Internet is no substitute for a library, and it's silly even to think so. Perhaps if the Web ran the statement — the Internet Is No Substitute for a Library — in an endless loop as a foot or header (or both) on every page, we might be able to succeed in making some value out of the Web while still preserving what has always led us to knowledge. It may be too much to hope that we would respond, not with our usual one-best-way, silver bullet approach, but with a thoughtful, careful assessment of what we have before we lose it. We need not let libraries pass to see their value. And we need not let others who fail to see their value let it go because they are too busy surfing to see. If any hopeful sign exists it is in the very content the Web provides. So much of it is of such dubious merit that it may sink of its own stink. Acting beyond one's limits — what the Greeks called *hubris*— often leads to a fall, not of a personal level, but of a cosmic one.[35]

As with most important issues, it's hard to find a better voice than G.K. Chesterton, the great English essayist. In 1926, he wrote,

> In the matter of reforming things, as distinct from deforming them, there is one plain and simple principle; a principle which will probably be called a paradox. There exists in such a case a certain institution or law; let us say, for the sake of simplicity, a fence or gate erected across a road. The more modern type of reformer goes gaily up to it and says, "I don't see the use of this; let us clear it away." To which the more intelligent type of reformer will do well to answer: "If you don't see the use of it, I certainly won't let you clear it away. Go away and think. Then, when you can come back and tell me that you *do* see the use of it, I may allow you to destroy it."[36]

This is precisely the point. We are unable to make a distinction between forming a new thing, the Web, without deforming an old one, the library. Elsewhere Chesterton points out that "nine out of ten of what we call new ideas are simply old mistakes ... blind alleys and bad roads ... all the ways have been shown to be worthless by the best of all evidence: the evidence of those who have gone down them."[37] It is possible to form a new thing while preserving an old one, but we haven't so far been able to do that. Do we really have to go down yet another blind alley or bad road just to prove it cannot be done?

We can use the best that *both* have to offer without destroying either. We can have both work to our advantage without trying to make one a panacea. We can, in short, create the future we want and need to have, rather than accepting a future merely because we cannot see beyond today, beyond the now. It will take time and effort and a great deal of restraint. It will also require us to change when necessary, and resist change when it is not required. We need not, as Tennyson wrote, "let the great world spin for ever down the ringing grooves of change." Change is exhilarating; it is also very dizzying and disorienting, and all too often it is the condition of change wherein we accept the next glittering thing only because it glitters, only because it "wows" like nothing old we know. It's only when we try to cash in that fool's gold that we begin to realize our mistake.

It is also how we lose those things that matter most.

Chapter Notes

Introduction

1. Michael Gorman, *The Enduring Library: Technology, Tradition, and the Quest for Balance* (Chicago: American Library Association, 2003), ix. Gorman recounts the delightful scholarship about George Eliot's *Middlemarch*.

2. The point is, we have always been prone to *overestimate* the ability of technology to accomplish human tasks. It can do human tasks faster; it is rare that it does them *better*.

3. It may surprise readers how television forced its way into the library but there it is. See "Media in Academic Libraries: Steps and Fumbles," *Library Journal* 100 (December 1, 1975): 2200; "CATV and Circulation Hookup Will Provide Online Catalog," *Library Journal* 104 (December 1, 1979): 2508–9; "Get into CATV Picture, ALA Urges Libraries," *Library Journal* 96 (November 15, 1971): 3709–10; B.K.L. Genova, "Video and Cable: Emerging Forms of Library Service," *Library Trends* 26 (Fall 1979): 297–309.

4. The sad story is now well known and can be read in Nicholas Baker's *Double Fold*. Yes, many librarians have found fault with Mr. Baker. It's true that Mr. Baker can be impugned on a number of points. Still, his basic premise remains inexpugnable. Those who should have known better did not do better.

5. We are never told why size matters in these cases but apparently it does. Moreover, it matters in a less-than-intuitive way: *smaller* is better, ostensibly.

6. Indeed, in ancient Israel, prophets, under the authority of Moses, who were proved wrong were to be stoned to death.

7. George Eliot, *Middlemarch* (London: Zodiac Press, 1950), 83.

8. See United States National Commission on Excellence in Education, *A Nation at Risk: The Full Account* (Cambridge, MA: USA Research, 1984); or, http://www.ed.gov/pubs/NatAtRisk/risk.html (accessed January 2006).

9. Frederick Taylor, *The Principles of Scientific Management* (New York: Harper and Brothers, 1911).

Taylor (1856–1915) strove to change business by coming up with what later came to be called "the one best way." Taylor tried to adapt this way to every business in every context, regardless of product, type or delivery. For a good critique of this and the Taylor history, see Robert Kanigel, *The One Best Way: Frederick Winslow Taylor and the Enigma of Efficiency* (New York: Viking, 1997).

10. William W. Bishop, "Training in the Use of Books," *Sewanee Review* 20 (July 1912): 280.

11. Charles A. D'Aniello, "Cultural Literacy and Reference Service," *RQ* 28 (Spring 1989): 370–280.

12. For more, see Charles Sykes, *Dumbing Down Our Kids* (New York: St. Martin's Press, 1995); William J. Bennett, *The De-Valuing of America: The Fight for Our Culture and Our Children* (Summit Books, 1992); and Arthur Schlesinger, *The Disuniting of America* (New York: Norton, 1992). The most depressing such book is Diane Ravitch and Chester Finn, *What Do Seventeen Years Olds Know?: A Report on the First National Assessment of History and Literature* (New York: Harper and Row, 1988, (c)1987).

13. Gerry Harrington, "Seven Dwarfs vs. Supreme Court Justices," United Press International, http://license.icopyright.net/user/viewFreeUse.act?fuid=MT UyOTYz (accessed August 2006).

14. Regna Lee Woods, "Open Letter," *National Review*, September 30, 1996, p. 49.

15. See, for example, National Association of Scholars, *The Dissolution of General Education: 1914–1993* (National Association of Scholars, 1996). While this report is now a decade old, recent shorter surveys by the National Association of Scholars have proved that this trend is now a trait of GenXer, NetGens and whatever other monikers the current generation has assumed.

16. Jeffrey Ghassemi, "I said, 'Not While You Study!'" *Washington Post,* Tuesday, September 5, 2006, HE 01ff.

17. Books that come to mind chronicling both the poor teaching in America's high schools, colleges and universities and the subsequent neglect on at least one

professional front, teaching, are listed here. The sampling, I should hasten to point out, includes authors of all ideological persuasions: liberal, moderate, and conservative. William J. Bennett, *The De-Valuing of America: The Fight for Our Culture and Our Children* (Summit Books, 1992); John Chubb and Terry Moe, *Politics, Markets and America's Schools* (Brookings, 1990); Dinesh D'Souza, *Illiberal Education: The Politics of Race and Sex on Campus* (Free Press, 1991); Joni Finney, *At the Crossroads: Linking Teacher Education to School Reform* (Denver: Education Commission of the States, 1992); Calvin Frazier, *A Shared Vision: Policy Recommendations for Linking Teacher Education to School Reform* (Denver: Education Commission of the States, 1993); E.D. Hirsch, *The Schools We Need and Why We Don't Have Them* (New York: Doubleday, 1996); William Kilpatrick, *Why Johnny Can't Tell Right from Wrong* (New York: Simon and Schuster, 1992); Roger Kimball, *Tenured Radicals* (New York: Harper and Row, 1990); Rita Kramer, *Ed School Follies: The Miseducation of America's Teachers* (Free Press, 1991); Diane McGuinness, *Why Our Children Can't Read: And What We Can Do About It* (New York: Free Press, 1997); George Marsden, *The Soul of the American University: From Protestant Establishment to Established Nonbelief* (Oxford: Oxford University Press, 1994); Arthur Schlesinger, *The Disuniting of America* (New York: Norton, 1992); Theodore Sizer, *Horace's Hope: What Works for the American High School* (Houghton Mifflin, 1996); Thomas Sowell, *Inside American Education: The Decline, the Deception, the Dogmas* (Macmillan, 1993); Sandra Stotsky, *Losing Our Language: How Multicultural Classroom Instruction Is Undermining Our Children's Ability to Read, Write, and Reason* (Free Press, 1999); Charles Sykes, *Dumbing Down Our Kids: Why America's Children Feel Good About Themselves but Can't Read, Write, or Add* (St. Martin's Press, 1995); Frederick Wirt, *Schools in Conflict: The Politics of Education* (McCutchan, 1989).

18. One of the best such books on this topic is Alan Sokal and Jean Bricmont, *Fashionable Nonsense: Postmodern Intellectuals: Abuse of Science* (New York: Picador, 1998). The authors have spleen to vent against just about everyone in the academy from the right, to the moderate, to the left. Their point is a sobering one: when ideologies interfere, education ceases. They show that in their specialty, physics, the problem is reaching critical mass.

19. Without delving too far into the political and so stir up a mare's nest, it is important to make a distinction here. Republicans, especially conservative Republicans, are often lumped together with Libertarians. While it's true that the two will find points on which to agree, Libertarians are far more at home with social Democrats than with any type of Republican. Indeed, voting patterns bear out that Libertarians will side more often on more issues with liberal Democrats than with Republicans, save on fiscal issues. There they side with fiscally conservative Republicans. But fiscally conservative Republicans still want government, albeit smaller than the one we now have. Fiscally conservative Republicans may want smaller government, but Libertarians want it microscopic, at least from a funding perspective. As it

touches upon libraries, Libertarians pose a much more formidable threat to librarians than conservative Republicans. The latter wish to maintain the culture that libraries have historically striven to store. Libertarians only want something if you, the individual citizen, wish to fund it personally, not through taxation, but literally through your own funds. For more on this see Lawrence Lessig, *The Future of Ideas: The Fate of the Commons in a Connected World* (New York: Random House, 2001), v–x. See also J. Burnett and Michael Gorman, "The Economic Crisis in Libraries: Causes and Effects," in Richard J. Abel, *Scholarly Publishing: Books, Journals. Publishers and Libraries in the Twentieth Century* (New York: John E. Wiley and Sons, 2002), 260–271.

20. Lessig, 47–48; 70–72. Throughout the Lessig book there is a return to the idea that the more complex the Web becomes, the more ideas it makes available, the less free it will become. While the idea of an Internet tax is dormant at this writing, it would be foolish to think it is a dead issue. See also Siva Vaidhyanathan, *The Anarchist in the Library: How the Clash Between Freedom and Control Is Hacking the Real World and Crashing the System* (New York: Basic Books, 2004). Vaidhyanathan tackles this question throughout but especially in his chapter "The Perfect Library."

21. Apparently public libraries in the UK may well be a thing of the past owing to the Web and other pressures. See Simon Fraser, "Love It or Lose It," *BBC News,* June 29, 2006, http://newsvote.bbc.co.uk/mpapps/pagetools/print/news.bbc.co.uk/1/hi/magazine/5105580 (accessed June 2006).

22. Harold Billings, "The Wild-Card Academic Library 2013," *College and Research Libraries,* March 2003, 105–109. The quote is from p. 109.

23. Michael Gorman makes a similar point in his book, cited above, p. 4. His emphasis is slightly different from my own, however.

24. The quote is from William Y. Arms, a computer guru who is also a putative expert on digital libraries. Arms's view is that libraries have outlived their useful and it's time to move on. See his *Digital Libraries* (Boston: MIT Press, 2001). (The quote may also be found in Gorman, p. 32. Gorman spends several pages effectively debunking Arms's distorted view of traditional libraries.) Other evidence abounds, as in Provost Fred Heath's decision to eliminate 90,000 books at the University of Texas at Austin's undergraduate library, mentioned in the text and cited below. See also Norman D. Stevens, "The Fully Electronic Academic Library," *College and Research Libraries,* January 2006, pp. 5–14. Stevens is of course known for his facetiae, and is pulling a leg here. What dismays, however, is how many academicians will read it as a good thing. At a conference at the University of Clemson in 2000, I argued against the digitization of libraries *in toto,* raising as objections certain obstacles to it we have not yet begun to resolve. My point wasn't that we could not overwhelm these objections eventually but whether we *should.* I was in the minority. Moreover, the biggest proponent was a librarian form the University of Michigan. Finally, consider my poster, "Reasons Why the Internet Is No Substitute for a Library" (see www.winthrop.edu/dacus). Before

selling this poster on my own (there are now more than 3,000 of these posters throughout the world, literally), I offered It to ALA as a poster it could use to raise funds (clearly I was right that it could be used as such). It was not turned down as poorly done, but as "being too negative about automation." Apparently automation is now the new "true believer" religion in my own profession.

25. Andy Burnett, *Libraries, Community, and Technology* (Jefferson, NC: McFarland, 2002), 3, 9.

26. Katherine Mangan, "Packing Up the Books," *Chronicle of Higher Education,* July 1, 2005 (accessed via Lexis-Nexis, December 2005). It's hard to know if this is "news" on the order of the famed one-eyed kitten, or news, in the sense of "we need to move forward with this!"

27. Fred Heath, "Libraries, Information Technology and the Future," *Resource Sharing and Information Networks* 10, no. 1/2 (1995): 1–20.

28. *Ibid.*, 16.

29. Christopher Conkey, "Libraries Beckon, but Stacks of Books Aren't in the Pitch," *Wall Street Journal* CCXLVIII, no. 95 (October 21–22, 2006): A1, A7. To give some idea of the proportion of budgets electronic sources now consume, a few years ago Yale was spending not even half a million on electronic access. Yale spent more than *five million* during its more recent fiscal year. But of course, all this electronic "stuff" is cheaper!

30. Consider what the *New York Times,* which many call the paper of record, ran in response to this story: Ralph Blumenthal, "College Libraries Set Aside Books in Digital Age," *New York Times,* May 14, 2005, late edition (accessed via Lexis-Nexis, December 2005).

31. *Ibid.*

32. Robert Brumfield, "Wireless Technology About to Get a Boost," *eSchool News Online,* www.eschoolnews.com/news/showStoryts.cfm?ArticleID-6063 (accessed January 2006).

33. For a good analysis, see Michael Gorman, "Living and Dying with 'Information': Comments on the Report Buildings, Books, and Bytes," *APLIS* 11, no. 1 (March 1998): 22–28.

34. The evidence of this is everywhere. See my *At the Core of the Problem* (OAS, 2001). Although this deals specifically with the state of Oklahoma, it is easily generalized. For that which reveals the whole depressing general trend see any of the following: E.D Hirsch, *The Schools We Need and Why We Don't Have Them* (Doubleday, 1996); William Kilpatrick, *Why Johnny Can't Tell Right from Wrong* (Simon and Schuster, 1992); Roger Kimball, *Tenured Radicals* (Harper and Row, 1990); Rita Kramer, *Ed School Follies: The Miseducation of America's Teachers* (Free Press, 1991); Diane McGuinness, *Why Our Children Can't Read: And What We Can Do About It* (Free Press, 1997); Sandra Stotsky, *Losing Our Language: How Multicultural Classroom Instruction Is Undermining Our Children's Ability to Read, Write and Reason* (New York: Free Press, 1999).

35. Harvard researcher Sandra Stotsky argues that poor reading comes from poor reading methods and also from the way we teach teachers to teach reading

(i.e., avoid phonic and phoneme awareness). See Sandra Stotsky, "Why American Students Do Not Learn to Read Very Well: The Unintended Consequences of Title II and Teacher Testing," *Third Group Review* 2, no. 2 (May 20, 2006), www.tegr.org/Review/Articles/v012/v2n2.pdf (accessed June 2006). This 37-page report is "must" reading for anyone interested in this subject.

36. See www.education-consumers.com for more information.

37. Jim Milliot, "NEA Finds Rapid Decline in Reading," *Publishers Weekly,* July 12, 2004 (accessed via Lexis-Nexis, December 2005).

38. *Ibid.* Percentages have been rounded up. See also "Pleasure Reading Plunges," *Publishers Weekly,* July 12, 2004 (accessed via Lexis-Nexis, December 2005).

39. National Endowment for the Arts, *Reading at Risk: A Survey of Literary Reading,* Research Division Report #46 (Washington: NEA, 2004), vii.

40. *Ibid.*, ix.

41. Debra Lau Whelan, "Librarians Respond to Decline in Reading," *School Library Journal,* September 1, 2004 (accessed via Lexis-Nexis, December 2005).

42. Mark Bauerlein, "A Very Long Disengagement," *The Chronicle of Higher Education* 52, no. 18 (January 6, 2006): 15–18 (accessed via Lexis-Nexis, January 2006).

43. *Ibid.*

44. See Robert Bellah, *Habits of the Heart: Individualism and Commitment in American Life* (Berkeley: University of California Press, 1985); Quentin J. Schultze, *Habits of the High-Tech Heart: Living Virtuously in the Information Age* (Grand Rapids, MI: Baker Academic, 2002); and Robert D. Putnam, *Bowling Alone: The Collapse and Revival of American Community* (New York: Simon and Schuster, 2000). All three books make very compelling cases that we are becoming a nation of loners — not individuals. This may clash with the current information coming to us that NetGen-ers like to work in groups, but I don't think so. The argument here is not that they are anti-social. Many are quite affable. But this affability is not an enduring cultural trait. They would much rather meet online than in person.

45. Mark Bauerlein, "A Very Long Disengagement," *The Chronicle of Higher Education* 52, no. 18 (January 6, 2006): 15–18 (accessed via Lexis-Nexis, January 2006).

46. John Crace, "Children Are Less Able than They Used to Be," *The Guardian,* January 24, 2006. www.education.guardian.co.uk/cgweekly/story/0,,1692929 52,00.html (accessed January 2006).

47. Only one voice crying in the wilderness: Christina Sommers, *The War Against Boys: How Misguided Feminism Is Harming Our Young Men* (New York: Simon and Schuster, 2000). The irrepressible Sommers points out failings in math and elsewhere and also points to the sad lack of our nation comprehending, much less understanding this risk. The famous Coleman Report worried over this and many other things more than fifty years ago. The change today among young men, however, is stark, so utterly

different from their predecessors that everyone should be taking notice. To be fair, however, I should point out that some complain that we shouldn't care about this intellectual decline in boys. They're just lazy.

48. Richard Whitmire, "Boy Trouble," *The New Republic* 234, no. 4749 (January 23, 2006): 15–18. The article does not address as specifically here the Web issues as others cited, but the trouble is that almost no attention has been paid to this report. Whitmire points out that a search of Lexis-Nexis reveals that only five news stories could be found that even reported the results of this study.

49. Samuel P. Huntington, *The Clash of Cultures and the Remaking of the World Order* (New York: Simon and Schuster, 1996), *sic passim*, but especially chapter 6. Huntington makes clear that we have inherited a global culture so *unlike* all other cultures before it that, as was said of Hamlet, "'since nor the exterior nor the inward man / Resembles that it was....'" Multiple minority groups have emerged that also are victims of poor readings skills. Indeed, bilingual education is so much more abysmal than education for the native-born as to defy belief. Whereas before when non-English speaking peoples came to this country they learned the language via language immersion and so were able to function quite well, programs proliferate to make them comfortable in a language that will doom their success. Language immersion, at least for two decades, was so discredited that it took speakers of English as a second language to beg to have it reapplied, too late, however, to help those "lost" generations. Even though language immersion is back, somewhat, it is still widely fought against, and so non-native English speakers still struggle to learn how to read restaurant menus.

Chapter 1

1. Students in these classes were from all levels, freshmen through seniors. For worries about those not yet in college, see Roger Riddell, "'Wiki' Tests Students Research Skills: 'Information Literacy' Is Key in Dealing with Online Sources," *eSchool Newsonline*, www.eschoolnews.com/news/PFshowstory.cfm?ArticleID=6069.

2. An editorial in *USA Today* broke the original story. See below for other references.

3. Daniel Terdiman, "Tracking Down the *Wikipedia* Prankster," http://news.zdnet.com/2100-9588_22-5996542.html. Of course many other such stories could be mentioned but I cite this one as representative. To present both sides, however, I should add that there are many touting *Wikipedia* as a great resource: Kinley Levack, "If Two Heads Are Better than One, Try 7,000 with *Wikipedia*," *Information Today* 26, no. 4 (April 2003): 112–13; Mick Oleary, "*Wikipedia*: Encyclopedia or Not?" *Information Today* 22, no. 8 (September 2005): 49, 53; Peggy Anne Saltz, "Power to the People: Do It Yourself Content Distribution," *Information Today* 28, no. 6 (June 2005): 36–41. O'Leary makes the important point that most places on the Web are known for their insipidities, not their facts. *Wikipedia* deigns to pass itself off as an encyclo-

pedia and so cannot afford to be wrong. My point is similar but more strident. As a primary information resource nonsense cannot be allowed for any reason. In a print edition of, say, the nature of *Britannica*, it never would.

4. I am referring to James Frey's *Million Little Pieces*, an Oprah Book Club selection that sold well over a million copies. The Web site Smoking Gun first raised the objection that story was not a memoir but a fictional story about addiction and redemption. The Web site's concerns have since brought the book down, but it is still selling well. Indeed, Mr. Frey has a new book on the *New York Times* Bestseller List even as I write this in March 2006.

5. Daniel Terdiman, "Study: *Wikipedia* as Accurate as Britannica," http://news.com.com/Study+*Wikipedia*+as+accurate+as+Britannica/2100-1038_3-5997332.html. The title is disingenuous. The study reveals that *Wikipedia* does not make as many mistakes when tested against *Britannica* on *science* articles. Still, this is something of a relief.

6. Katie Hafner, "Growing *Wikipedia* Revises Its 'Anyone Can Edit' Policy," *New York Times,* June 17, 2006 at www.nytimes.com/2006/06/17/tecnology/17wiki.html (accessed June 2006).

7. Yes, of course Grove's is a putative dictionary, now at 20 volumes. Its size belies its title.

8. Brock Read, "Can *Wikipedia* Ever Make the Grade?" *Chronicle of Higher Education* LIII, no. 10 (October 27, 2006): 31–37.

9. But not always even adults. As the election cycle heats up, many candidates are discovering much to their dismay that their Web-based biographies have been written by their enemies.

10. "Thomas Friedman, author of *The World Is Flat: A Brief History of the Twenty-First Century*." Book-TV, C-Span, March 24, 2006. See also the book cited.

11. Center for Strategic and International Studies and the Global Strategy Institute, *Seven Revolutions*, 2006. See http://www.7revs.org/sevenrevs_content.html for more information. While the Web site will give readers much to think about, those wishing the full impact of this excellent series will have to order the video session for their institutions or campuses.

12. Quoted in Phillip J. Calvert, "Scholarly Misconduct and Misinformation on the World Wide Web," *The Electronic Library* 19, no. 4 (2000): 232.

13. Kenneth Chang, "On Scientific Fakery and the Systems to Catch It," *The New York Times,* October 15, 2002, LE Section F, col. 5, p. 1; "In the Matter of J. Hendrik Schon," *Physicis World,* November 2002, http://physicsweb.org/articles/world/15/11/2.

14. See Joyce Lee Malcolm, "Disarming History," *Reasononline,* March 2003, http://www.reason.com/0303/fe.jm.disarming.shtml (accessed March 2006). The story is an interesting one. Bellesiles argued, contrary to reason, that Colonial America had few guns and most did not use them, implying that our contemporary "worship" of guns comes late. A team of scholars eventually discovered that the research had been cooked. This is a case of "science" bringing to the facts the philosophy it claims the facts presented. The case did take a great deal of time — more than 16

months — before Bellesiles's work proved fraudulent, the book was pulled from Knopf and the prestigious Bancroft Award Bellesiles won was rescinded. The case is not dissimilar to Joseph Ellis at Mount Holyoke, who found that writing award-winning books about Vietnam was not enough. So, he claimed to have been there, and with General William Westmoreland. Ellis's case was not fraudulent Web-based scholarship but a fraudulent persona.

15. Calvert, 233–234.

16. Peter Hernon, "Disinformation and Misinformation through the Internet: Findings of an Exploratory Study," *Government Information Quarterly* 12, no. 2 (1995): 133–9.

17. Amy E. Schwartz, "...And Fools for the Net," *The Washington Post*, April 8, 1997, 15.

18. *Ibid.*

19. Paul S. Piper, "Web Hoaxes, Counterfeit Sites, and Other Spurious Information on the Internet," in *Web of Deception: Misinformation on the Internet*, Anne P. Mintz, ed. (Medford, NJ: CyberAge Books, 2002), 7–8. Fox News also reported the story in January 2002.

20. Eva Perkins, "John Hopkins's Tragedy: Could Librarians Have Prevented a Death?" *Information Today, Inc.*, August 7, 2001, http://www.infotoday.com/newsbreaks/nb010806-1.htm (accessed March 2006). The description which follows comes from this article. See also Susan Levine, "Hopkins Researcher Faulted in Death," *The Washington Post*, July 17, 2001, (accessed via *Lexis-Nexis*, February 2006).

21. See my *Genetic Engineering* (Greenwood Press, 2005).

22. See also Richard Monastersky, "Panel Says South Korean Researcher Fabricated All Cloned Stem-Cell Lines," *Chronicle of Higher Education* 52, no. 20 (January 20, 2006): 23; Lila Guterman, "A Silent Scientist under Fire," *Chronicle of Higher Education* 52, no. 22 (February 3, 2006): 15; Lila Guterman, "The Taint of Misbehavior," *Chronicle of Higher Education* 52, no. 25 (February 24, 2006): 14.

23. Susan M. Detwiler, "Charlatans, Leeches, and Old Wives: Medical Misinformation," in *Web of Deception: Misinformation on the Internet*, Anne P. Mintz, ed. (Medford, NJ: CyberAge Books, 2002), 25.

24. Hasci Horvath, AIDS Heresies: From Maverick Science to Conspiracy Theories," *WebMD*, http://www.cnn.com/HEALTH?AIDS/9909/15/aids.health3/index.html, 3.

25. *Ibid.*, 5.

26. David Wilson, "Pigs Just Won't Fly, No Matter What the Internet Says," *Business Post*, August 28, 2002, 13 (accessed via *Lexis-Nexis*, March 2006).

27. Quoted in Richard Spinello, *CyberEthics: Morality and Law in Cyberspace* (Jones and Bartlett Publishers, 2003), 29.

28. *Ibid.*, 30.

29. Wilson, 2.

30. Robert McChesney, "So Much for the Magic of Technology and the Free Market," in *The World Wide Web and Contemporary Cultural Theory* (New York: Routledge, 2000), 8.

31. *Ibid.*, 28. McChesney argues that the Web has no discernible democracy and so has a weakened claim to one of its highly touted benefits. The Web is closer to a kakistocracy, or mob-rule.

32. MySpace.com is a good case in point. As many parents are sadly learning, young people are putting highly personal, incriminating matters on these spaces. Many comments are of a sexual nature, but some involve underage drinking and illegal drug use. College-age young people are putting up information that business experts argue will damage their future. How can any of this be a good thing?

33. For more on the Web's internecine influence on citizenship, see Vincent Mosco, "Webs of Myth and Power," in *The World Wide Web and Contemporary Cultural Theory* (New York: Routledge, 2000), 38–52. See also Robert Putnam, *Bowling Alone: The Collapse and Revival of the American Community* (New York: Simon and Schuster, 2000).

34. Andrew Shapiro, *The Control Revolution: How the Internet Is Putting Individuals in Charge and Changing the World We Know* (New York: A Century Foundation Book, 1999), ix–x (emphases mine). Shapiro is more sanguine than I about the future of the Web. This is also the theme of Thomas Friedman's *The Earth Is Flat: A Brief History of the Twenty-First Century* (New York: Farrar, Straus and Giroux, 2005).

35. Jodi Dean, "Webs of Conspiracy," in *The World Wide Web and Contemporary Cultural Theory* (New York: Routledge, 2000), 64.

36. For an interesting discussion see Andrew Herman and John Sloop, "Red Alert!" in *The World Wide Web and Contemporary Cultural Theory* (New York: Routledge, 2000), 77–98.

37. Clay Risen, "Degree Burns," *The New Republic* 234, no. 4749 (January 23, 2006): 13–14. I am indebted to my associate dean, Larry Mitlin, for pointing out this reference.

38. *Hate Groups: Opposing Viewpoints*, Mary E. Williams, ed. (San Diego: Greenhaven Press, 2004), 10–12. See also Kevin W. Saunders, *Saving Our Children from the First Amendment* (New York: New York University Press, 2003), 179–197; Anne P. Mintz, "Lies, Damned Lies, and the Internet," in *Web of Deception: Misinformation on the Internet*, Anne P. Mintz, ed. (Medford, NJ: CyberAge Books, 2002), xvi–xix.

39. In *Hate Groups: Opposing Viewpoints*, Mary E. Williams, ed. (San Diego: Greenhaven Press, 2004), 77–78.

40. *Ibid.*, 79. See also United States Senate, *Hate Crimes on the Internet: Hearing Before the Committee on the Judiciary. Ramifications of the Internet on Today's Children, Focusing on the Prevalence of Internet Hate, and Recommendations on How to Shield Children from the Negative Impact of Violent Media*, 106 Congress, First Session (September 14, 1999). Serial no. J-106-48 (Washington: U.S. Government Printing Office, 2001).

41. See Hugh Hewitt, *BLOG: Understanding the Information Reformation That's Changing Your World* (Nashville, TN, 2005), 154–155. Hewitt is very energetic in touting only the benefits of the Web. His book underscores the many good blogs that are out there and offers a list of how many of those are changing the way we see the news. He underscores the value of bloggers in unraveling the Bush National Guard

controversy during the last election. The book is a fine read but it does not take into account (except for the "black blogs") that for every one excellent blog (like Hewitt's own, Glenn Sanders's marvelous *Instapundit*, or Charles Johnson's *Little Green Footballs*) there are scores more that spread hatred like a cancer. See also pages 106–110 of Hewitt's book for more on the better blogs that everyone should read.

42. Spinello, 70.

43. *Ibid.*, 70–71.

44. See Spinello, 71. The selling of swastikas and other objects of racial hatred is outlawed there. The judge in the case ruled that Yahoo! had violated French law on a US Web site that made them available for sale. Yahoo! was ordered to install filtering technology or face a $13,000 a day fine even though it claimed that no such blocking was technically possible. Remailers, discussed in the following paragraph, are also discussed here.

45. Carol Ebbinghouse, "Deliberate Misinformation on the Web!? Tell Me It Ain't So!" *Information Today, Inc.* 8, no. 5 (May 2000): 63 (emphases added) (accessed via *Academic Search Premiere*, March 2006). I use the classifications that appear in this article here. See also her article "Medical and Legal Information," *Searcher* 8, no. 9 (2000): 18–35.

46. National Fraud Information Center, "Internet Scams Fraud Trends, January—December 2005," http://www.fraud.org./internet/internet_scams_half year_2005.pdf.

47. Anne P. Mintz, "Lies, Damned Lies, and the Internet," in *Web of Deception: Misinformation on the Internet,* Anne P. Mintz, ed. (Medford, NJ: CyberAge Books, 2002), xix.

48. Federal Trade Commission, "Cross-Border Fraud Trends, January–December 2004," March 9, 2005, www.ftc.gov/bcp/conline/edscams/crossborder/PDFs/Cross-BorderCY-2004.pdf.

49. Carlos Bergfeld, "Counting Up Click Fraud's Tool," *Business Week Online,* July 7, 2006. http://www.businessweek.com/print/technology/content/ju12006/tc20060707_842584.htm (accessed June 2006).

50. National Fraud Information Center. See also Anne P. Mintz, "Lies, Damned Lies, and the Internet," in *Web of Deception: Misinformation on the Internet,* Anne P. Mintz, ed. (Medford, NJ: CyberAge Books, 2002), xix–xii.

51. Senate Special Committee on Aging, "Prepared Statement of the Federal Trade Commission on Efforts to Fight Fraud on the Internet," March 23, 2005, www.ftc.gov/os/2004/03/bealsfraudtest.pdf. (accessed March 2006).

52. Anne P. Mintz, "Lies, Damned Lies, and the Internet," in *Web of Deception: Misinformation on the Internet,* Anne P. Mintz, ed. (Medford, NJ: CyberAge Books, 2002), xvii. Also in the same book, see Paul S. Piper, "Web Hoaxes, Counterfeit Sites, and Other Spurious Information on the Internet," 9–10. Piper report the number of Internet scams that sprang up after the September 11, 2001, tragedy.

53. Ebinghouse, 64.

54. *Ibid.*, 65.

55. Helene Kasler, "It's a Dangerous World Out There: Misinformation in the Corporate Universe,"

53, and Anne P. Mintz, "Lies, Damned Lies, and the Internet," xviii, in *Web of Deception: Misinformation on the Internet,* Anne P. Mintz, ed. (Medford, NJ: CyberAge Books, 2002).

56. Carol Ebbinghouse, "Medical and Legal Information," *Searcher* 8, no. 9 (2000): 3. See also Susan M. Detwiler, "Charlatans, Leeches, and Old Wives: Medical Misinformation," in *Web of Deception: Misinformation on the Internet,* Anne P. Mintz, ed. (Medford, NJ: CyberAge Books, 2002), 34–38.

57. *Ibid.*, 4. See also note 42. Piper argues there (note 46 above) that medical misinformation on the Web is perhaps the most troublesome information of all.

58. Paul S. Piper, "Better Read That Again: Web Hoaxes and Misinformation," *Searcher,* September 2000, 43.

59. *Ibid.* The Gates sites mentioned in the next sentence also come from this article.

60. See "Cybersquatting: What It Is and What Can Be Done about It," www.nolo.com (accessed March 2006).

61. *Ibid.*

62. Helene Kasler, "It's a Dangerous World Out There: Misinformation in the Corporate Universe," in *Web of Deception: Misinformation on the Internet,* Anne P. Mintz, ed. (Medford, New Jersey: CyberAge Books, 2002), 65. Amazon refunded a total of about $21,000, about $3 per customer, to reestablish its good name. Don't you feel better now?

63. Anne P. Mintz, "Lies, Damned Lies, and the Internet," in *Web of Deception: Misinformation on the Internet,* Anne P. Mintz, ed. (Medford, NJ: CyberAge Books, 2002), xix. The pro-choice group took the pro-life group to court and won easily.

Chapter 2

1. Edward O'Neil, Brian F. Lavoie and Rick Bennett, "Trends in the Evolution of the Web," *D-Lin Magazine* 9, no. 4 (April 2003): 3, www.dlib.org/dlib/april103/lovie/041avoie.html (accessed February 2006).

2. Edward Tenner, "Searching for Dummies," *The New York Times,* March 26, 2006 (accessed via *Lexis-Nexus,* March 2006).

3. "Researchers from 2 Universities Seek Ways to Find Credible Information Online," *Chronicle of Higher Education* LII, no. 31 (April 7, 2006): A44.

4. Chris Sherman and Gary Price, *The Invisible Web: Uncovering Information Sources Search Engines Can't See* (Medford, New Jersey: CyberAge Books, 2001), xv.

5. *Ibid.*, xviv.

6. While it isn't the only such book, the one I cite here (Sherman and Price, *The Invisible Web*) is one of the best on the invisible Web.

7. Sherman and Price, 53.

8. The Web and the Internet are not synonymous though they have become so in common parlance. Rather that try to swim upstream keeping the two separate, I have chosen to use them interchangeably. The Internet is, of course, made up of protocols or rules that let computers "talk" to each other. The Web or

the World Wide Web, on the other hand, is made up of software protocols that run on top of the Internet and that lets users see and access files stored on other computers. For more on this distinction, see Sherman and Price, chapter 1, a book that I cite here extensively.

9. Sherman and Price, 6.

10. Michael Dahn, "Spotlight on the Invisible Web," *Online* 24, no. 4 (July/August 2000): 57.

11. Sherman and Price, 23.

12. I have relied on points made in Sherman and Price, pp. 24–26, but have adapted them for use here.

13. See Bonnie Snow, "The Internet's Hidden Content and How to Find It," *Online* 24, no. 3 (May/June 2000): 61. Snow makes a similar point about the Web.

14. Anne P. Mintz, "Lies, Damned Lies, and the Internet," in *Web of Deception: Misinformation on the Internet,* Anne P. Mintz, ed. (Medford, New Jersey: CyberAge Books, 2002), xxiii.

15. Sherman and Price, 31, 51

16. *Ibid.*, 69.

17. Susan Feldman, "This Is What I Asked For? The Searching Quagmire," in *Web of Deception: Misinformation on the Internet,* Anne P. Mintz, ed. (Medford, New Jersey: CyberAge Books, 2002), 195.

18. Erika Chavez, "Google Bombs: Graffiti or Activism," *Sacramento Bee,* September 30, 2005, A-1ff (accessed via *Lexis-Nexis,* March 2006).

19. Mick O'Leary, "Online Searchers and Online Managers," *Online* 27, no. 6 (November/December 2003): 26–46.

20. Sherman and Price, 35.

21. *Ibid.*, 112. This has to do with the way search engines search for information, for example, the practice of relevancy ranking, wherein a page gets one ranked position in a set of results until it's bumped by something more "relevant" later.

22. See chapter one about the problems with Web-based medical information in general.

23. O'Neill, et al., 4–7.

24. A number of articles treat this phenomenon: Erika Chavez, "Google Bombs: Graffiti or Activism," *Sacramento Bee,* September 30, 2005 (accessed via *Lexis-Nexis,* March 2006); Eugene Wee, "It's a Blast: Google Bombs Subvert the Net to Air Political Views for Just a Laugh," *The Strait Times* (Singapore), January 4, 2004 (accessed via *Lexis-Nexis,* March 2006); John Hiler, "Google Time Bomb: Will Weblogs Blow Up the World's Favorite Search Engine?," http://www.microcontentnews.com/articles/googlebombs.htm; Saul Hansell, "Foes of Bush Enlist Google to Make a Point," *New York Times,* December 8, 2003, www.nytimes.com (accessed March 2006); Neil McIntosh, "Google Bombs Target Failure Bush," January 23, 2004, *Lexis-Nexis* retrieved March 15, 2005 (accessed March 2006); Verne Kopytoff, "Google Targeted by Pranksters; Web Site Operators, Bloggers Skew Results," *The San Francisco Chronicle,* January 26, 2004 (accessed via *Lexis-Nexis,* March 2006).

25. John Hiler, "Google Blogs: How Weblogs Influence a Billion Google Searches a Week," February 22, 2002, http://www.miccrocontentnes.com/articles/googleblogs.htm.

26. For more on this see Mac J. Rosenberg, *E-Learning: Approaches and Technologies to Enhance Organizational Knowledge, Learning, and Performance* (San Francisco: Pfeiffer, 2006), 5–8. Rosenberg, however, does point out the many failings of e-courses and e-learning and why we haven't moved very much father ahead from where we were a decade ago.

27. Susan Feldman, 177.

28. Martin Frank, "Access to the Scientific Literature — A Difficult Balance," *New England Journal of Medicine* 345, no. 15 (April 13, 2006): 1552–1555. I am indebted to my friend Eric Johnson, M.D., for pointing out this article.

29. Unfortunately this very valuable Web site is undergoing a 50 percent reduction in funds and its existence on the Web is anything but certain.

30. See Sherman and Price, 96–103, for these and many others.

31. See Francine Egger-Sider, "Beyond Google: The Invisible Web in the Academic Library," *Journal of Academic Librarianship* 30, no. 4 (July 2004): 265–269.

32. Chris Sherman and Gary Price, "The Invisible Web: Uncovering Sources Search Engines Can't See," *Library Trends* 52, no. 2 (Fall 2003): 283. This article was adapted from their book by the same title. (Emphases in the original.)

33. *Ibid.*, 286.

34. *Ibid.*, 291.

35. The announcement came to me in an e-mail during the week of 11 April 2006.

36. While admittedly far afield, consider the problem of welfare. If one can make more money by collecting it than one can by working, why would anyone want to work? One does not have to be a genius — or a liberal or a conservative — to see that such unintended consequences are almost impossible to overcome.

37. See David Kohl, "Where's the Library?" *Journal of Academic Librarianship* 32, no. 2 (March 2006): 117–118.

Chapter 3

1. In order to discuss this chapter in a manner that portrays accurately the nature of this beast, it is necessary to bring before the reading public matters that some will find offensive. Those who feel this way should skip this chapter.

2. The phrase "wall of separation" is nowhere to be found in the Constitution. It comes from a letter Thomas Jefferson wrote to Anabaptists in Danbury, Connecticut. Not only did Jefferson write this about a specific matter, but he approved himself the use of federal funds to proselytize Native Americans. To argue today that Jefferson meant there to be a literal or even metaphorical "wall" is to rely on, in Einstein's fine phrase, a "montage of tropes." Clearly, Jefferson cannot be considered religious in the definitions we use today. Jefferson was a deist at best and denied the deity of Christ, a point of view that would not sit well with any religious conservatives I know. But he also did not mean to favor or create our current alienation of religion from government, or anything government does.

Jefferson would not have favored the "naked public square" (to use a phrase Richard John Neuhaus made famous by a book of the same title) we have erected today where pornography is tolerated and religion excoriated in the public market place (and both to the public's peril).

3. Movie critic Michael Medved has discussed this oddity. G-rated movies do two and three times better at the box office than PG, PG-13, R or NC-17 movies. Yet producers make five or even six times as many of the PG, PG-13, R and NC-17 movies than the G-rated ones that earn so much more money.

4. The story is repeated in Siva Vaidhyanathan, *The Anarchist in the Library: How the Clash between Freedom and Control Is Hacking the Real World and Crashing the System* (New York: Basic Books, 2004), 25.

5. Jerry Ropelato, "Internet Pornography Statistics," http://internet-filter-review.toptenreviews.com/internet-pornography-statistics.html (accessed April 2006). All statistics are from this source unless otherwise noted.

6. Some of the best books for discussing the philosophical underpinnings of pornography and its deleterious effects on all of society are as follows: Robert P. George, *The Clash of Orthodoxies: Law, Religion, and Morality in Crisis* (Wilmington, Del.: ISI Books, 2001); Pamela Paul, *Pornified: How Pornography Is Transforming Our Lives, Our Relationships, and Our Families* (New York: Times Books, 2005); Roger Shattuck, *Forbidden Knowledge: From Prometheus to Pornography* (San Diego: Harcourt Brace, 1997); United States House of Representatives, Committee on Energy and Commerce, Subcommittee on Commerce Trade, and Consumer Protection, *Online Pornography: Closing the Door on Smut: Hearing before the Subcommittee on Commerce, Trade, and Consumer Protection of the Committee on Energy and Commerce, House of Representatives*, One Hundred Eight Congress, Second Session, May 6, 2004 (Washington: U.S. Government Printing Office, 2004). Paul's book is good because Paul is herself a First Amendment die-hard and a *Times* reporter. Shattuck's thesis is that there are things that we can do that we should not, and no better example exists than the widespread availaby of pornography. That is, just because we *can* do something doesn't mean we *should*.

7. Other sources indicate that in 2005, almost 75 percent of searches worldwide were for pornographic material.

8. House of Representatives, *Stumbling onto Smut: The Alarming Ease of Access to Pornography on Peer-to-Peer Networks: Hearing before the Committee on Government Reform*, House of Representatives, 108th Congress, March 13, 2003, 1. KaZaA and Gnutella are two of many file sharing sites. Others include Morpheus, BearShare and Grokster.

9. *Ibid.*, 26. Interestingly, MediaDefender is not itself able to visually verify the child pornography since that would be illegal, another case where our laws favor criminals. See page 59 of this same report.

10. *Ibid.*, 29.

11. *Ibid.*, 41.

12. *Ibid.*, 49.

13. *Ibid.*, 2.

14. Dorothy Field, "Pornography? Not in Our Library!" *American Libraries,* November 1997, 63.

15. Gary Dean, "Public Libraries, Pornography, and the Damage Done: A Case Study," *Library Administration and Management* 18, no. 1 (Winter 2004): 8–13. The case study is of Canada's (once) most respected public library system. See also David Isaacson, "Discriminating Librarians," *Library Journal* 125, no. 19 (November 2005): 40–41. Isaacson is a strong proponent of free speech yet strongly desires to eliminate smut. Bear in mind that none of what is talked about in this chapter would *ever* appear in libraries in *print*; hence, my contention that because it is delivered over the Web, librarians now act differently about selection and collection development practices.

16. Juris Dilevko and Lisa Gottlieb, "Selection and Cataloging of Adult Pornography Web Sites for Academic Libraries," *Journal of Academic Librarianship* 30, no. 1: 36–50. In what appears to be an if-you-can't-lick-them-join-them approach, the authors argue that cataloging according to genre (oral, anal, bestiality, erotic asphyxiation, etc.) would be a step forward since pornography is now being studied in some universities. Besides, they argue, pornography is a social construct. See page 44 ff, especially.

17. The story was reported by Fox News during the month of May 2006. See also Michael Beder and Steven Giegerich, "Teachers Are Disciplined over Attack on Girl, 8," *St. Louis Post-Dispatch,* May 9, 2006, www.stltoday.com/stltoday/news/stories.nsf/stlouiscitycounty/story/19EFF0B6B6657328625716A00180C4B?OpenDocument (accessed May 2006).

18. House of Representatives, *Stumbling onto Smut,* 67.

19. For example, in the case of alar, a public "menace" that brought the likes of Meryl Streep to Washington to testify, an individual had to eat 70 alar-treated apples *every day* for *seventy years* to ingest enough of the putative carcinogen to make it dangerous. Of course alar-treated apples were removed from shelves, all but destroying the apple industry for one year. Contrast that with our tolerance of pornography.

20. Various estimates place libraries as providing 30–35 percent of all other online access outside the home. No other online access comes close for those who do not have Internet access in the home.

21. While this chapter is not the place to argue the merits and defects of filtering, I do want to refer to a recent report: Marjorie Heins, Christina Cho and Ariel Feldman, *Internet Filters: A Public Policy Report,* Free Expression Policy Report, 2nd ed. (Brennan Center for Justice, 2006), available at www.fepproject.org (accessed May 2006). The authors are eager to debunk filters of all kinds but put forward the same tiresome arguments: that filters do not work 100 percent of the time, all the time. Imagine if this standard were used to assess Google's searching ability, when it searches only 40 percent of the Web. Over- and under-blocking complaints are lodged, as are sites that filters overlook or block and at precisely the wrong times. But even the authors are forced to admit that these failures are rare and happen in only a small percentage of

the total. My contention about filters is that we hold them to a standard of functionality and conditions that we do not require of any other software. This is disingenuous at best, mendacious at worst. See for example page 26 of the report where, horror of all horrors, one filter blocked searches on eating disorders. Stop the presses! The authors worry about children who need this information while they are ostensibly oblivious to those millions of other children put at risk owing to the ubiquity of pornography. This is straining at a gnat while swallowing a camel.

22. Numerous places are available to view a discussion of *Miller*. See Richard A. Spinello, *CyberEthics: Morality and Law in Cyberspace* (Boston: Jones and Bartlett Publishers, 2003), 56 ff.

23. *Ibid.*

24. *Ibid.*, 57–58.

25. For example, one Web site, the Sexy Librarian, has made available nude women holding books or even shelving. Another site shows women in nun's habits engaging in sex of various kinds. The list could go on and on but the underlying theme is exclusively prurient interests.

26. Dick Thornburgh and Herbert S. Lin, eds., *Youth, Pornography and the Internet* (Washington, D.C.: National Academy Press, 2002), 4–12.

27. The literature speaks of both CHIPA and CIPA as proper acronyms for the Children's Internet Protection Act. The FCC refers to the act as CHIPA but others writing about it refer to it as CIPA. For more on this burning question see Jim Tyre, "The (Not So) Great Debate: Is It CHIPA or CIPA?" http://censoreware.net/articles/01/05/18/0522238.shtml (accessed May 2006). CIPA is codified at 20 U.S.C. 9134 (2001) and 47 U.S.C 254(h) (2001) while COPA is codified at 47 U.S.C. 213 (1999).

28. Thornburgh and Lin, 4–15.

29. Minow and Lipinski, 135.

30. Jonathan Bick, "Surfing at the Library Could Get Less Restrictive," *New Jersey Law Journal,* January 30, 2006 (accessed via Lexis-Nexis, April 2006)

31. Thornburgh and Lin, 4–17. See also South Carolina State Budget and Control Board, *A Report to the Legislature: Evaluation of Pilot Programs to Assess the Feasibility of Installing Internet Filtering Software in Public Schools, Public Libraries or Institutions,* December 1, 2001, 3 ff.

32. *Ibid.*, 10–4.

33. Lawrence Lessig, *The Future of Ideas: The Fate of the Commons in a Connected World* (New York: Random House, 2001), 184.

34. *Ibid.*

35. This is not merely hyperbole or simply a meaningless statement. The pornography on the Web is unbelievable. At the risk of sickening some, it's important to understand what we are talking about. Some I fear think that "pornography" means something like *Playboy* in the fifties. A random search of pornographic sites reveal (no pun intended) women eating feces, women urinating (on themselves and others), oral and anal sex, the same *with animals,* photographs of what appear to be speculum-like exams, snowballing (you'll have to look that one up), necrophilia (ostensibly simulated), incest, rape, all sorts of ostensibly

non-consensual sex, and the saddest, most cruel photographs inflicted on humans I've ever seen. (I have never viewed child porn but of course we know that is there as well.) It is inconceivable, not only that such things are done, but that we as a nation equivocate about putting an end to it. And remember, this is what I found without trying. All of these examples have been judged obscene by some jury somewhere in this country. Still, all of it persists on the Web. See Mary Minow and Tomas A. Lipinski, *The Library's Legal Answer Book* (Chicago: American Library Association, 2003), 128.

36. Kevin Saunders, *Saving Our Children from the First Amendment* (New York: New York University Press, 2003), 169.

37. COPA, Section 213, no. 1, www.epic.org/free_speech/censorship/copa.html (accessed June 2006). Also quoted in Saunders, 169.

38. Spinello, 60.

39. Thornburgh and Lin, xiii. For much of the same kinds of information, see David Burt, *Dangerous Access 2000 Edition: Uncovering Internet Pornography in America's Libraries* (Washington, D.C.: Family Research Council, 2000), 5–7, 23–27.

40. Thornburgh and Lin, ES-3.

41. Rebecca Hagelin, "Porn, Pedophiles, Our Kids and MySpace," www.townhall.com/opinion/columns/rebeccahagelin/2006/05/30/199114.html (accessed June 2006).

42. Stephanie Dunnewind, "Schools Trying to Prevent Harassment in Cyberspace," *The Seattle Times,* October 17, 2006, http://seattletimes.nwsource.com/html/living/2003292713_schoolspace07.html.

43. See United States National Commission on Excellence in Education, *A Nation at Risk.* Although the report is now nearly a quarter of a century old, its argument, that we are in a "rising tide of mediocrity," has, sadly, yet to be reversed.

44. For a good and complete discussion of this fear, see Kevin Saunders, *Saving Our Children from the First Amendment* (New York: New York University Press, 2003), 2–5, 50–51, 114–115.

45. Saunders, 164–166.

46. For a similar discussion, see Siva Viadhyanathan, *The Anarchist in the Library: How the Clash Between Freedom and Control Is Hacking the Real World and Crashing the System* (New York: Basic Books, 2001), 26–28.

47. Derek Law, "Parlor Games: The Real Nature of the Internet," www.uksg.org/serials/law.asp (accessed January 2006).

48. Katie Hafner and Matt Richtel, "Google Resists U.S. Subpoena of Search Data," *New York Times,* January 20, 2006, www.nytimes.com/2006/01/20technology/20google.html (accessed January 2006). (Registration required.)

49. Justice Douglas's words are from *Griswold vs. Connecticut,* and run thusly: "specific apparatus in the Bill of Rights have penumbras, found by emanations from those guarantees that help give them life and substance." No better example of a circular argument exists. There are these coruscations from the Bill of Rights, and it is the shadows emanating from them that give substance and life to the apparatus that we

think we see there. As Gertrude Stein once said, there is no there, there.

50. See note 13.

51. Saunders, 132.

52. Thornburgh and Lin, 5–1.

53. Saunders, 128.

54. Thornburgh and Lin, 5–17.

55. *Ibid.*

56. Jerry Ropelato, "Tricks Pornographers Play," http://internet-filter-review.toptenreviews.com/tricks-pornographers-play.html (accessed May 2006).

57. *Ibid.* This has since been corrected.

58. *Ibid.* All of these have since been corrected, too.

59. *Ibid.*

60. The pop-ups themselves are invidious as they generally run through a series of photos, first of nude women, then women engaged in various forms of sexual intercourse (oral, anal, etc.). The idea appears to be, "Does this interest you? Does this? How about this?"

61. Ropelato.

62. *Ibid.*

63. *Ibid.*

64. Thornburg and Lin, 5–18.

65. *Ibid.*, 7–18.

66. Attorney General's Commission on Pornography, *Final Report,* 1986 (Washington, D.C.: U.S. Government Printing Office, July 1986). Closing statements of the Meese Commission's final report. Also quoted in Thornburg and Lin, 7–17.

67. Robert S. Peck, *The First Amendment and Cyberspace: What You Need to Know* (Chicago: American Library Association, 2000), x.

68. *Ibid.*, 30.

69. Frederick Stielow, "Reconsidering Arsenals of a Democratic Culture," in *Libraries and Democracy: The Cornerstone of Liberty*, ed. N. Kranich (Chicago: American Library Association, 2001), 9.

70. *Ibid.*, 91.

71. House of Representatives, *Stumbling onto Smut: The Alarming Ease of Access to Pornography on Peer-to-Peer Networks*, 105.

Chapter 4

1. Sir Walter Scott, *The Antiquary* (New York: Macmillan, 1895), 43.

2. Anthony Grafton, *The Footnote: A Curious History* (Cambridge, MA: Harvard University Press, 1997).

3. See, for example, Grafton, above, 1–2.

4. *Ibid.*, 8.

5. For the so-called "hybrid" collections, see Mark Rowse, "The Hybrid Environment: Electronic-Only versus Print Retention," *Against the Grain,* April 2003, 24–28. The problem of lost titles is this: an aggregate database can contain 100 titles in September and 100 in May. The trouble is they are not the *same* 100 titles. Many libraries come to know about these lost or vanishing titles only after patrons come to them complaining that what they saw last month isn't there this month. For more, see later in this chapter.

6. Andrea L. Foster, "Elsevier's Vanishing Act: To the Dismay of Scholars, the Publishing Giant Quietly Purges Articles from Its Database," *The Chronicle of Higher Education,* January 10, 2003 (accessed via *Lexis-Nexis* May 2006). In this case, the article may have been pilfered, but Elsevier removed it without warning or explanation. It represents yet one more "Catch-22" in the e-world. Scholars often complain there is no "digital" trail, and cases like this to explain why.

7. Carol Tenopir, "Disappearing Databases," *Library Journal* 127, no. 20 (December 2002): 38. Tenopir raises another issue with respect to a once regnant vendor, in this case Dialog, slowly becoming less and less a factor in the e-delivery, as format, delivery, etc., passed them by. Who's to say this will not happen in five or ten years with many other vendors?

8. Michael Bugeja and Daniela V. Dimitrova, "The Half-Life of Phenomenon: Eroding Citations in Journals," *The Serials Librarian* 49, no. 3: 117.

9. Scott Carlson, "Scholars Note the Decay of Citation to Online References," *The Chronicle of Higher Education,* March 18, 2005, A30. Also cited in Bujega and Dimitrova.

10. Bugeja and Dimitrova, 121–122.

11. Some experts claim re-mastering is required every *three* years.

12. For more on the elusive paperless society see Michael Gorman, *Our Own Selves: More Meditations for Librarians* (Chicago: American Library Association, 2005), 137–138.

13. Michael Gorman, *The Enduring Library: Technology, Tradition, and the Quest for Balance* (Chicago: American Library Association, 2003), 114–116; Richard Abel, "The Change of Book and Journal Infrastructure: Two Publishers, Consolidation, and Niche Publishing," in *Scholarly Publishing: Books, Journals, Publishers and Libraries in the Twentieth Century* (New York: John Wiley and Sons, 2002); Stephanie Oda, "Growth and Change in Trade Book Publishing: What I Learned from the Numbers," in *Scholarly Publishing: Books, Journals, Publishers and Libraries in the Twentieth Century* (New York: John Wiley and Sons, 2002).

14. For a similar point made in a different manner, see Shelley Phipps, "Rafting the Rapids 2005: Searching for Our Future Purpose," *College and Research Library News,* February 2005, 114–117.

15. Scott Carlson, "Library Construction Focuses More on Books than on Technology, Study Finds," *Chronicle of Higher Education,* December 19, 2003, 33.

16. Ken Wissoker, "Scholarly Monographs Are Flourishing," *Chronicle of Higher Education,* September 12, 1997, B4 ff; Stephanie Oda, "Growth and Change in Trade Book Publishing: What I Learned from the Numbers," in *Scholarly Publishing: Books, Journals, Publishers and Libraries in the Twentieth Century* (New York: John Wiley and Sons, 2002).

17. It should be pointed out here that companies like Questia *rely* on large libraries remaining around for the foreseeable future, otherwise their plan would not work. Even if Questia and others were able to produce e-braries of 100,000 or more texts, these would only represent a very small percentage of the total available. Many who might use an e-brary to find

citations, Google included, would repair to a library to find the actual text.

18. Wissoker, B4.

19. Scott Carlson, "Do Libraries Really Need Books?" *Chronicle of Higher Education,* July 12, 2002, 31.

20. Scott Carlson, "Students and Faculty Members Turn First to Online Library Materials, Study Finds," *Chronicle Of Higher Education,* October 18, 2002, 37.

21. I add libraries as becoming a thing of the past because the present culture argues that *place* is no longer important. The electronic medium is about no place. Libraries, having been about ownership and therefore place for most of their history, are in contradistinction to the e-culture they now serve. Marrying the two may be as likely as the proverbial "friendly" divorce.

22. Op. cit.

23. Karen J. Winkler, "Academic Presses Look to the Internet to Save Scholarly Monographs," *Chronicle of Higher Education,* September 12, 1997, A18.

24. Susan Lyons, "Persistent Identification of Electronic Documents and the Future of Footnotes," *Law Library Journal* 97, no. 4 (Fall 2005), 681 (accessed via Lexis-Nexis May 2006).

25. *Ibid.,* 681.

26. *Ibid.,* 683.

27. Scott Carlson, "Here Today, Gone Tomorrow. Studying How Online Footnotes Vanish," *Chronicle of Higher Education,* April 30, 2004, A33. Also cited in Lyons.

28. Lyons, 686.

29. Every effort has been made in this book to cite a paper document source, but that has not always been possible.

30. While the following discussion is not meant to be a complete explanation — the matter is complex — it provides a workable thumbnail sketch of PURLs.

31. See Keith Shafer, Stuart Weibel, Erik Jul and Jon Fausey, "Introduction to Persistent Uniform Resource Locators," http://purl.oclc.org/docs/inet 96.html (accessed June 2006). Lyons, 689, cites in footnote 41 the summary version of this document and so has a different order of authors.

32. For example, the library where I work uses Innovative Interfaces (III) as its automated system. III produces a report on PURLS that our technical services staff must check regularly.

33. Shafer et al., 2.

34. Shafer et al., 1.

35. Not everyone agrees that paper is, or should be, the "gold standard." For example, see Mary Rumsey, "Paper versus Electronic Sources for Law Review Cite Checking: Should Paper be the Gold Standard," *Law Library Review* 97, no. 1 (January 2005): 31–48. Rumsey bemoans the fact that many law review editors make staff members check electronic citations before publication. Rumsey thinks that this practice should cease. Obviously, I disagree with Rumsey as I do not think electronic materials a medium stable enough to rely upon so far. Thankfully, as Rumsey points out, the *Bluebook* editors were planning at the time of the publication of her article to retain the "paper only" rule.

36. Carlson, "Scholars Note 'Decay' of Citation to Online References," 30.

37. For more on the South Sea Bubble, one of the grandest and intriguing crashes of any stock market, see Charles Mackay, *Extraordinary Popular Delusions and the Madness of Crowds* (London: Richard Bentley, New Burlington Street, 1841), 46–88. It is most instructive about the natural human tendency to hyperbolize almost any potential business venture.

38. Susan Davis Herring, "Use of Electronic Resources in Scholarly Electronic Journals: A Citation Analysis," *College and Research Libraries* 63, no. 4 (July 2002): 334. (The authors are not related.)

39. *Ibid.,* 336.

40. Carol Tenopir, "Electronic Publishing: Research Issues for Academic Libraries and Users," *Library Trends* 51, no. 4 (Spring 2003): 614.

41. *Ibid.,* 632.

42. Jia Mi and Nesta Frederick, "The Missing Link: Context Loss in Online Databases," *The Journal of Academic Librarianship* 31, no. 6: 578.

43. Tony McSeán, "Research Libraries and Journal Publishers: A Marriage in Trouble which Both Sides Would Like to Save," *Logos* 16, no. 1 (2005): 27, 29.

44. Rosemary Streatfield and Darlene Hildebrandt, "Special Issues in the Sciences: The Case of Bibliographic Access," *The Journal of Academic Librarianship* 27, no. 5 (September 2001): 399.

45. Sam Brooks, "Academic Journal Embargoes and Full Text Databases," *The Library Quarterly* 73, no. 3 (July 2003): 243–260.

46. The whole point of Brooks's article, above, is to defend publishers' embargoes, a view I do not entirely share.

47. It should be added that while ARTstor and JSTOR are marvelous electronic sources that avoid many of the frustrations mentioned here, they are hardly purchases all libraries can afford to make (one-time membership fees for *each* for a college or university of 6,000 FTE students is $49,000). As we wade deeper into cyberspace, they may well become purchases libraries of *any* size can ill afford to be without.

48. For more on this, see Alexandra de Luise, "Full Text or Not? All Illustrations or Not?" *Art Documentation* 22, no. 2 (2003): 20–5.

49. For more on LOCKSS and other possible solutions, see Nia Butkovitch, "Libraries in Transition: Impact of Print and Electronic Journal Access," *Against the Grain* 15, no. 2 (April 2003): 32–24.

Chapter 5

1. For more on BackRub see Google Corporate Information, "Google Milestones," n.d., www.google.com/corporate/histor1.html (accessed February 2006). Some readers may object that Google is being picked on throughout this book but it isn't Google, per se, but any entity in which all the digitization eggs are placed in only one virtual basket. So far, only Google holds that basket.

2. *Ibid.*

3. The phrase is Michael Novak's. For more on

democratic capitalism see his *The Spirit of Democratic Capitalism* (New York: Simon and Schuster, 1982).

4. I suppose this should be called the G-6 with the addition of the University of California. See the next note. Others come on board as this goes to press.

5. For the Stanford addition, see Scott Carlson, "U. of California Is in Talks to Join Google's Library Scanning Project," *Chronicle of Higher Education* LII, no. 49 (August 11, 2006): A29.

6. For more on open access and its related subjects, and for a more hopeful view than my own, see William S. Arms, "Automated Digital Libraries: How Effectively Can Computers Be Used for the Skilled Tasks of Professional Librarianship?" *D-Lib Magazine* 6, no. 7/8 (July/August 2000), http://dlib.org/dlib/july00/arms/07arms.html (accessed April 2006). Arms is hopeful about digital libraries but admits they will come at the expense, even the disarming, of traditional ones. The Newman Project may well provide a new model for Open Access or Open Content to work, or to work better than it has so far. The idea is to scan millions of books in the public domain as soon as possible by working with libraries. See Jonathan Bengston, "The Birth of the Universal Library," *NetConnect Library Journal*, April 15, 2006, http://www.library journal.com/article/CA6322017.html (accessed June 2006).

7. For one of the best and most honest looks at the nuts and bolts of a digitization project, see Eileen Mathias, "Anatomy of a Digitization Project," *Netconnect*, Winter 2004, 2–7. Mathias raises many of the same concerns that I raise here.

8. This chapter is not meant to be a "how-to" chapter for those interested in creating a digital library. For the how-to part there are a number of texts cited in these notes for the wary but interested to pursue. This chapter raises questions about the rush to digitization and whether we have the will, the way and the resources required to make it work.

9. My apologizes to William F. Buckley Jr., who used the phrase far more appositely with respect to turning the tide of history from its mad dash to Marxist-cum-Leninism from democratic capitalism.

10. Anjana Bhatnager, "Digitization in Academic Libraries," *Information Studies* 12, no. 1 (January 2006): 35.

11. Quoted in Bhatnager, 36. See also D. Lee Stuart, *Digital Imaging: A Practical Handbook* (New York: Neal-Schuman Publishers, 2001), 3.

12. This is an overly generous number of years. See below.

13. The story is retold in Lorna Hughes, *Digitizing Collections: Strategic Issues for the Information Manager* (London: Facet Publishing, 2004), 35.

14. Bob Thompson, "Search Me?" *Washington Post*, August 13, 2006, D01.

15. For more on the opt-in versus the opt-out argument, see Trudi Bellardo Hahn, "Impacts of Mass Digitization Projects on Libraries and Information Policy," ASIS&T *Bulletin*, October/November 2006, www.asis.org/Bulletin/Oct-06/hahn.html (accessed October 2006).

16. *Op cit.* Thompson reports that many publishers see this not as an altruistic venture on Google's part, but a money-maker even larger than Google is now. The "pay-per-view" is my own worry.

17. Trudy Levy, "Managing a Digitization Project," *Visual Resources Association Bulletin* 31, no. 2 (Winter 2005): 36.

18. U.S. National Commission on Libraries and Information Science (NCLIS), *Mass Digitization: Implications for Information Policy,* Report from "Scholarship and Libraries in Transition: A Dialogue about the Impacts of Mass Digitization Projects," March 9, 2006, symposium held on March 10–11, 2006 (University of Michigan, Ann Arbor), 16. The concern is a widely held one, too.

19. Bhatnager, 37–39. See also Hughes, 189–193; Stuart, 46- 48, 116–126; Stephen Chapman, "Techniques for Creating Sustainable Digital Collections," *Library Technology Reports,* September–October 2004, 18.

20. For more on this, see also Anne R. Kenney, "Digital Benchmarking for Conversion Access," in *Moving Theory into Practice: Digital Imaging for Libraries and Archives,* Anne R. Kenney and Oya Y Rieger, eds. (Mountain View, CA: Research Libraries Group, 2000), 54; Jill Marie Koelling, *Digital Imaging: A Practical Approach* (Walnut Creek, CA: AltaMira Press, 2004), 3–4.

21. JPEG 2000, a dynamic JPEG delivery that allows for rotating, zooming and panning images, is yet another format that could become more widespread if adopted. It has still not caught on everywhere though it is increasingly more common. Adoption of JEPG 2000 as a standard format would create new and different issues. See Chapman, 58–59.

22. *Ibid.*, 50.

23. See my *Genetic Engineering* (Greenwood Press, 2006) for more.

24. See, for example, Anne R. Kenney and Oya Y. Rieger, "Moving Theory into Practice," in *Moving Theory into Practice: Digital Imaging for Libraries and Archives,* Anne R. Kenney and Oya Y. Rieger, eds. (Mountain View, CA: Research Libraries Group, 2000), 2–3; Stephen Chapman, "Techniques for Creating Sustainable Digital Collections," *Library Technology Reports,* September–October 2004, 10; Lynn Silipigni Connaway, Edward T. O'Neill, and Chandra Prabha, "Last Copies: What's at Risk?" *College and Research Libraries,* July 2006, 370–379. This article is especially important because the authors address last copies, and their fugacious fate, in light of mass digitization projects.

25. Levy, 50–53.

26. *Ibid.* Stuart also points out this problem (78–82).

27. See Hughes, 155.

28. *Ibid.*, 53–54. See also Anne R. Kenney, "Digital Benchmarking for Conversion Access," in *Moving Theory into Practice: Digital Imaging for Libraries and Archives,* Anne R. Kenney and Oya Y. Rieger, eds. (Mountain View, CA: Research Libraries Group, 2000), 42–46; Jill Marie Koelling, *Digital Imaging: A Practical Approach* (Walnut Creek, CA: AltaMira Press, 2004), 1.

29. See Levy's checklist of outsourcing concerns and questions (62). See also Stuart, 130–136; Koelling, 18–20.

30. See Stuart, 6–7. Stuart says that "one of the hard facts of digitization that needs to be confronted early on is that it is extremely expensive to undertake." To be fair, Stuart is also forthcoming on the advantages of digitization, 22–23.

31. Levy offers very useful formulae (59–60). See also Stuart, 92–98.

32. Bhatnager, 42.

33. Stuart, 138. Stuart also goes on to say that the "commonly held views on the throughput of OCR are often widely optimistic." This could well be a descriptive sentence for the enterprise called mass digitization!

34. For more see Stuart, 139–148. See also U.S. National Commission on Libraries and Information Science (NCLIS), *Mass Digitization: Implications for Information Policy,* 3, 7–11. See also Paula deStefano, "Selection for Digital Conversion," in *Moving Theory into Practice: Digital Imaging for Libraries and Archives,* Anne R. Kenney and Oya Y Rieger, eds. (Mountain View, CA: Research Libraries Group, 2000), 11–13; Koelling, 23–24.

35. See, for example, the controversy at the University of California at San Diego and Cornell where the Association of American Publishers has been challenging e-reserves and leading to a possible litigation controversy. The argument in both cases has to do with AAP's contention that e-reserves mimic course packs. Most libraries with which I am familiar have some level of e-reserves, most of them linking to full-text databases, the safest way. But many others scan articles and "lock" them under certain areas on the college or university's intranet. While the case is still under review, it deserves notice with respect to the conversation about digitization and copyright. See Andrew Albanese, "Battle Brews over E-Reserves," *Library Journal,* May 15, 2005, http://www.library journal.com/article/CA601047.html (accessed August 2006). The Cornell matter was referred to me via e-mail.

36. For more on the Tasini problem, see *New York Times Co. v. Tasini (00-2-1)* 533 U.S. 483 (2001), 206F.3d 161, affirmed, http://supct.law.cornell.edu/supct/html/00-201.ZS.html (accessed September 2006).

37. Another personal example. While searching for something on the Web I saw my name and did not recognize the associated Web site. I clicked on the site and, lo and behold, there was one of my articles on the site, for which I had not given permission.

38. Claudia Perry, "Education for Digitization: How Do We Prepare?" *The Journal of Academic Librarianship* 31, no. 6: 524. See also Anne R. Kenney and Oya Y. Rieger, "Moving Theory into Practice," 6.

39. *Ibid.,* 528–529. Perry offers online examples, workshops and courses (and where offered) for those interested.

40. For the necessity of quality control, see Jenn Riley and Kurt Whitsel, "Practical Quality Control Procedures for Digital Imaging Projects," *OCLC Systems and Services International Digital Library Perspectives* 21, no. 1: 48–8. See also Stuart, 42–45. See also Oya Y. Reiger, "Establishing a Quality Control Program," in *Moving Theory into Practice: Digital Imaging for Libraries and Archives,* Anne R. Kenney and

Oya Y. Rieger, eds. (Mountain View, CA: Research Libraries Group, 2000), 61–82.

41. *Ibid.,* 42.

42. See Stuart (103–106) for more on the importance of metadata and the concerns that it raises. See also Carl Lagoze and Sandra Payette, "Metadata: Principles, Practices, and Challenges," in *Moving Theory into Practice: Digital Imaging for Libraries and Archives,* Anne R. Kenney and Oya Y Rieger, eds. (Mountain View, CA: Research Libraries Group, 2000), 84–104.

43. See Richard A. Lanham, "What Is Happening to the Book?" in *Development of Digital Libraries: An American Perspective,* Danna B. Marcum, ed. (Westport, CT: Greenwood Press: 2001), 41–42.

44. John Markoff, "Robots Digitizing Libraries: New Technology Helps Turn Books into Images," *New York Times,* May 19, 2003, SFgate.com, http://sfgate.com/cbi-bin-article.cgi?file=c/a/2003/05/19/BUS5255 (accessed May 2006).

45. *Ibid.*

46. Stuart D. Lee, "Digitization: Is It Worth It?" *Computers in Libraries* 21, no. 5: 30.

47. Although the issue of rescanning is only alluded to here, it is a major issue when it comes to the cost of digitization, as scanned images do not last forever. For a chilling case-in-point see Deborah Woodyard, "Refreshing: Lessons Learned in a Library," in *Moving Theory into Practice: Digital Imaging for Libraries and Archives,* Anne R. Kenney and Oya Y Rieger, eds. (Mountain View, CA: Research Libraries Group, 2000), 147–148.

48. Marie Kennedy, "Reformatting Preservation Departments: The Effect of Digitization on Workload and Staff," *College and Research Libraries* 166, no. 5 (November 2005): 544.

49. *Ibid.,* 546.

50. *Ibid.,* 550–551.

51. Marcum writes best about the requirements of any digital project, and they strike me as also many of the obstacles that face us in all of the mass digitization projects to date: integrity, completeness, accuracy, and usability. See Deanna B. Marcum, "Government Records in a Digital World," in *Development of Digital Libraries: An American Perspective,* Deanna B. Marcum, ed. (Westport, CT: Greenwood Press, 2001), 179–182.

52. Lorna M. Hughes, *Digitizing Collections: Strategic Issues for the Information Manager* (London: Facet Publishing, 2004), 7.

53. Jeffrey Young, "Book 2.0: Scholars Turn Monographs into Digital Conversations," *Chronicle of Higher Education* LII, no. 47 (July 28, 2006): A23.

54. By this I mean the delight in the new for its own sake. It reminds one of the passage in the New Testament where listeners only want something new because they have "itching, burning ears." We may well be trying new things for the sake of the new and nothing else, but at the expense of something very valuable.

55. For Fathom see Hughes, above, 21.

56. In case some thought my earlier note about stem cell research was off base, consider now the further similarity. Adult stem cells have shown great promise but embryonic stem cells, which have an astonishing rate of failure, continue to be touted as the

new medical panacea. Of course the failures do not mean success is impossible, but why put all the eggs in the basket with an open or false bottom?

57. Hughes, 46. There are others. For a grim list of would-be successes except that they failed, see Anne R. Kenney, "Projects to Programs: Mainstreaming Digital Imaging Initiatives," in *Moving Theory into Practice: Digital Imaging for Libraries and Archives,* Anne R. Kenney and Oya Y Rieger, eds. (Mountain View, CA: Research Libraries Group, 2000), 172–173. Kenney writes that while advances are being made and successes are occurring, "to date there is little hard evidence that they will succeed." Of course some will complain that her statement resonates but only to the time at which it was written, the year 2000. "That was then," they will argue; "this is now." But is that the case? When Google announced its plan in 2004, many thought it would be well on the way by now. It is still hung up for some of the very reasons given in this chapter. This is no reason to quit, of course, but plenty of reason to give us all pause.

58. For more on this, see Hughes, 24.

59. I am not the first to raise this question; see Stuart Lee's article, note 26.

60. Hughes, 171. Failure here is defined by running over budget, not completing the project on time, or not meeting stated goals and objectives.

61. U.S. National Commission on Libraries and Information Science (NCLIS), *Mass Digitization: Implications for Information Policy,* 11. The "good enough" phrase also appears here. In the same report, however (p. 18), the fear is suggested by another that "good enough" may well prove to be *not* good enough.

62. Ian Youngs, "Libraries Fear Digital Lockdown," *BBC News,* February 3, 2006, http://news.bbc.co.uk/go/pr/fr/-/1/hi/technology/4675280.stm (accessed February 2006).

63. *Ibid.,* 13. The speaker is Mary Sue Coleman of the University of Michigan. Ms. Coleman is far more sanguine about mass digitization projects than I, and I do not mean to associate her with my views. Yet I do question the ideal, again, one I have not see in librarianship before. A new ideal is by no means a reason for rejection. But a new ideal that represents something of a *volte-face* in this profession must be examined carefully, and its impact fully understood, before setting it up as the new ideal. Obviously I do not think we have thought all these things through enough to know if this is the right pursuit right now.

64. Ann J. Wolpert, "The Library as Provider of Digital Resources for Teaching and Scholarship," in *Development of Digital Libraries: An American Perspective,* Deanna B. Marcum, ed. (Westport, CT: Greenwood Press, 2001), 85.

65. Hahn, 5. The fear is that the price of books will be so low that only Google will be able to compete. Apparently when Wal-Mart does this in a community they are demonized above all other demons. If this turns out to be true about Google and the elimination of small and even medium-sized publishers, my guess is that Google will be hailed with the usual unthinking hurrahs that have so far greeted everything else Google has done. Again, if it's on the Web, or delivered thereby, it *has* to be right.

Chapter 6

1. To be honest, eBooks have been promised for the last *fifty* years. See Jennifer Adamec, "EBooks in the College Classroom," unpublished thesis (n.p.: MS Publishing, 2006), 2.

2. See Scott Carlson, "Library Renovation Leads to Soul Searching at Cal Poly," *Chronicle of Higher Education* LIII, no. 2 (September 1, 2006): A59–61, where professors and librarians complain about the shift from print to online exclusively, and where print is considered so passé.

3. Malcolm Gladwell, "Chip Thrills," *The New Yorker* LXXII, no. 43 (January 20, 1997): 7–8. The subway example is from this article. Gladwell gives the Kraus quote and the Tenner reference, too.

4. This page-turning feature is making a comeback in Hiero Interactive Digital Flip Books. Many think the "authentic" page turning experience in Hiero's eBooks will make readers flock to it (see Fox citation below). Of course the question must be repeated again and again: why simulate a page-turning experience when you can really have one? Could it be this eBook-emperor really doesn't have on any clothes?

5. For more on this, see Lawrence Lessig, *The Future of Ideas: The Fate of the Commons in a Connected World* (New York: Random House, 2001), 6–8.

6. *Ibid.,* 122. The "relatively" is curious here for one is hard-pressed to relate to something else that carries information but is *more* durable. Does Lessig mean relative to pyramids? Sure, those walls do contain information that is more durable, lasting now some 5,000+ years. But what other portable, durable, functional or practicable source is he implying?

7. Some newly touted technology is Sony's E Ink screen, for example (see the end of this chapter for more). It may well help solve this problem but our collective breaths should not be held.

8. Rudolf Bultmann, *History and Eschatology: The Presence of Eternity* (New York: Harper Torchbooks, 1957), 1. I chose this book randomly from my personal library. While I recognize Bultmann as a major figure in his field, I endorse neither his interpretation of theology nor his eschatology.

9. The text I have before me is 155 pages of amply spaced lines.

10. Lessig answers yes, resoundingly (133). I am not so sure that many others are that delighted. Some I suspect are persuaded *only because* they are recommended. In order for the program to work, it must be broad-based, so much so that almost every title in that genre is recommended. If it is narrow, few would be represented and not very often.

11. International Digital Publishing, "Ebook User Survey, 2006," International Digital Publishing Forum, February 2006. See survey question 3 about why individuals did not want to buy eBooks. The top three are price, content and standardization. One cannot make much of this survey, however. It was sent to 6,000 eBook readers (users of www.ereader.com and www.fictionwise.com) and of that number, just over 11 percent responded. For more statistical data on eBook usage, see Primary Research Group, *Libraries'*

Use of eBooks: A Report from Primary Research Group (New York: Primary Research Group, 2003). PRG reports little different from the 2006 survey.

12. A similar sentiment is found in Andy Barnett, *Libraries, Community and Technology* (Jefferson, NC: McFarland, 2002), 98. Barnett makes the astute observation: "In the 1950s, enthusiasts proclaimed that nuclear power would be so cheap that it would not even be metered, just provided as a public service. In the 1990s, the descendants of those prophets declared that knowledge and wisdom would flow like milk and honey."

13. Deborah Stafford, "Will eBooks Replace pBooks?" *Book Report* 20, no. 4 (Jan/Feb 2002): 22. Her answer, too, is no.

14. The first academic library I worked in had less that 100,000 volumes, several hundred of which were the Loeb texts, made available many years before I came to head it up. Citing the text required the actual volumes for reasons mentioned in chapter 3, with respect to footnotes.

15. For the claim, see www.questia.com. To be fair, Questia does not claim that it is a "substitute for a traditional bricks-and-mortar library" (see Nancy Buchanan, "It's Academic; It's Online," *The Chronicle of Higher Education* LII [14] [November 25, 2005]: 17). The examples cited here and below are representative. In addition to Questia and netLibrary, there are also ebrary and many publisher-specific eBooks offerings, such as Greenwood, Safari, Pearson, McGraw-Hill and Cambridge.

16. Pitch made to the author by Questia representatives, spring 2001. See also Calvin Reid, "EBooks Go to School," *Publishers Weekly* 252, no. 22: 29. Reid says that Questia managed to survive the "digital hubris," a nice description. Questia grew to 300 employees in 2001, fell to 24 by 2002. It had managed to come back to some 74 employees by the end of 2005. In response to a piece I wrote for *The Chronicle of Higher Education* in which Questia was similarly portrayed, its president argued that this comeback meant that Questia could not be characterized as having failed.

17. An interesting pilot of Questia occurred in the city where I live. A high school used Questia as a resource for its students. Questia charged the students a very low fee. The students used the resource but afterwards the vast majority complained that they missed the actual books, and still preferred to use them. The pilot was considered a success and now has moved to other high schools in the area. If students are required to sign up for a nominal fee, you can bet that funding for print-base libraries will not be long for this world.

18. Less than 1 percent of all users, according to our most recent figures, spring 2006. Using the report feature for SOLINET's delivery of netLibrary to the Southeast, I have not found in a five year survey any title used more than 102 times, two used more than 65, about a dozen used more than 30 but less than 35, and a half dozen used more than 25 but less than 31. By far the bulk of the titles are use either 0, 1 or 2 times. This is at best *underwhelming*.

19. It should be pointed out that this is the model that netLibrary had in place when it fell into Chapter 11. Once a book was "check out" by a user, it was locked out to others until it was "returned."

20. These problems have been highlighted before. See James Litchenburg, "What Can Publishers Learn from Librarians? *Publishers' Weekly* 248, no. 12 (March 19, 2001): 17. I have adapted some of his points for my own purposes here.

21. netLibrary, for example, offers about half commercial and half academic. The service is too expensive for an individual to purchase on his or her own.

22. International Digital Publishing, "Ebook User Survey, 2006," February 2006, International Digital Publishing Forum, survey questions 7–8.

23. The new Sony Reader makes this claim but so far many experts do not yet agree. See further in this chapter.

24. Lynn Silipigni Connaway, "Electronic Books (eBooks): Current Trends and Future Directions," *DESIDOC Bulletin of Information Technology* 21, no. 1 (January 2003): 13. Connaway is far more hopeful about eBook developments than am I.

25. Even in the case of academic libraries, patrons who have not matriculated can walk into a public university's library and use its resources free of charge. Most library databases are not password protected within the library building though most are from off site, in compliance with contractual agreements.

26. See for example, Rosie Croft and Shailoo Bedi, "eBooks for a Distributed University: The Royals Roads University Case," *Journal of Library Administration* 41, no. 1/2 (2004): 113–117. This would appear to be a good case in point, where 80 percent of the university's learners are working on Web-based online courses. While the study shows increasing usage, it does not show overwhelming support as one would expect to find. The authors cite approvingly another researcher's claim that "Electronic books are unlikely to replace printed books" (p. 118). In the university where I work, we routinely stress eBook availability (even making searching them quick, easy and intuitive) but cannot seem to get students to use them with anything approaching regularity. One of the conclusions of the study cited here is that even business learners (where the eBook content was the highest) remained reluctant to use them. It would seem, to ape the familiar song, that if eBooks can't attract users there, they may not well make it with any other user group anywhere. See also Connaway, cited below.

27. From the most recent statistics from same, www.bowker.com (accessed August 2006).

28. The other area where eBooks should have taken off is in textbook publishing. The cost of publishing a textbook by conventional means is enormous, yet through digital means, astonishingly inexpensive. eBooks as textbooks have not yet caught on either. One hates to be cynical, but if textbook publishers passed along the savings, costs to student would drop by at least 50 percent. SafariX WebBooks did just this and offered the Pearson line of textbooks at 50 percent less than the printed editions. Other companies have followed suit but it has not so far caught on. See Adamec, 10, 16,18.

29. See for example Ron Miller, "EBooks Worm

Their Way into the Reference Market," *Econtent* 28, no. 7/8 (July/August 2005): 30–34. The phrase "tipping point" has been made famous by Malcolm Gladwell's book by the same title and refers to some event that causes a thing that has not caught on before to suddenly catch fire, so to speak.

30. *Ibid.*, 31. Says one eBook CEO, "People had been writing off eBooks as a tool that didn't fill a need, but there has been a resurgence on the corporate and academic side, although it's nothing like a major trend." See also Frances C. Wilkinson and Linda K. Lewis, "Reference eBooks: Does an eBook on the Screen Beat One on the Shelf," *Against the Grain* 17, no. 4 (September 2005): 1, 18, 20, 22.

31. Sheri Myers, "eBooks and the Academic Library," *Kentucky Libraries,* Summer 2004, 5, emphasis added.

32. Problematic, because of the lack of uniform standards among outsourcers and electronic content placed on the Web. Some of the materials are easy to access, other much less so.

33. Karen Coyle, "CHAOS: eBooks: Where Have All the Standards Gone?" *Against the Grain* 17, no. 1 (February 2005): 84. This is a superb article on all the efforts made toward this elusive standard.

34. Megan K. Fox, "Product Pipeline," *Library Journal,* April 15, 2006, (http://www.libraryjournal.com/article/CA6324217.html) (accessed August 2006).

35. *Ibid.*

36. For example, the 2001 Joint Information Systems Committee's book working group annual survey of publishers found that only 4 percent of surveyed publishers offered 100 percent of their content. Doubtless it is much higher today, but even if it's 400 percent better, it is still very small. See Meyers, 6.

37. Lynn Silipigni Connaway, "Transaction Log Analyses of Electronic Book (eBook) Usage," *Against the Grain* 17, no. 1 (February 2005): 86, 89. Connaway examined netLibrary usage during the same day of the week over a three year period. As time with the eBooks grew, it never made it past twelve minutes and the average number of pages viewed did not exceed twenty, lending some credence to the charge that individuals are not "reading" eBooks.

38. This is particularly bewildering since publishers can expect a fully digital book to cost about 50 percent less than a book produced through digital means. See Adamec, 5.

39. For more features and converters, see Terrence Cavanaugh, "EBooks: Expanding the School Library," *Library Media Connection,* February 2005, 56, 59

40. Imagine some student with only dial-up having to read *Pride and Prejudice* at home.

41. Take a personal example. The library where I work offers one computer for the visually impaired. Only in 2005 were we able, through our office for the disabled, to offer one special reading machine for those who cannot see at all. Some will argue that this has always been a problem, but when in college, my work-study included reading to the visually impaired. I was one of dozens. While some schools must still offer this, it is not as widespread as it once was.

42. Coyle, 84.

43. *Ibid.*, 85.

44. *Ibid.*, 89.

45. Quoted in Lynn Silipigni Connaway, "Transaction Log Analyses of Electronic Book (eBook) Usage," *Against the Grain* 17, no. 1 (February 2005): 85.

46. See "CONFU: The Conference on Fair Use," www.utsystem.edu/ogc/INTELLECTUALPROPERTY/confu.htm (accessed September 2006), for this long day's journey into night.

47. Miller, 32.

48. Ron Miller, "Can the Sony Reader Push eBooks into the Mainstream?" *Econtent* 29, no. 3 (April 2006): 13.

49. *Ibid.* Why "page turns"? Why not "clicks" and simply live in the new world such devices are trying to create?

50. *Ibid.*

51. Fox.

52. *Ibid.*

53. See www.irextechnologies.com/products/iliad for more that this e-Book has to offer.

54. Michael Rogers, "EBooks Struggling to Find a Niche," *Library Journal* 131, no. 11 (June 15, 2006): 25.

55. Fox.

56. Rogers.

57. Fox.

58. Rogers, 26.

59. Lesley Williams, "Making 'E' Visible," *Library Journal* 131, no. 11 (June 15, 2006): 41–42.

60. A report of this experience is forthcoming from our unit later.

61. The line is a great one but is not original. It comes from the preface to Johnson's grand dictionary.

62. See for example Jeffrey Young, "Scholars Turn Monographs into Digital Conversations," *Chronicle of Higher Education* LII, no. 47 (July 28, 2006): 20–24. Here some enterprising scholar has made his forthcoming book a blog-like experience. A young scholar, McKenzie Wark, has taken his next monograph, placed a draft online, and is soliciting comments. Some of these he will use, others he will not. Some comments have simply been harsh while others might really improve the text. In the end, however, it stands as yet another relic of the digital curiosity shop that will last as long as it's there. Would he not be better served by sending it to experts in his field for comments?

63. "Rice U. Will Start First All-Digital University Press," *Chronicle of Higher Education,* July 28, 2006, A23.

64. Steven Bell, "Electronic Libraries Can't Be Academic," *Chronicle of Higher Education,* September 30, 2005, 14.

Chapter 7

1. Robert J. Samuelson, *Untruth: Why Conventional Wisdom Is (Almost Always) Wrong* (New York: AtRandom.com, 2001), 218.

2. My favorite edition is the Vintage edition published in 1977, reprint of the 1932 Everyman edition. The book was of course published in 1621 and is a

towering monument to scholarship of the highest, best and most humorous kind, though not many critics see the latter. I cannot help but point out that he, in addition to spending a lifetime on this book, was also a college librarian.

3. The survey, though hardly scientific, asked the question, "What could you not live without?" and listed cell phones, computers/Internet, music, television, movies, newspapers and video games. Happily, books won by a large margin. I do not say surprisingly, because the contention in this book all along has been that most people are much more comfortable around paper than the computer commissars who wish us to go paperless right now.

4. Mark Kirby and Nancy H. Evans, "The Network Is the Library," *EDUCOM Review* 24, no. 3 (Fall 1989): 16. Also quoted in Karen M. Drabenstott, *Analytical Review of the Library of the Future* (Washington, D.C.: Council on Library Resources, 1994), 9.

5. Landoni Monica, Nadia Catenazzi and Forbes Gibb, "Hyper-Books and Visual-Books in an Electronic Library," *Electronic Library* 11, no. 3 (June 1993): 176. Also quoted in Karen M. Drabenstott, *Analytical Review of the Library of the Future* (Washington, D.C.: Council on Library Resources, 1994), 10.

6. Drabenstott, *Analytical Review of the Library of the Future*, 11, 15, 20, 27.

7. *Ibid.*, 47.

8. *Ibid.*

9. *Ibid.*, 65, 132.

10. Also quoted in Walt Crawford and Michael Gorman, *Future Libraries: Dreams, Madness, and Reality* (Chicago: American Library Association, 1995), 4.

11. "Robert Theobald," *Earthbeat with Alexandra de Blas,* Radio National, 24 October 1998, www.abc.net.au/rn/science/earth/stories/s14248.htm (accessed September 2006).

12. "Ipswich, Inc., Warns that Spam Continues to Rise," August 31, 2006, http://www.ipswitch.com/company/press_releases/060831_spamometer.asp (accessed September 2006).

13. Crawford and Gorman make a similar point, 4.

14. For the Mead allusion, see Derek Freeman, *Margaret Mead and Samoa: The Making and Unmaking of an Anthropological Myth* (New York: Pelican, 1986).

15. For a similar argument, see Crawford and Gorman, 17–18.

16. *Ibid.*, 20.

17. *Ibid.*, 61.

18. *Ibid.*, 63.

19. Michael Buckland, *Redesigning Library Services: A Manifesto* (Chicago: ALA, 1992), 124–125.

20. OCLC Online Computer Library Center, *College Students' Perceptions of Libraries and Information Resources* (Dublin, Ohio: OCLC Online Computer Library Center, 2006). This is a companion piece to an earlier report mentioned in this book, *Perceptions of Libraries and Information Resources,* 2005.

21. *Ibid.*, 1–1.

22. *Ibid.*, 1–2, 1–4, 1–7.

23. *Ibid.*, 1–8.

24. *Ibid.*, 1–11.

25. *Ibid.*, 1–12. Total respondents claim Google provides worthwhile information (55 percent) to the library (33 percent). The library outdistanced Yahoo by only 1 percent.

26. *Ibid.*, 2–10.

27. *Ibid.*, 2–13. In order for librarians to match search engines, "very satisfied" and "satisfied" must be combined. When measuring only the very satisfied against each other, librarians do not come out as strongly. I blame this on the execrable state of teaching in library school today.

28. Elinor Mills, "Most Reliable Search Tool Could Be Your Librarian," *C/net News.com,* September 29, 2006, http://news.com.com/Most+reliable+search+tool+could+be+your+librarian/2100-1032_3-6120778.html (accessed October 2006).

29. This is average for the most recent figures, 2005. It represents 20 new academic library buildings. But the figure is only a talking point as each region in the country has its own square footage. The high in this particular year was $352 in Minnesota, the low, $116 in Arkansas. Of course not only do states differ, but the total square footage also intrudes on the average price. See Bette-Lee Fox, "A Storm Rains on Our Parade," *Library Journal,* December 2005, 46

30. I follow Ovid's *Metamorphoses,* trans. Mary M. Innes (Middlesex, England: Penguin Books, 1955), 242–245. Hippomenes forgets to thank the goddess for help and so they both end as lions, scavengers of the forest.

31. See, for example, OCLC Report, 3–1.

32. Some will complain that I have forgotten about the famous "READ" posters that ALA sells in its online store. No, I have not. Forgive me if I think it unwise to use famous Hollywood celebrities and famous athletes to tout reading, two groups that do not generally come readily to mind as prolific readers, though surely some in both camps are.

33. See, for example, Kris Axtman, "Academic Libraries Empty Stacks for Online Centers," *Christian Science Monitor,* August 23, 2005.

34. *Ibid.*

35. Scott Carlson, "Library Renovation Leads to Soul Searching at Cal Poly," *Chronicle of Higher Education* LIII, no. 2 (September 1, 2006): A59–60.

36. *Ibid.*, A60.

37. *Ibid.*, A61.

38. JSTOR did not emerge as a viable alternative until later in the game, in the 1990s. Librarians and scholars realized that most proprietary databases added a new year by dropping years at the beginning of the "storage," meaning that most online journals rarely made available more than 10 or 15 years at a time. But JSTOR makes available only about 2,000 of the more than 100,000 journals subscribed to by academic libraries in North America. The problem is not really space but the cost of these often hugely overpriced journals to libraries. For example, about a half dozen key science journals can add up to a cost of more than $30,000 annually for a library. Although a science professor may be able to buy them for a fraction, literally, of that cost, it is illegal for that professor to make them available in the library for students to use until the current year for each has passed. Typically, the cost

to libraries is often three four and even five times what it is to the individual.

39. Vijaay Kuman, "Role of University Libraries in Efficient Resource Management," paper presented in an international seminar, "Higher Education Administration in Developing Countries," held in Calcutta, February 4–6, 2006, at the University of Calcutta, www.caluniv.ac.in (accessed September 2006).

40. I should add that while I cannot extrapolate for all libraries, the one where I work has increased in usage over the last seven years. Moreover, our door count, a measure of physical presence, has also increased.

41. F. Wilfrid Lancaster, "Second Thoughts on the Paperless Society," *Library Journal* 124, no. 15 (September 15, 1999): 48. See also his article "The Paperless Society Revisited," *American Libraries* 16, no. 8 (September 1985): 553–555.

42. *Ibid.*

43. *Ibid.* (Emphases mine.)

44. *Ibid.*

45. I would not want to suggest that his comment here *contra* electronic everything is the only reason, or even a primary one, that Lancaster himself has had troubles of late, but the timing is surely right. Only recently he has to step down as the editor of *Library Trends*, a move that was not only not of his making, but also not of his liking. It strikes me that the "trends" portion of that journal's name may well not like the idea that its editor is not fully on board with the current electronic *uber alles* trend. See "Lancaster Steps Down from *Library Trends* but Not by Choice," *Library Hotline,* August 14, 2006, 3.

46. *Ibid.*, 49.

47. *Ibid.*, 50

Chapter 8

1. I am not the first to raise this issue. See Sven Birkerts, *The Gutenberg Elegies: The Fate of Reading in an Electronic Age* (Boston: Faber and Faber, 1994). Birkerts's book was prophetic, foreseeing more than a decade before it could be seen most of what I record here.

2. See K. Rayner, B.R. Foorman, E. Perfetti, D. Pesetsky and Mark S. Seidenberg, "How Psychological Science Informs the Teaching of Reading," *Psychological Science in the Public Interest* 2, no. 2 (2001); William Honig, *Teaching Our Children to Read: The Role of Skills in a Comprehensive Reading Program* (Thousand Oaks, CA: Corwin Press, 1995); Diane Ravitch, *The Language Police: How Pressure Groups Restrict What Students Learn* (New York: Knopf, 2003).

3. For an examination of some of the complexities, see for example Michael Shaughnessy, "An Interview with Dr. Marion Blank: About New Ways to View Reading and Reading Instruction," *EducationNews,* www.educationnews.org/writers/michael/An_Interview_with_Dr_Marion_Blank.htm (accessed September 2006). The interview examines the process of reading without respect to the Web.

4. Michael Skube, "Writing Off Reading," *Washington Post,* August 20, 2006, B3.

5. While some words may be admittedly hard in a given text I assign, *all* of them are in standard dictionaries. What I find dismaying is the complete lack of interest in learning a new word. Students at all three colleges and universities where I have taught are indifferent to new words: they simply don't want to learn them.

6. Figures for what follows have come from William P. O'Hare, *Trends in the Well-Being of America's Children* (New York: Russell Sage Foundation, and Washington, DC: Population Reference Bureau, 2004), specifically "Achievement/Proficiency." See also Tom Loveless, *How Well Are American Students Learning?* The 2006 Brown Center Report on American Education (Washington: The Brooking Institution, 2006), 8–11.

7. It isn't part of this argument about libraries and literacy, but it is interesting to note that the Brown report cited in note 6, above, also points out that not only do students not do better if they are happy (i.e., have strong self esteem) but that trying to make learning relevant not only does not improve learning but may also very well impede it (Loveless 13–18).

8. *Ibid.*, 326.

9. *Ibid.*, 327–330.

10. *Ibid.*, 353.

11. I'm not discounting the fact that *some* children could be helped by using the Web in certain controlled contexts. I am arguing that the unfettered Web, to which most young people have the widest access, does not improve reading abilities and may well further erode already weak reading skills.

12. National Accessible Reading Assessment Projects, *Defining Reading Proficiency for Accessible Large-Scale Assessments: Some Guiding Principles* (Minneapolis, MN: February 17, 2006), 1, available at www.narap.info (accessed September 2006).

13. *Ibid.*, 3. The changes are in response to standards made tighter by the NCLB Act. While flexibility is stressed, it is flexibility not in what defines proficiency but in what a child is able to read.

14. *Ibid.*, 6.

15. Jeffrey Goldfarb, "Google Launches Literacy Project," *Boston.com,* October 4, 2006, http://www.boston.com/business/articles/2006/10/04/google_launches_literacy_project_to_link_resources/ (accessed October 2006).

16. Siva Vaidhyanathan, "A Risky Gamble with Google," *The Chronicle of Higher Education* LII, no. 15 (December 15, 2005): B7.

17. *Ibid.*, B7.

18. For the digital rights management issue, see Karen Coyle, "The Automation of Rights," *Journal of Academic Librarianship* 32, no. 3 (May 2006): 326–329; Donald Walters, "Managing Digital Assets in Higher Education: An Overview," *ARL* 244 (February 2006): 1–10. The DRM is not a concern for the Googles of the world per se, but for the licensing of information in proprietary databases. Should this change radically, it could spell the end of reliable online information. No one expects it to change radically, but many fear its eventual resting place will

make libraries' provision of access too exorbitant to continue. What does concern Google, however, would be the digital rights with respect to mass digitization projects, for which see Jessica Dye, "The Digital Rights Issues: Behind Book Digitization Projects," *Econtent* 29, no. 1 (January/February 2006): 32–4, 36–7; and Chen Xiotian, "Scribes of the Digital Era," *Chronicle of Higher Education* 52, no. 1 (January 26, 2006): 34. Here the copyright issue raises its beautiful/ugly head (depending on whether you are a publisher or Google) and the unraveling of the matter could well unravel Google's plans. If Google would adopt both Microsoft and Yahoo's approach, it would save everyone time and money. Of course, it would require some backtracking on Google's part, some lost revenues and some crow-eating.

19. Vaidhyanathan, B7. See also Adam Cohen, "What Google Should Roll Out Next: Privacy Upgrade," *New York Times*, November 28, 2005, A18 (L).

20. *Ibid.*

21. *Ibid.* This is the Publisher Program part of Google Print.

22. Center for Academic Integrity, http://www.academicintegrity.org/.

23. Quoted in Julie Coiro, "Reading Comprehension on the Internet: Expanding Our Understanding of Reading Comprehension to Encompass New Literacies," *Reading Teacher* 56, no. 5 (February 2003): 458.

24. "MacArthur to Invest $50 Million in Digital Learning," *eSchoolNewsOnline*,www.eschoolnews.com (accessed October 2006). Talk about throwing good money after bad ideas. The study will examine how video games, social networking sites (like MySpace and Facebook) and other digital media can be used to help students learn. The tried and proven failure of trying to meet students where they are instead of leading them where they should be will once again waste millions of dollars. Try to get even $500,000 for new books and no foundation in the US will even consider the proposal. Gee, perhaps we can use some of the more violent sites to teach young boys math: "If Bob shoots more men than women while Shelia more women than men..."

25. It reminds me of so-called educational television. Students fled from that until we could devise shows that were more entertaining than educational, defeating the intended purpose.

26. Coiro, 458.

27. "Almost everyone," because I am not unaware that this is an argument made by those wanting to eliminate the death penalty.

28. The book that lifted the lid on this Pandora's Box is William Honig's *Teaching Our Children to Read: The Role of Skills in a Comprehensive Reading Program* (Thousand Oaks, CA: Corwin Press, 1995). Honig was the California superintendent of education when Whole Language was introduced there.

29. Nancy Mitchell, "Innovative School Stirs Anger of Some," *Rocky Mountain News*, October 13, 2006, www.rockymountainnews.com/drm/education/article/0,1299DRMN_957_5063375,00.html (accessed October 2006).

30. Coiro, 462.

31. *Ibid.*, 464

32. Elizabeth Schmar-Dobler, "Reading on the Internet: The Link between Literacy and Technology," *Journal of Adolescent and Adult Literacy* 47, no. 1: 2003, 80. The 50 percent figure is updated from the article.

33. *Ibid.*, 81.

34. *Ibid.*, 83

35. U.S. Department of Education, *Toward a New Golden Age in American Education* (Washington, D.C.: U.S. Department of Education, 2004), 6.

36. Every test, every study, and every bit of data we have so far collected indicates that students cannot master these simple skills despite our grand movement forward on the information superhighway.

37. U.S. Department of Education, *Toward a New Golden Age in American Education*, 10.

38. *Ibid.*, 12.

39. *Ibid.*, 15.

40. *Ibid.*, 17–18.

41. *Ibid.*, 19. Emphasis added.

42. *Ibid.*, 21.

43. Robin Goodfellow, "Online Literacies and Learning: Operational, Cultural and Critical Dimensions," *Language and Education* 18, no. 5 (2004): 380. While some of what Goodfellow argues here agrees with my conclusions, he, too, is more hopeful about the future of Web-based learning than am I.

44. For a good discussion of path-based learning see John E. McEneaney, *Learning on the Web: A Content Literacy Perspective*, ERIC, ED 442 098 (International Reading Association, 2000). The author is a great deal more sanguine about the prospects of this than am I, and I in no way mean to imply that he agrees with any of my conclusions here. He does make the case that learning from a subject area "involves focusing on both the text's content and on the processes students apply as they work to acquire, organize, an integrate that content." I agree whole-heartedly with this assessment and it is my contention that students who do not read well to begin with will have a devil of time doing the cognitive work required to master either path-based or hypertext-based learning.

45. *Ibid.*, 8–9.

46. This is an adaptation of a brilliant title by C.S. Lewis, *Pilgrim's Regress* (Grand Rapids, MI: William B. Eerdmans), 68.

47. McEneaney, 14.

48. *Ibid.*, 17.

49. Quoted in Goodfellow, 379.

50. *Ibid.*, 382.

51. A.W. Bates, *Technology, Open Learning, and Distance Education* (London: Routledge, 1995), 21.

52. Pete Weaver, "Preventing E-Learning Failure: Ten Common Pitfalls and How to Avoid Them," *T+D*, August 2002, 45–50, 75. While some of these are my own, I have also adapted and revised some of Weaver's points but follow them closely nonetheless.

53. Before such "invisible" chains were added, libraries routinely loss about 33 percent of their collections annually.

54. By far the most recent, the largest and the most comprehensive to date is Texas Center for Educational Results, *Evaluation of the Texas Technology Immersion Pilot: First Year Results* (Austin, TX: Texas Center for

Educational Research, 2006). Results reported in the paragraph are from this report, specifically 71–82.

55. *Ibid.*, i.

56. *Ibid.*, 77.

57. *Ibid.*, 80.

58. *Ibid.*, 81.

59. Will Fitzhugh, "Bibliophobia," *Education Week*, October 4, 2006, 33.

60. About ten days after I wrote these words, I ran across this: Vicki Haddock, "After Years of Teachers Piling It On, There's a New Movement to ... Abolish Homework," SFGate, http://www.sfgate.com/cgi-bin/article.cgi?f=/c/a/2006/10/08/ING0FLHNM21.D TL&type (accessed October 2006). The idea here is to abolish homework even at the AP and IB levels. See also Greg Toppo, "Homework Load Doesn't Add Up," *USA Today*, October 1, 2006, usatoday.com, http://www.usatoday.com/news/nation/2003-10-01-home work-study_x.htm (accessed October 2006).

61. Pew Internet and American Life Project, *The Future of the Internet II* (Washington, D.C.: Pew Internet and American Life Project, September 24, 2006), v.

62. *Ibid.*, vi. The author of the words is Robert Eller.

63. Elinor Mills, "Most Reliable Search Tool Could Be Your Librarian," *C/net News.com*, September 29, 2006, http://news.com.com/Most+reliable+search+tool+could+be+your+librarian/2100-1032_3-6120778.html (accessed October 2006), 1.

Chapter 9

1. World Internet Usage Statistics News and Population Stats, "Internet Usage Statistics — The Big Picture," www.internetworldstats.com/stats.htm (accessed October 2006).

2. Blissfully unaware of the Web but painfully aware of everything else. Darfur is a case in point where malicious governments threaten starving populations who cannot begin to defend themselves. Yes, the world may be flat one day, but can we take care of starving populations under murderous regimes first?

3. *Op cit.*

4. Marilyn Deegan, "The Spectrum of the Digital Objects in the Library and Beyond," in G.E. Gorman, *The Digital Factor in Library and Information Services* (Lanham, MD: Scarecrow Press, 2002), 16. The citation here quotes another source that contends that about 85 percent of the world hasn't made a phone call, but I have chosen here to refer to land lines subscriptions. I doubt the "phone call" assertion because it does not take into account that some could use another's phone. Using the most recent census figures, teledensity is right below the 20 percent figure worldwide so that is the figure I use here. See www.census.gov/cgi-bin/ipc/popclock and www.itu.int/ITU-D/ict/statistics/at_glance/KeyTelecom99.com for more.

5. *Ibid.*, 17.

6. Quoted in Denice Adkins, "The Digital library

and Younger Users," in G.E. Gorman, *The Digital Factor in Library and Information Services* (Lanham, MD: Scarecrow Press, 2002), 136–137.

7. Lorna Peterson, "Digital Versus Print Issues," in G.E. Gorman, *The Digital Factor in Library and Information Services* (Lanham, MD: Scarecrow Press, 2002), 27.

8. *Ibid.*, 37.

9. Stephen M. Mutula, "Web-Based Reference Services: Design and Implementation Decisions," in G.E. Gorman, *The Digital Factor in Library and Information Services* (Lanham, MD: Scarecrow Press, 2002), 179.

10. See the previous chapter. See also Catherine Sheldrick Ross, "Reading in a Digital Age," in G.E. Gorman, *The Digital Factor in Library and Information Services* (Lanham, MD: Scarecrow Press, 2002), 91–95.

11. Adkins, 141.

12. Suzy Bausch and Lelani Han, "U.S. Teens Graduate from Choosing IM Buddy Icons to Creating Elaborate Social Networking Profiles," Nielsen/NetRatings, http://www.nielsen-netratings.com/ (accessed October 16, 2006).

13. *Ibid.*

14. *Ibid.*

15. As pointed out in an earlier chapter, the following comes from Wikipedia's "cite" pages: "Most educators and professionals do not consider it appropriate to use tertiary sources such as encyclopedias as the sole source for any information — citing an encyclopedia as an important reference in footnotes or bibliographies may result in censure or a failing grade. Wikipedia articles should be used for background information, as a reference for correct terminology and search terms, and as a starting point for further research. As with any community-built reference, there is a possibility for error in Wikipedia's content — please check your facts against multiple sources and read our disclaimers for more information." This note should accompany every Web page, substituting the words "The Web" for "Wikipedia."

16. See also Andrew Abbott, "Professionalism and the Future of Librarianship," *Library Trends* 46, no. 3 (Winter 1998): 430–431, who uses the same story to make a similar point.

17. Jorge Louis Borges, "The Library of Babel," in *Labyrinths: Selected Stories and Other Writings* (New York: New Directions, 1962), 54, 52.

18. *Ibid.*, 55.

19. "IMLS College Libraries Panel," December 15, 2005, http://www.libraryworkforce.org/tiki-page.php?pageName=opinion_papers (accessed September and October 2006), 7. The site is still a work in progress. Many such opinion papers may be found here and I have cited those referenced.

20. *Ibid.*, 10.

21. *Ibid.*, 16, where the point is made but in a different context.

22. "IMLS Task Force on the Future of Libraries in the Workforce — University Libraries," December 8, 2006, 2. For full citation see note 19 above.

23. "IMLS College Libraries Panel," 18. For full citation, see note 19 above.

24. "IMLS Task Force on the Future of Libraries in the Workforce — University Libraries," 4. For full citation see note 19 above.

25. *Ibid.*

26. *Ibid.*, 17.

27. Michael Gorman, interview with Dick Kaser at VNU's Online Information Conference, www.info-todayblog.com (accessed October 2006). Click on "December 02, 2005" for the interview. Also quoted in George R. Ploskere, "Where We Are Now with Content and Technology," *Online* 30, no. 3 (May/June 2006): 50.

28. See also Andy Barnett, *Libraries, Community, and Technology* (Jefferson, NC: McFarland, 2002), 47–50.

29. Veronica Reyes, "The Future Role of Academic Librarians in Higher Education," *Libraries and the Academy* 6, no. 3 (2006): 302.

30. *Ibid.*, 303. Reyes has a less negative view.

31. Bill Crowley, "Suicide Prevention: Safeguarding the Future of the Professional Librarian," *Library Administration and Management* 20, no. 2 (Spring 2006): 76.

32. W. Lee Hisle, "Reference Questions in the Library of Future," *Chronicle of Higher Education* LII, no. 6 (September 30, 2005): 6.

33. For one such "put on a happy face" approach, see Robert E. Renaud, "Shaping a New Profession: The Role of Librarians When the Library and Computer Center Merge," *Library Administration and Management* 20, no. 2 (Spring 2006): 65–71, 74.

34. Derek Lee, "Parlour Games: The Real Nature of the Internet," www.uksg.org/serials/law.asp (accessed January 2006). While nearly ten years old, many of the complaints about the Internet Law are still at issue. See also Lawrence Lessig, *The Future of Ideas: The Fate of the Commons in a Connected World* (New York: Random House, 2001), 160–165. Lessig fears more those entities that control the Web, such as bandwidth, Internet providers and so on.

35. See Louise Mabille, *The Rage of Caliban: Nietzsche and Wilde Contra Modernity* (Bethesda, MD: Academica Press, LLC, 2006), 10, note 5.

36. G.K. Chesterton, *Why I Am a Catholic,* G.K. Chesterton: Collected Works, vol. 3 (San Francisco: Ignatius Press, 1990), 157. Barnett, cited above, also makes use of part of this quote in a different context.

37. *Ibid.*, 129.

Index